THE SCIENCE OF INVESTMENT

PROFESSOR FRANK GEORGE

First published in 1984 by

ABACUS PRESS

Abacus House, Speldhurst Road, Tunbridge Wells, Kent TN4 OHU

British Library Cataloguing in Publication Data

George, F. H.
The science of investment.
1. Investments
I. Title
337.6 HG4521

ISBN 0-85626-422-9

BSDCS7

Printed and bound by Woolnough Bookbinding,
Wellingborough, England

SERIES PREFACE

The purpose of this series is to promote a "systems viewpoint" with respect to a whole series of different subjects. In a sense, the systems viewpoint is concerned with looking at problems holistically and in terms of information science. It is closely related to Cybernetics, Artificial Intelligence and Computer Science and is closely bound up with information science in general terms. It is also related to problem solving, planning and decision taking which, as has been rightly said by Newell, Shaw and Simon, are equivalent to each other at more abstract levels, or even identical in their logic.

The systems viewpoint could, in some respects, be identified with the application of scientific method to any material or data at all from history to football. But in general we shall leave it to the reader to decide how and where the most useful applications are made.

The series of books is intended to be introductory but the belief is that the implications for the future are of the utmost importance.

FRANK GEORGE
BEACONSFIELD
1983

PREFACE

In this book, the first of the series on Information Technology, I have tried to take a systems approach to Investment.

I have treated Investment in broad terms and linked it closely to corporate strategy in business and to the use of tree-searches and aspects of artificial intelligence.

The undertaking is introductory in the sense that both the Investment aspect and the systems aspect are themselves familiar to specialists in each of those subjects. The difficulty implicit in trying to weld, as it were, two subjects together in this manner is that you cannot avoid over-simplifying one aspect for one section of the readers. On the other hand I have presumed that readers will in some cases - perhaps most - be unfamiliar with both the systems approach and the investment problem.

I have intentionally repeated some mention of certain central matters such as Risk Analysis and Random Walk which are central to the pilgrimage and I can only hope that the repitition does not irritate those who are already thoroughly familiar with their importance. In a sense this monograph represents, at least for the author, an experiment. Although one is continually involved in the cross-fertilisation of ideas, on this occasion the gulf between the two fields of activity is, at least for this author, wider than usual.

There is, in spite of what I have said, a background tradition for the scientific treatment of investment, and no-one has contributed to it more than Clarkson and Granger respectively. Their work has been of the highest quality and I only hope that I have managed to reflect some of their major contributions in a fair and accurate manner. I can only hope that a few readers will find the monograph useful and even fun to read, certainly it has been fun to write.

I have also to acknowledge a great deal of help I have received in the production of this book, not only from the Abacus Press, but also from the Pengelly typing agency, from my daughter Mrs. C.E.Smith for help with many aspects of the text, chapter headings and the like and from Miss Shevanthi da Silva for her drawings that were essential to the text.

I would also like to acknowledge the help shown by The Financial Times and Moodies Services Ltd., the publishers of Moodies Investment Handbook for permission to reproduce information from their respective publications. I would like to thank the Cambridge University Press, Gordon and Breach and Lexington Books for permission to reproduce material from the work of M.J.C.Surrey, A.Ghosal and C.W.J.Granger and O.Morgenstern respectively.

References to all these books appear in the text. I would especially like to draw attention to that excellent Financial Times Business Information Publication, A Guide to Financial Times Statistics, which I have also drawn on.

Finally, I would like to thank a number of people, including my wife, who have read and made helpful and constructive comments on the text itself. As is usual in these cases, the final responsibility for what appears rests with the author.

FRANK GEORGE
BEACONSFIELD
1983

CONTENTS

CHAPTER 1
INTRODUCTION

It will be assumed that you wish to make an investment with a view to making money, at least a "certain amount" of money; it will be easiest if we write from this point of view. We are carefully avoiding assuming, at least in the first instance, that you wish to hit "the jackpot" in the sense of winning £1,000,000 overnight. No one doubts that you would almost certainly be pleased to achieve such a goal, but there are many other (more realistic) goals which you might wish to achieve such as getting a 20% increase in your income or acquiring a £10,000 capital gain. It goes without saying that the more modest your ambition, the greater chance of its success. But however you tackle the subject, you must play your cards correctly. The main point is, however, that it can be done. But it requires the use of statistics, logic and scientific method. It is indeed one of many applications within the general field of information technology.

By statistics, we mean very little more than an average and a standard deviation. It is clear that if you are going to invest in a company, one of the things you would want to know is its average profit over the years. Is it decreasing or increasing? You will want, of course, to know a great deal more than that, but at least to acquire the average is a basic statistic. More can follow quite simply.

If you are to invest in order to make money you have to make a forecast of some sort and you have to take a certain risk. You can forecast by tossing a coin or throwing a die, but in general this is far too primitive a method of forecasting, so you need to add something else, and that something else is a degree of insight into whatever you are trying to forecast, and the correct methods for making that particular forecast. One well known and well established method of making money is by investing in the stock exchange, and since this will be our principal theme, let us look at that immediately, but only for the first time; it is a theme we shall return to later more than once and treat in ever increasing detail. We must not forget that when we look at the stock exchange, we will be looking at such things as average profits over the years.

We shall say something later, very briefly in passing, about forms of commodity dealing and other forms of investment and even mention gambling, since many of the same principles are involved. Indeed right from the start I would like the reader to accept analogies with horse racing, football pools, dog racing and even casino games. We will try not to overstress the considerable resemblance that exists between them, but investing in anything (particularly stocks and shares) is similar in many ways to betting on a horse race.

If you think of investment very generally as <u>any part</u> of a business activity in which you make an acquisition, diversify, etc., you are on rather different grounds from what we are considering at the moment, although we shall come to consider such variations later, since it is all part of what you need to know to be a successful investor. Before we turn to the first and most fundamental feature of investment in the stock market which is forecasting, let me just make an important point about value. The value of an investment lies in its cash value, present or future, and is concerned with the minimum investment at minimum risk, with maximum potential payoff, where the payoff may, according to the investor's needs, be either short or long term.

Investments then can vary in three ways:

1. In their degree of liquidity
2. In the return one can expect
3. In the level of risk involved in the investment.

An investment is said to be liquid if one can convert it in to cash almost immediately whenever one wishes. Examples of liquid assets are shares and Premium Bonds. However some assets are not liquid; some life insurance policies are very non-liquid as one cannot regain the deposits until an agreed number of years have passed. An investment in a physical object such an an antique or a picture or some other "personal" property is not necessarily liquid, as one cannot always find a buyer at exactly the right moment. The ability to sell such investments with little delay is known as the marketability of the commodity.

Investments such as shares in most large companies are liquid only because there are so many people involved in the market that they are therefore easily marketed, but a large holding in a minor company may well be difficult to sell at any given moment. The same is true of commodities: most are easily marketed, but some are not so at all times. Thus if one is particularly concerned with liquidity it is better in invest in the more popular commodities, which are generally the most liquid.

In this chapter we are thinking strictly of investing in the stock market. This is open to the public and to any investor. It is true that investment is also a part of total business involvement, but only a part. Now we can think of it as a "game", since it is in some ways similar to a 1-person game (indeed, as we have said already, it is like football pools, horse racing and dog racing, and these are 1-person games) in that it involves risks and yet it is not, in general, what is often called "a game against nature" (this is exemplified by sciences like physics and chemistry) in so far as the "nature" of a 1-person game can be in some considerable measure affected by our bets. As a scientist observing nature (certainly as a physicist or a chemist), he does not significantly change what he observes, but here in the stock market he certainly could. We shall say more about games later.

To make the last point clear it is necessary to consider two different aspects of forecasting. As examples let us, in the first case, consider weather forecasting and in the second case economic forecasting. Whatever my forecast of the weather may be, it will not change what happens (this is an example of a game against nature), in the case of economic forecasting however, what I forecast may lead governments to act in a way that wholly changes my forecast. This is a 2-person game in which both the forecaster and the government (or whoever makes economic policy) are both active. This is, of course, the cause of many complaints by econometricians to the effect that their influential forecasting actually makes their own forecasting wrong. In this sense investment can perhaps be thought of as a 2-person game.

The "form" in stocks and shares is a little more difficult than the form of a horse or dog, partly in that we, in some greater measure, supply the form ourselves as punters by showing confidence in (or otherwise) our team: i.e. the stocks and shares we select. There is, of course, an interaction in the other cases too, since the odds there change according to our betting, but also according to (presumably) the actual form of the horse; in a sense, there is less form and more questions of confidence that constrain the stock market.

There is one further point about stocks and shares that should be mentioned immediately. The need for large amounts of information is very great, and that means that the need for access to a computer is now considerable. If we may continue to borrow on the comparison with horse racing, we can say that there are many more different shares to invest in than there are horses to select from, in any one country, and that makes the use of the computer that much more important. We shall be discussing the sources of information in a later chapter in some detail.

To process quickly all the information required to make a successful investment calls for a sizeable data base, as will become apparent. The words 'data base' are used here intentionally to associate the whole process with the computer, although it can of course (logically) be done without. It should perhaps be made absolutely clear that the main role the computer plays, at this stage, is to process quickly large quantities of data. This can be of the utmost importance in conditions of urgency. The computer may also be used, as we shall see, to evaluate the data.

The sort of measures we have of the Stock Exchange (the bookmaker, the Tote, and Ladbrokes all rolled into one) are much the same sort of measures that we have of a horse's form: weight carried, the going, the jockey, the history of the horse, the trainer, etc., which are all mirrored by factors such as outstanding overdraft, the market, the chairman and board, the financial history of the company, and so on.

This, above all, is still gambling in that you are taking, hopefully, a calculated risk and placing a bet (making an investment) and hoping in time (short or long) to sell out at a profit, or perhaps acquire a steady income (your goal has to be made explicit). So let us look at the situation. Our equivalent to the Sporting Life's racecards is the Financial Times' share prices. Look at the following brief sample: our problem is now to produce a collection of share investments (a so-called portfolio) which will go up in value and yield a capital gain on sale, or yield a good and secure income, or whatever is required by the customer.

To judge the best way to do this requires that we know the "form" of the company and the following column from the Financial Times illustrates exactly (but briefly) the information available daily to a financial tipster. Our example, is taken at random from the Financial Times and shows information about a typical set of stocks and shares:-

Garages and Distributors

122	93	Adams Gibbon..	116	......	†4.63	2.7	5.7	7.6
11½	8	Alexanders 10p	9	......	—	—	—	—
37	25	Appleyard Grp..	34	......	—	—	—	—
156	98	Arlington Motor..	143	......	6.5	2.6	6.5	(6.7)
21½	9	BSG Int. 10p....	19	......	0.1	—	0.8	—
180	138	Bramall (C. D.).	163	......	†d6.0	2.9	5.3	9.4
*212	150	Brit. Car Auct. 10p	191	−2	b5.0	2.1	3.7	18.2
142	112	Caffyns 50p......	116	......	4.5	—	5.5	—
90	34	Cowie (T.) 5p...	34	−2	d2.0	1.8	8.4	(7.7)
113	72	Davis Godfrey...	72	......	h3.2	2.1	6.4	10.8
69	49½	Gates (F.G.).....	57	......	d3.0	2.9	6.0	6.5
38	31	Glanfield Lawr.	34	......	—	—	—	—
31	16	Hanger Invs. 10p.	29	......	—	—	—	—
70½	53½	Harrison (T.C.).	60	......	h2.2	3.6	5.2	4.6
102	80	Hartwells.........	83	−1	4.4	2.6	7.6	6.1
116	78	Henlys 20p.......	83	+5	0.1	—	0.2	—
92	55	Hurst (Charles)	83	......	d3.58	4.3	6.2	4.1
76	38	Jessups	73	+1	t3.0	2.1	5.9	(14.4)
*112	77	Kenning Mtr.....	107	......	g6.5	2.1	8.7	(7.8)
368	150	Lex Service......	325	......	†8.1	2.4	3.6	13.6
85	55	Lookers...........	81	+2	3.85	2.1	6.8	(8.1)
15½	8½	Manor Nat. Group 20p..	13	......	B—	—	—	—
103	82	Perry (H.) Mtrs...	86	......	3.75	2.8	6.3	7.1
51	31	Quick (H. & J.) 10p..	45xd	......	1.45	—	4.6	—
188	103	Tate of Leeds...	170	......	♦1.25	25.0	1.0	3.9
63	39	Western Mtr. ...	50	......	—	—	—	—
60	21	Young (H.).......	50	−1	—	—	—	—

NEWSPAPERS, PUBLISHERS

290	170	Ass. Book P. 20p.	290	......	6.5	2.9	3.2	12.1
418	138	Assoc. News.....	380	−3	10.4	2.1	3.9	17.5
102	74	BPM Hldgs. 'A'	100	......	5.78	0.1	8.4	—
230	96	Benn Brothers..	208	......	♦4.2	1.5	2.9	32.6
203	133	Black (A. & C.).	200	......	7.5	3.2	5.4	6.3
290	220	Bristol Post......	285	......	16.0	1.1	8.0	15.8
340	240	Collins William.	330xd	......	g8.5	2.9	3.7	(11.0)
*308	190	Do. "A"	295xd	......	g8.5	2.9	4.1	(9.8)
785	395	Daily Mail 'A' 50p.	735	......	†31.0	1.0	6.0	24.6
77	51	E. Mid. Allied 'A'	67	......	h2.0	2.2	4.3	14.7
*129	23	Fleet Hldgs.	124xd	......	2.25	φ	2.6	φ
117	90	Gordon & Gotch	110	−2	7.5	1.5	9.7	10.0
210	170	Haynes Pub 20p..	195xd	+10	11.0	φ	8.1	φ
115	65	Home Counties.	100xd	......	5.0	0.9	7.1	22.9
*128	82	Independent.....	123	......	Q56.9%	1.6	9.0	8.9
690	402	Int. Thomson‖..	688	−2	gQ25c	—	2.4	-
473	313	Link House 20p	473	......	†12.3	2.1	3.7	17.9
185	138	L'pool D. Post 50p	180xd	......	†10.2	1.1	8.1	16.2
147	120	✠Metal Bulletin 10p.	123	......	6.0	1.7	7.1	11.7
315	108	News Int. Sp. Div..	310xd	−5	6.71	φ	3.1	φ
433	348	Octopus Publishing	427	......	‡8.0	2.3	2.6	20.4
158	116	Portsm'th & Sund.	158	......	3.75	4.8	3.4	7.0
180	130	Routledge & KP..	150	......	—	—	—	—
455	315	Sharpe (W. N.) Hldgs...	315	......	†9.0	4.3	4.1	8.0
270	168	Utd. Newspapers.	255xd	+5	¶13.0	1.4	7.8	(13.6)
104	38	Websters Grp. 5p	101	......	2.7	2.6	3.8	14.2

PAPER, PRINTING ADVERTISING

103	62	✠Aidcom Int. 10p	75	−1	g0.6	3.4	1.2	35.6
*93	57	Assoc. Paper....	89	......	t4.2	2.8	6.9	6.7
70	26	Ault & Wiborg..	36	......	‡1.25	1.5	‡	(16.4)
213	141	Bemrose	210xd	......	†10.0	1.9	6.8	(9.4)
370	295	Boase Massimi Pollitt	365	+10	b4.5	2.6	1.8	30.8
118	77	Brit. Printing....	104	......	§5.0	1.4	6.9	10.2
173	119	Brunning Grp....	138	......	4.72	2.1	4.9	13.9
150	84	Do. Restric. Vtg.	128	......	4.72	2.1	5.3	12.9
368	217	Bunzl	365xd	......	†9.0	2.6	3.5	13.7
353	215	Carlton Communications...	353	+3	t4.0	1.5	1.6	34.5
65	29	Causton (Sir J.)	60	......	2.13	2.1	5.1	13.5
215	125	Chapman Inds. 50p...	210	......	7.5	2.5	5.1	10.7
89	63	Clay (Richard)..	83xd	......	†3.0	1.7	5.2	16.3
83	53	Clondalkin Group.	82	......	Q35.7%	φ	8.5	φ
31	23	Cradley 10p......	29	......	d0.79	2.8	3.9	13.4
188	100	Cropper (James).	183	......	3.5	4.3	2.7	9.2
98	25	Delyn Pack 20p	95	......	1.5	5.9	2.3	8.0
116	81	DRG...............	109	......	6.0	1.0	7.9	(17.2)
60	44	East Lancs. Por	48	......	3.5	1.9	10.4	(6.1)
255	160	Eucalyptus	250	......	—	—	—	29.1
97	87	Ferry Pick 10p.	97	......	2.6	3.7	3.8	8.2
330	225	✠Fitch & Co. 10p.	270xd	......	g4.2	2.1	2.2	30.3
41	17	G.B. Papers......	38	......	1.5	3.3	5.6	6.2
204	150	Geers Gross 10p..	154	......	4.0	2.5	3.7	14.2
225	96½	Good Relats 10p..	220	−5	†h2.33	2.1	1.5	45.4
120	85	Harrison Cowley..	108	......	4.2	1.2	5.6	21.0
157	85	✠Hunterprint Grp..	135	......	g3.15	3.7	3.3	(8.8)
41	24½	✠L.C.A. Hldgs. 8p.	37	......	0.2	6.4	0.8	29.1
293	220	McCorquodale 50p	268	......	†9.0	2.2	4.8	11.0
90	65	More O'Ferr 10p	65	......	2.96	2.0	6.5	10.8
£38⅞	£27⅛	Ogilvy & M. $2.	£31¾	+½	Q$1.64	—	3.5	-
36	18	Olives Paper 20p.	27	......	Z0.35	-	1.8	87.9
525	406	Saatchi 10p.....	485	+5	†h5.8	3.1	1.7	27.0

102	52	Runciman (W.).	93	+3	5.0	1.5	7.7	11.2
£20	£14½	Sea Containers 12½p...	£17½	+⅜	Q42c	—	1.6	—

SHOES AND LEATHER

117	67	FII Group.........	94	......	d5.04	1.5	7.8	12.0
106	60	Garnar Booth...	96xd	......	†6.65	1.7	9.9	(7.3)
43½	37	Headlam, Sims 5p.	39	......	3.0	1.6	11.0	8.2
155	96	Lambert Hth. 20p	150xd	......	h4.79	3.3	4.6	9.6
63	37	Newbold & Burt'n.	56xd	−1	†3.78	1.3	9.6	11.8
61	42	Pittard Grp.......	57	−4	4.0	—	10.3	—
67	27	Strong & Fisher	62	−5	‡1.67	—	‡	—
134	100	Stylo..............	120	......	3.5	1.5	4.2	(20.1)

SOUTH AFRICANS

185	124	Abercom R0.30	158	......	Q16c	—	6.2	—
£20	£14¼	Anglo Am. In. R1.	£18	......	Q180c	2.5	5.9	6.8
*807	504	Barlow Rand R.10c..	790	−2	Q70c	2.4	5.2	8.0
405	200	Checkers Stores 'A' 50c	250	+10	Q5c	—	‡	—
206	104	Gold Flds. P. 2½c	196	+2	Q20c	φ	6.0	8.8
420	232	Messina R0.50.	390	−12	Q50c	5.1	7.5	2.6
£16¼	950	OK Bazaars 50c	£14½	......	Q142c	1.5	5.8	11.5
580	300	Rex Trueform 'A' 50c	580	......	Q55c	φ	5.8	φ
502	304	S.A. Brews. 20c..	455	−2	Q35c	1.7	4.5	13.0
£21	£11¼	Tiger Oats R1...	£19¾	......	tQ125c	2.8	3.7	10.5
345	190	Unisec 20cts.....	340	......	Q30c	1.3	5.2	14.9

TEXTILES

264	217	Allied Textile...	246	......	7.24	2.9	4.2	10.0
86	59	Atkins Bros.	82	......	5.0	0.6	8.7	(43.8)
108	61	Beales (J.) 20p.	95	......	3.0	2.5	4.5	(9.2)
86	75	Beckman A. 10p..	81	......	5.73	1.3	10.4	(9.3)
90	53½	Brit. Mohair.....	82xd	−2	4.2	2.1	7.3	8.6
53	37	Bulmer L'mb. 20p.	49	+1	3.82	—	11.1	—
83	11	Carpets Int. 50p..	62	+1	—	—	—	—
77	56	Coats Patons....	72	......	4.2	2.5	8.3	(5.4)
73	56½	Corah..............	57	−1	3.5	2.0	8.8	(6.8)
*105	69	Courtaulds........	93	−1	g3.25	2.8	5.0	8.3
£88	£80	Do. 7% Deb 82/7	£84½	......	Q7%	q23.6	e8.1	—
*32	18	Crowther (J.)...	27	−2	M1.0	—	5.3	—
173	132	Dawson intl......	157	......	6.5	2.2	5.9	9.1
112	66	Dixon (David)...	108	......	6.2	—	8.2	—
92	67	Don Brothers Buist	86xd	......	b3.5	2.7	5.8	9.3
24	17	Early's of Witney 10p...	22	−2	1.32	0.8	8.7	(24.7)
40	24	Foster (John)...	35	−1	1.5	1.2	6.1	(17.8)
87	48	Gaskell B'loom 20p.	85	......	3.5	2.5	5.9	9.7
90	35	Hicking P'st. 50p.	50	......	2.0	—	6.0	—
23	15	Ill'gworth M. 20p	17	......	♦—	—	—	—
13	9	Do. 'A' 20p.....	12	......	♦—	—	—	—
328	18	Ingram (H.) 10p..	300#	......	♦—	—	—	—
74	62	Jerome (Hldgs.)..	67	......	2.69	0.1	5.7	—
112	98	Leeds Grp	100	......	†hd3.75	2.9	5.4	8.1
47	30	Lister..............	34	......	0.1	6.0	0.4	(41.5)
49	29	Lowe (Robert H.)	30	......	‡3.27	—	‡	—
106	83	Lyles (S.) 20p..	97	+1	6.25	1.4	9.2	9.6
67	44	Mackay Hugh...	64	+2	4.0	1.0	9.3	(14.8)
64	41	Martin (A.) 20p	45	......	t2.0	2.4	6.4	(7.5)
65	47	Miller (F.) 10p.	47	......	h1.35	3.0	4.1	11.7
47	18	Montfort.........	39	−1	♦—	—	—	—
*47	35	Munton Bros 10p.	43½xr	+½	3.0	1.3	9.9	(11.0)
250	190	Notts. Manfg....	190	−2	†5.1	3.4	3.9	9.1
95	51	Nova Jersey 20p..	55	−1	4.0	1.8	10.4	(6.3)
79	47	Parkland 'A'.....	73	......	3.7	1.9	7.2	(8.9)
44	22	Reliance Knit 20p	37	......	1.75	2.7	6.8	(6.3)
27	19	Richards 10p....	23	......	0.6	—	3.7	—
86	62	S.E.E.T. 20p....	75	......	3.5	φ	6.7	φ
29	13	Sekers Int. 10p.	19xd	......	m—	—	—	φ
18	10	Shaw & Marvin 10p.	11½	......	—	—	—	—
38	22	Shaw Carpets 10p.	35	......	1.5	0.9	6.1	24.9
192	164	Sirdar	190xd	+2	5.05	φ	3.8	φ
65	40	Small & Tidmas	60	......	—	—	—	—
35	20	Smallshaw R. 10p.	29	......	1.8	2.3	8.9	(5.6)
53	31	Sn. Viscosa L1200	47	......	—	—	—	—
24	17	Spencer (Geo.).	19xd	......	0.1	—	0.8	—
16	7½	Stoddard 'A' 10p.	14	......	—	—	—	—
98	74	Stroud Riley Dr'd	75	......	2.25	3.8	4.3	6.8
11½	6½	Sumner (F.) ...	9	+½	—	—	—	—
46	18	Sunbeam Wolsey.	35	−1	†Q16.4%	2.6	9.2	5.7
79	58	Text'rd Jrsy. 10p.	67	......	4.0	1.3	8.5	(11.6)
195	100	Tomkinsons......	173	......	4.2	3.7	3.5	8.4
37	29½	Tootal	34	+1	2.35	1.7	9.9	(7.1)
119	94	Toray Y50........	112	......	tQ11½%	2.1	1.4	34.3
440	330	Yorklyde 20p....	330	......	18.0	3.1	7.8	5.9
17	3½	Youghal	13½	......	—	—	—	—

TOBACCOS

185	130	BAT Inds..........	133	......	h6.88	3.6	7.4	4.2
131	108	Imperial	116xd	......	7.25	2.0	8.9	7.3
132	98	Rothmans 12½p..	111	......	5.3	6.2	6.8	2.5

204	180
91	68
78	60½
77	58½
72	59½
68	55½
230	191
118	87
115	80
88½	77½
84	72
625	500
89	68
318	272
68	40
38½	23½
29	22
12	7
228	138
143	115
227	182
140	128
142	112
226	178
409	262
130	76
97	76
141	106
231	154
91	34
233	186
83	73
102	73
159	118
£71⅛	£57¼
715	572
£69¾	£54
699	540
193	145
£47½	£41½
58	50
187	168
134	115
258	198
194	157
289	276
118	98
193	159
286	216
266	202
164	121
110	77
408	328
82	67
176	139
228	172
142	116
40	30
130	104
218	162
173	116
116	67
113	84
218	166
158	116
191	127
108	86½
148	115½
95	78½
86	71
36	30
202	172
165	137
160	142
240	182
144	111
159	117
75½	67
440	390
175	129
94	60
187	113
487	378
67	40
113	80
206	150
50	37
240	154

1983	
High	Low
326	298

All of this sort of basic data will be exhibited in more detail and studied more carefully later.

Beyond this point of tactical buying and selling, we are interested in providing a sort of model of the investment process and are, therefore, primarily concerned with the processing of information and the taking of decisions under conditions of uncertainty. The process involves the selection of a portfolio in the light of:

1. The philosophy involved, such as a customer's beliefs and his desire for maximising capital growth as opposed to income.
2. Uncertainty over market trends.
3. When to buy and sell, especially if the investment is short-term and usually therefore intended to provide a quick capital gain.

Let us next say a few words on risk.

RISK AND RETURN

The return on an investment is usually taken to be the gain (or loss) over some stated period measured as a percentage of the capital involved, i.e. to quote Granger.

$$\text{Return} = \frac{\text{Final value - Initial value of investment}}{\text{Initial value}} \times 100$$

We naturally prefer an investment that gives a high return to one that gives a low return, but unfortunately comparison of investments is complicated by the fact that there is also a level of risk to consider.

Risk Analysis is a standard method of measuring risk. You can think of it in terms of a simple matrix (see also appendix II):

$$\begin{array}{c} \\ A_1 \\ A_2 \\ A_3 \end{array} \begin{array}{c} \begin{array}{ccc} B_1 & B_2 & B_3 \end{array} \\ \begin{bmatrix} 2 & 10 & 30 \\ 4 & 1 & 1 \\ 8 & 12 & 7 \end{bmatrix} \end{array}$$

Where B_1, B_2, B_3, are events equally likely to happen. So to maximise our payoff we bet on A_1 rather than A_2 or A_3, which are our three choices. If we want to minimise our loss if we are wrong (the so-called Minimax Regret technique) we subtract each value of the column from the maximum value of that column, that in the above example gives:

$$\begin{bmatrix} 6 & 2 & 0 \\ 2 & 11 & 29 \\ 0 & 0 & 13 \end{bmatrix}$$

This means that the best course is still A_1. The point about risk is that you will be balancing risk of loss against the size of the investment, so you may be happy to go for the "jack-pot" with a mere £100 investment, but with a £10,000 investment you will be much more likely to assess the possible loss. This shifts your aims from attacking to defensive tactics. This also leads to diversification. In the above example we have assumed B_1, B_2, B_3 are equally probable (this is the uncertainty factor). If B_1 had the probability of happening (i.e. of shares or commodities going up in price) which was much greater than the probabilities for B_2 and B_3 together, say, then this would change the situation and would probably lead you to choose A_3 above. Even if we drop numbers altogether (they are often subjective probabilities and not particularly reliable) and look only in a general way and can only say:

1. Very likely to rise in price.
2. Likely to rise in price.
3. Not so likely to rise in price.
4. Unlikely to rise in price.
5. Likely to fall in price.

and suchlike classes of possible outcomes, based hopefully on some hypothesis backed by some evidence, then we should still think in exactly the same way about balancing our assessment of the risk against uncertainty.

Clearly risk is difficult to measure and depends on the attitudes of the individual as well as his financial state. To some an investment may seem risky if it cannot be converted immediately into cash at all times, so that a very specialised antique which is not necessarily readily sold would appear risky. However, to most, risk can be related to the possibility of making a loss. It is clear that risk arises because of uncertainty about what will occur in the future, but risk and uncertainty are not the same. Suppose one is given a bond and told that almost certainly one will get a return of x percent but that there is a possibility of getting 2x percent; either return is acceptable, the uncertainty is not a 'risk', in the usual sense of the word, since we are not implying the possibility of losing money.

Some risk is though normally involved in investment. Even a fixed-interest asset, such as a bank deposit account, which gives a certain return and may thus seem riskless, could in a period of inflation, if the return is measured in terms of its real value rather than the monetary value, be a loss. One has lost the opportunity of getting a positive return from a fixed-interest investment, this being called the opportunity cost of the investment. A share is obviously a risky asset, as it is very possible to make a loss over any prescribed period. Clearly one balances risk against return in terms of what one can afford to risk. One way of reducing risk is to spread one's investments (diversify) over several assets. The best way to build up a portfolio is a very complicated procedure that is attempted by very few investors, but a good rule is to put part of one's savings into a fixed-interest, low-risk asset and to spread the rest over three or four assets, such as shares, investment trust bonds and commodities, whose prices do not move together. This point will be made clear in our discussion of Clarkson in a later chapter.

THE MARKET PLACE

What we are looking for is an investment theory (some basis for making good investments), which is a theory of the Stock Market and its relations with investors which enables us to invest in the soundest possible way. The theory must be pragmatic and be effective; there are many such theories and we shall be considering some of them. One well known such theory is the Dow theory of the New York Stock Exchange.

The Stock Exchange Market is the market place where buyers and sellers come together (just as a market place for food, antiques, or anything at all). The buyers and sellers more or less agree standard prices which are the prices of the stocks and shares, and these can be found daily in the press. The go-between is the stockbroker who advises, sells and purchases and acts for a client at an agreed fee.

The <u>issuing house</u> is a financial firm which specialises in selling of new stocks and shares for the first time to the general public. It undertakes to sell all of a new issue and can insure itself against the possibility of failure.

We shall in this book be concerned with describing and comparing a number of theories of investment. These will apply primarily to a portfolio. This is a collection of shares held by an individual or an institution, and it is the selection of portfolios (rather than individual shares, although they will also be considered) that is our primary concern. This involves, although is not wholly dependent upon the forecasting of prices.

Before we go any further, a brief word must be said about the Stock Exchange. Although we have London primarily in mind, many of the same conditions exist in all other Western and many Eastern countries. It is our formal name for the market place, where the "commodity" sold is the share certificate. This enables the owner to partake in the profits of the company in whose name the share was issued. There are ordinary shares which form the majority of a company's shares, but there are also preference shares which are scarcer and give priviledge to the holder in the event of liquidation or bankruptcy, when whatever assets that remain are shared out.

The question of shares only arises in the joint stock company and does not in any "official" way apply to a one-man business or a partnership. The private limited liability company involves shares, but there is no Stock Exchange quotation. The public joint stock company is the one that features on the Stock Exchange. Besides ordinary and preference shares there are also debentures which is in the form of a loan to the company on which a fixed interest is paid, and this interest is paid before profit is assessed and a dividend declared for payment to shareholders. So we can concentrate on the Stock Exchange and public companies.

The Stock Exchange itself is made up of stock-jobbers of whom are about 700 in the London Stock Exchange and they fix the share prices.

There is a council of 36 members which controls the Stock Exchange, decides upon its rules, admits new members and considers offers for sale of new shares and the like. In raising new capital, a company will go to the issuing house and is paid immediately, leaving the job of selling the shares to the issuing house.

Besides issuing houses, there are accepting houses, some of which also act as issuing houses; there are some 18, almost all private or public joint-stock companies that are members of the Accepting Houses Committee. They are often called Merchant Banks. One of their roles is that of discounting. Discounting is really taking a post-dated cheque. For example, to receive £900 now may be more valuable to me than £1000 six months later. I could invest it and make up the difference or buy essential products for manufacturing (it could be £9,000 or £90,000 now for the equivalent later). In any event it is a form of credit which is sometimes carried out by accepting houses, but is especially done by discounting houses. There is a London Discount Market Association and there are some 12 member companies of this and all of the main ones are organised in the form of public joint-stock companies. One half of the assets of the discounting houses is in the form of treasury bills (like ordinary commercial bills) which are negotiable and offered weekly for sale to the highest bidder. The Bank of England undertakes this work for the treasury and they are redeemed at face value normally after three months. The government is, in effect, paying for a short-term loan.

The role of the clearing banks (in the "high street") is too well known to be described. Indeed no more will be said about the system, since anyone interested in more detail can get more such detailed descriptions from many different sources. We are concerned with making effective investments, but a little knowledge of the background should be some help to us, and is of some interest in its own right. If you were going to play roulette you would want to know something of the "set up" of the casino before you went.

The analogy of the casino is a useful one because stocks and shares are like "chips" and the Stock Exchange is similar in methods (although usually regarded as more "morally" acceptable) to the casino and its roulette tables. The ressemblance goes further in fact, since both the bank in roulette and the Stock Exchange in investment always win. That does not mean that you cannot win, but it does mean that you are winning (in both cases) other people's (other investors) money: those that do not use scientific methods. It is known that some people make a living out of both gambling and investment, so our aim is to show how it is done. So let us look now at investment.

The central problem of Investment Analysis is clearly share-price prediction. Which shares will go up and which will go down and when will the change come from one to the other? Share-prices can fluctuate rapidly since a week can produce major changes, and in exceptional cases, shares can "shoot up" or "fall flat" overnight.

Although the jobber fixes the price, he has to tread warily, since too great a change made too quickly could produce a demand which he cannot meet, or he could become overwhelmed by too many unsaleable shares. Needless to say, the jobber does not announce his views since it would make buying and selling easier for the investor and thus reduce the jobber's profits.

The investor is therefore left to make his own forecasts. We do not want to worry about how a broker thinks, although his problem is exactly the same as ours, and he too will make his forecast based on some investment theory, or he should do.

There is one crucial point about investment and it is really a psychological one. Once other people are seen to be buying and there is a belief that something worthwhile is happening, and there can be an avalanche of buying, a huge rise in the share price occurs. Sometimes this will be justified by events or rumours, but sometimes not. The famous "South Sea Bubble" and the more recent Poseidon Affair illustrates the complete failure of hasty buying in a huge way. The same thing, of course, often happens the other way around, where a false rumour of approaching bankruptcy will suddenly lower a share's value. In each case the forecast is self-fulfilling, and much of investment is a matter of confidence. Our main argument will be that the greater the knowledge and therefore the greater the forecasting ability then the greater the confidence. We must never leave these psychological factors out of our thinking, or out of our methods.

We shall also throughout this book be thinking of a man who is investing singlehanded, who may or may not have the help of a computer. With the development of microprocessors, so many will be able to write or run (or both) programs themselves that we shall frequently talk as if we intended to write a program. Such an attitude is desirable, whether or not we actually ever use a computer. Now let us begin our prilgrimage; first of all in quite simple terms.

BASIC INFORMATION

The following information is the very least that is needed for the purpose of providing a computer program, or even for building up a file for the purpose of making your investments:

1. A file of company types and particular companies in each relevant type. Their trading state and prospects are also obviously relevant. Here one must distinguish carefully between facts and opinions. One is guided by expert opinion, balance sheets, profit and loss accounts and, of course, share prices.

2. A file stating economic conditions and trends, the existing taxation regulations, the legal situation, etc. These all act as constraints on our selection procedures.

3. A search through a list of possible investments and the acquisition by selection and evaluation procedures of a list of probable investments.

4. This finally leads to the setting up of an actual portfolio.

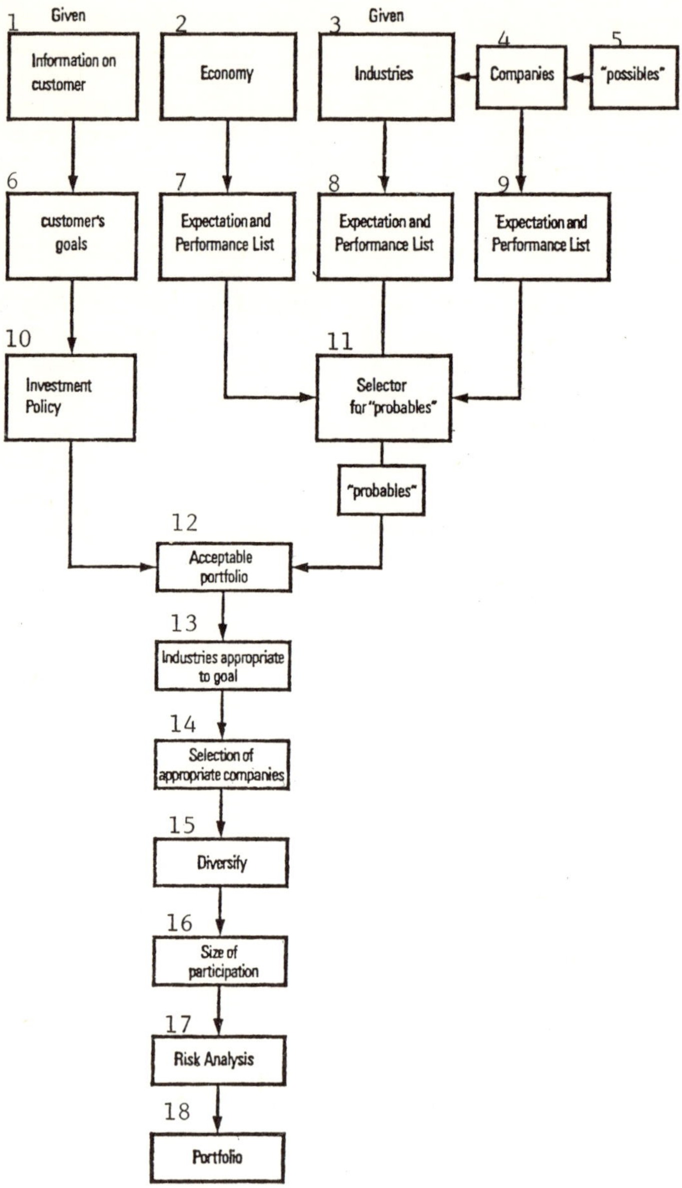

Figure 1 A general representation of the investment process.

Now we ought to explain some part of what is entailed in Figure 1. No detail will be gone into at this stage (we deal with that later), but at least we can outline the principles.

First of all (box 1) we see what information we have on the potential customer: for the individual investing this means a knowledge of his goals (e.g. income or capital). It also means a knowledge of balance sheet, profit and loss account, potential, etc. of the firm to be invested in (if only in very general terms) in the present economy (box 2), since it is this and its prospects (also political considerations) that will influence the choice of investment. We shall think here in terms of a complete portfolio, rather than a single investment. But as we have previously said, the same logic applies in both cases.

Box 10 involves investment policy and this may be the general philosophy of a multi-national company right down to the beliefs of an individual. Box 7 leads to an expectation of the future in the light of the past (a forecast in the light of the economy, the investor's philosophy and the performance of types of company).

Box 3 lists the industries and their more detailed characteristics, and into this are fed the categorised list of companies (box 4) which are "possible" investment sources (box 5).

Companies themselves, as well as industries, lead into an assessment of the future in the light of the past. So all three boxes 2,3 and 4 provide a list of industries, and then companies within any particular industries that meet the customer's requirements, or at least are likely (forecast) to do so.

We now return to box 6 and establish the customer's goals or aims: what is he trying to achieve? Income or capital are the most obvious objectives, but a mixture of the two and possibly other alternatives are possible. Box 10, which is the customer's investment policy, will be dictated by many considerations. These will be primarily his goals, but may also include beliefs that he holds that certain industries (or companies) provide a particularly good investment.

In the meantime, the expectations and previous performance considerations (details of how these are derived will be described later) are fed, with the contents of box 10, into what would seem to be a filter. The result is a portfolio, which specifies in rather general terms the type of industries (and companies within those industries) appropriate to the customer's goal (or goals). There is no guarantee that this will lead to a satisfactory end portfolio, and we may have to return to box 12 or box 13, according to the nature of the dissatisfaction with the proposed final portfolio (this will have to be spelt out in detail to answer the question in box 20).

In the meantime the process of selecting industries and companies is carried out, and clearly this is an operation that may be repeated many times according to the acceptability of the "final" portfolio. The details of the selection process stems directly from the adopted theory of investment, and this is one of the matters which we have to discuss in great detail. The next step, which is one of the key steps in deciding on the satisfactory outcome, is risk analysis. This too will require some later explanation, but here, since it is perhaps the least obvious step, in principle, can be outlined again immediately.

The role of risk analysis is simply to decide what the risk is in any investment or for any portfolio. This is really a check of the sensitivity of the portfolio. Could it be upset easily by a change of circumstances such as joining (or leaving) the EEC, the election of a new president, a recession or a boom, and so on and so forth? At this stage we can go back to our analogy with the gambling and say: here are the odds on the horses. What horse (or horses) will you bet on? The answer is clearly bound up with the amount of capital (especially "risk capital") you have available. If you have a small amount you will play with great care and be concerned with the defensive policy and not losing and hopefully making small gains. If you have a huge amount of capital you will balance some risk against some safety, and be prepared to adopt a strategy of increasing risk, either in the case of success or failure, as long as the losses are only a small percentage of your whole investment. In a sense, Figure 1 is slightly misleading in suggesting that risk only occurs before the implementation of the final portfolio, since it could, of course, also be used at other stages in the selection process. This might have the effect of short circuiting the whole operation, and feeding back to any earlier stage, after box 12, for example.

Figure 1 outlines the general principles involved then in selecting a portfolio. What we will need to do is to look at the various ways of carrying out the detailed steps which come within the boxes, and this will lead us into a comparison of theories of investment and a judgement as to which method is best.

A WORD ON PROBABILITY THEORY AND SCIENCE

We said right at the beginning of this chapter that a forecast could be made by tossing a coin or throwing a die. Let us in anticipation of just a few more probabilistic methods, notice what tossing a coin or throwing a die (or dice) entails.

If you toss a "fair" coin it can come down heads (H) or tails (T) and the chances of each are ½. The ½ is arrived at by saying that the probability of the event occurring, say H, is the top part of the fraction of all possibilities. So H = 1 and (H or T) = 2, therefore for either H or T the chances are ½, 50:50 or evens - these are all ways of expressing the same thing.

One difficulty is that, assuming it is a fair coin, that the probability is the same for each toss; they are independent of each other. So if you get a series of HHHHH, then the probability of T still remains (as does H) ½ for the next toss. Of course if you got 30 or 40 H's running you might well suspect that the coin was not a fair one and had H's on both sides. The fact also remains that if you go on long enough (say 1,000 tosses) then there will be a tendency for H's and T's to each occur about 500 times.

A die is slightly more complicated because there are 6 possibilities instead of 2. This means that the chance of throwing a 6 (or any of the numbers on the die) is 1/6. The chance of throwing an even number (2,4,6) is ½, and the same for an odd number. Treated this way the die is reduced to a coin. Now the only immediate and simple application of this to investment is in a situation where 4 probabilities exist in the 6 possibilities of the throw of the die. The chance of success is 4/6 (the same as 2/3) and therefore a good investment. If on the other hand the chance of success is 2/6 (the same as 1/3) then the investment is not likely to be a good one. 5/6 is the better case and 1/6 is the bad case and are even more extreme examples of a good and a bad investment, without going to the limits of positive or negative certainty. We shall have to extend these extremely simple beginnings to probability assessment just a little more as we go along.

We can also think of probability in ordinary language. We do not need to measure it numerically and sometimes cannot do so in any case. So we can say "what are the chances of it raining today?" Dark clouds and a weather forecast suggesting rain makes one answer "yes, it probably will". Similarly a blue sky and a good weather forecast may make your answer "no, I do not think it at all likely". Then we get the gradations of uncertainty in between. In broad terms there are usually about 7 grades of probability statement (a seven-valued logic):

1. Certain (or almost so)
2. Very likely.
3. Likely
4. Completely uncertain

5. Unlikely
6. Very unlikely
7. Certainly not (or almost so)

We can do just as well with these seven grades of probability as we can with "subjective probabilities" in which persons will say the probability is 1 in 5 or 1 in 6, etc. Such attempts to put "guesses" (even informed guesses) into numerical form gains nothing.

Before we conclude this first chapter, let us say a few words on the nature of science, as we shall think of it. Science is an extension of common sense, involving greater precision and often, because it wishes (or needs) to make distinctions we do not need in everyday life, it develops a great deal of new terminology, or jargon as some will call it. Science is a conjunction of hypothetico-deductive method with methods of explanation.

The general points of science are to make assumptions (with some evidence) and see what the consequences of those assumptions are. The other way around is to build up the assumptions as a result of observation, especially of things which happen together, or always follow each other. The assumption is usually made, with great care, that one thing causes the other, i.e. if I see a man kick at a ball then I am not surprised to see it fly through the air, because we say the kick caused the ball so to move. Similarly in investment the cause of the share price is caused by factors in the economy, the industry or the country that causes an increased profit or increased loss, and therefore a greater confidence (or otherwise) in their share value.

Logic clearly enters into science and we make logical inferences from assumptions to consequences, or vice-versa. But the most important point is that we can only determine whether our prediction is right or wrong if we know the results of our efforts. So we must find out whether the share prices went up or down, whether we predicted correctly, and what the reasons were. We want to be able to recognise the same circumstances if they occur again.

So much then for the start of proceedings. In the next chapter we get down one step into more detail.

REFERENCES CHAPTER 1

1. F.H.George, Precision, Language and Logic. Pergamon Press, 1979.

2. R.C.Jeffrey, The Logic of Decision, McGraw-Hill, 1965.

3. C.V.Negoita, Fuzzy Systems, Abacus Press, 1981.

4. C.W.J.Granger (Ed)., Trading in Commodities, Woodhead-Faulkner, 1974.

5. R.M.Thrall, C.H.Coombs and R.S.Davies. Decision Processes, Wiley, 1954.

6. G.P.E.Clarkson, 'Portfolio selection: a simulation of the trust investment process'. In Computers and Thought, E.A.Feigenbaum and J.Feldman (Eds)., McGraw-Hill, 1963.

7. F.H.George, The Science of Philosophy, Gordon and Breach, 1981.

8. C.G.Hempel and Paul Oppenheim 'The logic of explanation'. In Readings in the Philosophy of Science, H.Feigl and M.Brodbeck (Eds)., Appleton-Century-Crofts.

CHAPTER 2
THE RANGE OF INVESTMENT

We have already made clear that investment is not merely for increasing income, at least in the direct sense, but can also be for capital gains, which has though the same indirect sense of increasing income, if only ultimately. To increase capital one could save money, either by decreasing expenses or by putting aside unspent cash. The question which arises is as to what you will do with unused money? You have a whole range of choices as an individual which could be to spend more on the house and increase its capital value or to invest in some way in government bonds or in any of a whole host of ways; all of this we are going to try to decide about, and that is indeed the subject of this whole book (especially how to do it sensibly and efficiently, in fact scientifically).

But before we go any further we must realise that the economic state of the country is vitally important to the investor, and the first and most obvious manner of its importance is inflation. If prices (of materials) go up, costs (of production) go up (and vice-versa), wages go up, tax goes up, and the whole process spirals upwards. In these circumstances, money saved today will be worth far less tomorrow. Capital assets diminish and so on and so forth. Deflation is precisely the other way around, so that savings and assets increase in value. A somewhat similar situation arises over the exchange rate in the money market and as a result the British, in 1980, found it cheap to go to the USA for holidays, and in the years before that (and again since) the Americans find it cheap to come to Britain. It is simply that if you get $2.25 for each £1 when you go to Miami, you are much better off than if you only get $1.80.

These sort of simple arguments apply in exactly the same way in the business world where new factories may be needed, old ones improved and, as a result, you have to import raw materials and export finished goods, and so on and so forth. Inflation and Exchange Rates are vital features that no company can conceivably ignore.

It is of obvious interest that any country's government will seek to provide a balanced state of affairs. It can thus exercise some control by taxation of various kinds, and also on interest rates and the extent of the money supply. The former can take various forms, and the forms usually taken (whatever they are) are a subject of much dispute. The interest rates are like a brake that makes money cheaper or more expensive to borrow and thus directly influences the economy.

The problem for the business man, trying to raise money for his project, is to make the terms attractive to the investor, and also to provide a degree of security. Broadly speaking, higher rates of return to the investor mean higher risk and this is a matter that the investor has to decide upon and one way is, as we shall be discussing later, to diversify i.e. to put his money in everything from gilt-edged securities and so-called "blue chip" investments right down to high risk investment (what is often referred to as "risk capital"). The ratio of "what-to-what" depends upon the available capital and the investor's aims. The competitors in the field of the private business man, all encouraging investment and from which one must choose are:

Life Assurance
Pension Schemes
National Savings
Building Societies
Real Property
Mortgages (on property)
and
Marketable Securities

The first six of these are all fairly well-known and occur in various forms. We shall therefore concentrate our attention for the rest of this chapter on marketable securities in all its wide ramifications.

MARKETABLE SECURITIES

Marketable securities means precisely securities (assets of every kind in the shape of paper guarantees of a particular kind known variously as bonds, stocks, shares, etc). We already made clear in the last chapter something of the role of the Stock Exchange. This applies to London especially, but also to associated Stock Exchanges situated in the leading cities of the country, and indeed in other countries.

Lists of stocks and shares are available and we can get most of what we need in Britain from the daily press. The lists contain the name of each security, the bid price (the price at which it can be sold) and the offered price (the price at which it can be bought). These prices are necessarily approximate and refer to the state of affairs one hour before the close of business each day.

There is a vast range of securities quoted but there are many particularly nationalised industries - which get no quotation on the Stock Exchange. The dealing is done through the stockbroker or more rarely through a unit trust which I shall be describing later.

The jobber is a specialist who will deal with government stock, tobacco shares or whatever, and the stockbroker gets, on behalf of his clients, estimates from several of them in the form of two prices: the higher is his selling price and the lower his buying price. Included in his pricing will be his own charge.

The jobber's risk, and therefore potential gain, lies in selling shares on a "bear" market, where things are bad and he may not yet possess the shares, and the equivalent position, that of buying shares on a "bull" (good) market when he has no immediate buyer. The width of the price the jobber asks (difference between bid and offered prices) will be determined by the degree of public interest in the relevant shares. It is rather like trading in motor cars in a bull market as opposed to trading in rare antiques in a bear market.

PRICE OF MARKETABLE SECURITIES

The value or worth of any investment is dependent upon the income it is expected to yield (we shall be saying more on this subject in the next chapter). There are types of stock on which the capital is not redeemable and guarantees a fixed rate of interest. Such a fixed rate is called the par value (doubtless a reference to golf, or vice-versa) of the stock. It is also known as its face (or nominal) value. The rates of interest are controlled by the government and the Bank of England which can raise or lower the Bank rate and, by virtue of other controls, such as calling for special deposits, can influence the lending rates of the clearing banks. This takes us back on one hand to what we have already discussed under the title inflation, but here it is to be seen as the indicator of interest rates.

The buyer and seller of stocks is involved with the dividend paid up to the date of sale or purchase and this must be allowed for. In the case of ordinary shares this must be done after the dividend is declared, if indeed one is declared at all. Expenses involved in buying and selling are obviously also to be included.

The more intimate details of these transactions will be familiar to any investor, or, if not, can be discovered quickly from any one of a number of elementary texts, or from one's bank manager.

OTHER ECONOMIC FACTORS

The well-known Balance of Payments problem is relevant in any view one takes of the financial state of a country (obviously a vital factor to the investor).

Confidence is a major factor in economics and therefore in investing. We shall be reminding the reader of the South Sea Bubble and the Poseidon affair more than once. But equally, indeed more, important is the running battle to keep the country's currency one in which overseas customers and investors have confidence. If, for example, the currency is inflated, the demand is high at home, imports increase and exports decrease. This uses up financial reserves to purchase imports. The government then tries to control the situation by cutting down internal demand.

Furthermore, we can devalue (lower the exchange value of the pound or dollar, etc) and the effect is usually to destroy confidence and have a "run" (large sale of investment) on the pound; we are thinking here mainly of the U.K.

The results of these balancing acts are either that we have to pay too much for our imports when the pound's value is low and our products become uncompetitive (leaving aside the question of quality and efficiency) or if the pound's value is high we cannot compete because our completed products are still too high in price. Unless we can control internal demand, balance the import-export ratio, control the value of the pound and supply the right quality goods, then we are at a disadvantage. The cost of wages, loss of working time through strikes and lack of investment are all internal contributory factors to our uncompetitiveness which we should also bear in mind.

The picture is further complicated by the state of the world economy, which, if in recession, affects everyone, because of its interactive nature (naturally this could be a good time to buy shares) and the matter can become even more complicated if we have in the U.K. a high-value pound with respect to the dollar and a low value pound with respect to the other European currencies. The ultimate disaster occurs if you buy at a maximum price and try to sell "below quality" goods at a minimum price.

The effect on individual industries (e.g. the motor car industry, the textile industry) of all these factors must be taken into account by the investor. And even within an industry, the question of the most efficient companies is of vital importance. An economically bad sector can have one or two very profitable companies. This can happen if in a declining (temporary or otherwise) sector one company acquires almost all the business. Alternatively, in an expanding sector so many companies get on "the band waggon" that the result is that all cannot succeed and profit margins may become narrow.

A LITTLE MORE ON SECURITIES

The range of fixed interest securities is very great indeed and their yield, and therefore their value, varies accordingly. The principal classes involve Government loans, Local Authority loans and Public Authorities such as Docks and Water Boards. Also included are the Loan Debenture and Preference stocks of public companies (privately owned). These latter we are thinking of as U.K. registered companies, but foreign countries are a possible source of investment in ordinary shares and common stocks.

In the case of overseas ordinary stocks, they divide into American (of primary interest) and Commonwealth, where Canada is an exceptional case, not being a member of the sterling area. We shall return shortly to ordinary shares in general, but first let us say a little more on fixed interest securities.

The British Government securities are the result of the government's raising money by borrowing mainly by Funded Debt (where the government has no obligation to redeem), rather more on Internal Unfunded Debt which the government must at some time redeem, External Debt, and debt to the International Monetary Fund, which is the main international institution involved.

All, or virtually all, debts are publicly quoted under the names 2½ per cent Consols, 3½ per cent Conversion loan and the like (these are Funded). The unfunded arise from National Savings Certificates Defence Bonds and other such bonds, which are easily negotiable. It is the size of the undertaking in the case of the British Government which makes their bonds easily negotiable. One result of all this is that to buy or sell £1,000,000 or more of such stock may not change the price of the stock at all. Such could never be the case with other groups of stock, since a large proportion of (even the whole of) the <u>issue</u> of stock might be involved.

The advantages of government stock lie in their safety and easy negotiability, their compensating disadvantage lies in their low rate of interest. They make interesting comparison with Commonwealth Government Stock, because the latter are thought of as slightly less secure and have compensatingly better yield. As in the case of ordinary foreign or commonwealth shares they raise matters of a specialist kind and require specialist advice in general. Investors must carefully assess the news (especially in terms of economy, politics, trade and finance) and be able to assess these matters for themselves.

All these same arguments about confidence, negotiability and yield (and their interrelationship) apply to Local Authorities and Public Boards and Water Works. The largest are comparable to British Government Fixed Interest loans and the smallest to the smallest Commonwealth country's Government loans.

The Water Works Companies have often been regarded as of special interest because of their high yield and low "actual" risk. The risk involved is "theoretically" high, but the fact that they are monopolies greatly reduces that risk. It must be said though that as political, economic and other circumstances change, so degrees of confidence in different investments vary. In a sense, this is the whole matter of investment in a nutshell.

LAW AND TAXATION

Another factor which is of paramount importance to the investor is the legal situation - especially that of taxation. Capital Gains tax, which has been relatively recently introduced, is of considerable importance to the investor. In 1962, the short-term gains tax came into being, followed by long-term gains tax in 1965, and then the abolition of the short-term gains tax in 1971. The rates may change from time to time but are an essential consideration in investment; certain government securities, under certain circumstances, such as retention for more than a year, are exempt from Capital Gains tax. They are also, with Commonwealth, Local Authority and some Public Boards stocks, exempt from stamp duty, which is normally payable on transfer.

Another example of the effect of taxation is that of Preference stocks. They form part of a company's capital without voting rights (in general) and without the security of Debentures or the value of ordinary stock. Their one time relatively high yields have been off-set by the fact that companies have to pay Corporation tax on the profits on which Preference holders' dividends are paid.

In general, therefore, as of this time (but times change, or may do) the Preference Stock is usually regarded as a bad investment.

The reader will be aware that he must watch changes of law all the time since this could change the focus of his investment interest.

ORDINARY SHARES AND STOCKS

The ordinary shareholders in a company, (clearly distinguished from Debenture and Preference shareholders) own the company in proportion to the shares that they hold, and acquire the proportionate profits or losses. Because of the Companies Act's limited liability, they are not responsible for company's debts except to the extent of the capital subscribed, or promised capital already contracted to be subscribed.

The initiation of a company is not really our concern, but demands the formality of Issued Capital and perhaps Authorised Capital if the Issued Capital is to be increased, stamp duty is paid, and their shares are normally issued at a par value of £1. All this must appear on the company's Balance Sheet.

The raising of new capital may involve Debenture or Preference, with priority to existing shareholders; those shareholders who can acquire their shares on a rights basis can subscribe themselves or sell their rights to whom they choose. Large-scale Convertible Debentures or Loan stocks are sometimes offered to the public, and this can, of course, change the value of existing ordinary shares. Furthermore, any large-scale raising of capital (like the possibility of being "taken over" or "taking over" some other company) can be looked at by the investor, with, if not suspicion, the need for an explanation of why the company should need such large sums of money; it is usually where large sums are involved that the company goes directly to the public. All of what we have said in this section presupposes a knowledge of the layout and ability to read company accounts.

A few words about acquisition (take-over) and unit trusts will be sufficient to conclude this chapter, which is designed purely to expand upon some of the conditions laid out in Chapter One, especially in the boxes (of Figure 1) labelled economy (2), industries (3) and companies (4).

A company which is about to be acquired will, in general, be comfortably placed as far as the shareholder is concerned, since the share prices usually rise, because compensation is usually on the generous side. For the company making the acquisition, the shareholder's position is more difficult. He has the problem of assessing the value of the acquisition and, if opposed to it, has to "drum up" support from a sufficient number of shareholders in the face of what is apparently a unanimous decision of a Board of Directors.

The difficulty is that the conditions for acquisition are by no means clearcut (whether or not diversification - new products - are also involved or not) and there is no guarantee that a careful appraisal of the situation has been properly carried out. In fact, it is well-known that many appraisals have been quite inadequate and the result usually disastrous.

What the shareholder needs to know is the (hopefully) detailed analysis that has been made of the to-be-acquired company's profit record, market share, the market state for the industry, the degree of skill in management available, etc., both in the past, now and more "subjectively" in the future (forecasts). How, in particular, will it fit in with the company making the acquisition? We shall say a little more about this in Chapter Seven on Corporate Planning, but before we conclude this chapter let us briefly discuss Unit Trusts.

UNIT TRUSTS

This type of investment is not likely to be of the first interest to investors, but at least they ought to know of its existence and the implications they carry.

Unit Trusts are of much more recent origin than Investment Companies such as Limited Liability Investment Companies. The first of the British Unit Trusts date back to 1931 and apart from the important distinction between them and Investment Companies, which entail the investment companies being separate from their shareholders while the unit trusts are a mutual undertaking, there are two other main distinctions. They have as a rule no "gearing". The investor in the Unit Trust is making a straightforward purchase of a collection of shares which, after allowing for expenses, have exactly the value of money he is investing. There are also Trust Deeds and the Trust Deed lays down how each Trust is to be run. A Trustee, usually the Trustee Department of one of the large banks, holds the investments on behalf of the Unit holder, while a separate company whose powers and obligations and whose basis of remuneration are precisely defined in the Trust Deed, manages the investments. The basis of remuneration varies considerably, but in the case of most large Trusts consists of a preliminary charge of not more than 2% (included in the issue price of each unit) and an annual charge of no more than three-eights of 1% of the capital value of the Trust, which is taken out of the net revenue. This is a fairly typical guideline to their operation.

Unit Trusts in the early days were always Fixed Trusts. That is to say the portfolios of the Trusts were made up of a number of identical units of investment fixed in composition; the total value of a unit of investment might change, but it continued to be made up of the same specified and diversified securities. The investor therefore always knew in just what securities he had an interest. There were no problems of management, these having been decided when the Trusts were set up originally and the portfolio was settled.

The Fixed Trust was not a success since it involved the continued purchase of shares which, as conditions changed, many investors would not wish to continue buying and others which were improving and would well be worth buying. Furthermore as the prices of the Units change some shares might come to have a disproportionate influence on the portfolio. The new Trusts were therefore flexible and gave discretion to the managers to vary their investment portfolios according to changing circumstances.

In general, Unit Trusts confined their investments to Ordinary shares, and many important Trust groups have been able to show that an investment in its Trusts under these conditions provided an increase of some 10% in a period of some twenty years for the same fixed capital investment. The equivalent gilt-edged investor would do well to increase by half this amount. A good spread of investments (diversification) averages the losses as well as the gains of the investments chosen and this is ideal for the investor who seeks increased income. Investment dependability hinges on a well diversified portfolio of Ordinary shares; this has been shown again and again to be of great value, even vital to success.

For many years the Unit Trust movement aroused little interest, but it became active towards the end of 1958 with the formation of several new Unit Trusts. These provided no new services, but the development highlighted the advantages of this particular type of investment. It is desirable though that the hazards of Ordinary shares should not be obscured by this fresh interest.

In this monograph, we shall not be concerned to any extent with Unit Trusts, since given fairly large sums of money to invest the investor should be in a position to establish an Ordinary share portfolio of his own, and this is where the scientific application occurs. Provided he can secure good advice in the selection of individual Ordinary shares, he has no need of the services provided by either the Investment Company or the Unit Trust, unless of course, he is interested in them as individual investments in their own right. The special need which the Investment Company and the Unit Trust meets is the investment need of the small investor who does not have sufficient funds to establish a balanced Ordinary share Fund, and who also lacks the skill to make selections on his own account: this is rather like a football pool punter who can increase his stake by joining a syndicate. There is also the element of convenience too which applies equally to the large investor, since the investor receives a single dividend regularly every half year together, in the case of the Unit Trust, with a short report and audited account, telling him how his investment fared. Of the two kinds of investment - the general and private portfolio and the Unit Trust, the Unit Trust meets some of his needs best, not only because of the more speculative nature of the Ordinary shares of Investment Companies resulting from "gearing" but also because he can realise his investment at any time by going direct to the Unit Trust instead of having to find a buyer in the market. This latter advantage may be small in normal times but in time of recession, when it is most likely to be put to the test by investors wishing to realise their investments, it may be considerable.

The liquidity of the Unit Trust depends not merely on the public's interest in the particular Trust, but the public's interest in all the securities in which the Trust has invested its funds. To realise the sums invested in the Trust, it need only sell a portion of one of the many large and marketable securities in which its funds are invested. Alternatively, depending on market conditions, it can spread its sales over the whole range of securities in which it is interested to raise funds for the individual investor.

Both Investment Trusts and Unit Trusts are assessed for corporation tax at the full rate applicable to other companies and to capital gains tax at half the rate (of 15% as applicable to individuals). This is subject to the higher rates of tax as some of the investments are overseas. The capital gains tax rate of 15% represents a considerable concession to investors in Investment Trusts and Unit Trusts when taken in conjunction with the concession which entitles them to a credit of the same amount against the gains they secure when they dispose of their holdings. The actual taxation rates involved vary frequently enough, so that advice at the time of doing business of buying or selling investments is always necessary.

Unit Trusts now exist that cater for the varying needs of different classes of investors. There are Trusts which concentrate on income, on growth and on capital, Trusts which specialise in property, insurance, investment trusts, finance and raw materials, and also Trusts which concentrate on dollar and other overseas securities, but by and large we shall remain doubtful about the value of Unit Trusts for the reader of this book. The reason for our doubts is wholly bound up with the fact that, in effect, the Unit Trust Company is providing a service which this monograph is precisely intended to allow you to provide for yourself, although our interest is more in the methodology involved rather than the actual investing.

So we can leave this whole matter at this point, having hopefully provided a glimpse of the kind of rules and some of the implied strategies that apply in the investment game. This is a necessary preliminary to understanding the nature of investment.

REFERENCES CHAPTER 2

1. F.H. George, The Anatomy of Business, The Associated Business Press; Wiley-Halstead, 1974.
2. Robert K. Jaedicke and Robert T. Sprouse, Accounting Flows: Income, Funds and Cash. Foundations of Finance Series, Prentice-Hall, 1965.

CHAPTER 3
THE BEHAVIOR OF THE STOCKMARKET

We have already set the scene in some measure by our descriptions in chapters one and two as to how the stock market operates. We know who does what and how they do it in the "market place". The market place is, of course, not the market square where you once bartered pigs for cows and still buy and sell commodities of all kinds, although there is a huge international commodities market much like the stock exchange. In this monograph we shall not deal directly with the market place or even with the commodities market (although this will be mentioned in passing), since in spite of its similarities to the stock market, the differences are sufficiently great to demand a separate study.

Apart from the mechanics of the stock exchange and the various types of shares and economic environments we have described, we still need to say a little more, in perhaps a rather more abstract way, about stock exchange behaviour, before we can arrive at the study with which we are primarily concerned, the way to invest in stocks and shares, i.e. investment analysis.

The stock market is of vital importance to the nation's economy, and the results of the activities of the stock market are described primarily by the recorded price movements of stocks, and in some countries the total transactions of each and every price is also recorded. Information about the buyers and the sellers is usually only indirectly obtainable, and at irregular intervals, and is less dependable and less precise than the prices. As a consequence the stock market generates a great deal of what is, on the whole, reliable statistical material, readily available for analysis. The matter of information sources open to the investor will be discussed at the end of this chapter.

Since it is not possible to study all individual prices and transactions, a need for aggregation and sampling (the usual statistical methods) arises. It is surprising, in fact, that until recently the analysis of stock market prices has been intuitive rather than mathematical and scientific in character. This is now changing and we are intending to encourage further just such a change, and bring it into the realm of a "systems science".

A fundamental similarity among stock markets, as has already been made clear, is assumed. Not only are London and New York the largest markets in the world in turnover, but also the best documented. The difference between the two is that the stock market in London lists more stocks than the one in New York, but transactions are lighter in most of these London based stocks. This implies a concentration on London and New York.

The relative uniformity in trading of stocks is assured by institutional devices and the use of many rules of a wide variety. Hence there is no point in dealing with large samples of different industries.

The main assertions in economic theory according to Granger and Morgenstern (1970) are four:

"(a) The market assures the optional allocation of investible funds - if these search employment in stocks, especially by issue of new stock;
(b) The price movements on the stock market in their aggregate (as represented by various indices) are a predictor of subsequent fluctuations in the economy as a whole;
(c) The price of a share in the company is a function of past earnings assumed future earning power, expected dividend flows, and other characteristics of the respective enterprise;
(d) Future stock prices are predictable in a practically useful manner from their previous, mostly cyclical movements, either individually or in the aggregate".

These beliefs, strongly held by the authors to the point of conviction, are by no means universally agreed, but seem reasonably justified. Granger and Morgenstern (op.cit.)[2] also suggest the following principal common beliefs:

"(1) There are cyclical and noncyclical stocks: disproved.
(2) There are seasonal variations in stock prices, e.g. there is a "summer rise" and a "year-end rise", etc., : disproved.
(3) Certain stock price movements lead other stock price movements: disproved.
(4) Stock market price cycles lead general economic developments: since, as we will show, there are no cycles in stock market prices, this is disproved in general but there exist weak, temporary, parallel trends from time to time, too unreliable to guide either investment or economic policy.

(5) Stock prices can be predicted from "technical analysis" of price charts: disproved - as far as all currently used (linear) techniques are concerned.

(6) A high volume of transactions is needed to move price:"True only in the average".

These propositions by Granger and Morgenstern are ones that the investor should bear in mind all the time, since they are coupled to the reminder that prices vary with interest rates, expected profits, etc. and this is obviously, in some measure, true and the whole point of our pilgrimage is to discover what variations do occur and what do not. We have to distinguish two approaches. The first, and most usually, is the essentially empirical approach of making the present depend upon the past and the second is to have a theory that applies to the future but depends upon the present. This is identical to scientific method, where prediction depends upon near-repetitive or completely repetitive occurrences, and the second is an explanation (causal explanation if you like) which depends upon some understanding of the processes involved.

For the stock market, the first method is different since there are not enough records and because the stock market is subject to changes in regulations, practices, general trends so that the comparability of data over long periods might conceivably be impaired. The prediction might fail for that reason as will occur in science where we are observing changing phenomena without having a changing theory. This is the method used largely by most market analysts, and the example of Chartism is the best known such method. Predicting from a theory of the stock market depends upon the existence of such a theory, or at least some models, and these we shall be discussing in chapters eight and nine especially. The only model that can generally be derived from the evidence of price changes and from the characteristics of the speculative market is that prices follow a Random Walk. There the proper prediction of tomorrow's price is to state that it will be the same as today's. Such predictions prove to be the best predictions in the vast majority of cases.

As long as our knowledge of any or all phenomena was more rudimentary than it is now, it was also the safest (scientific) prediction to say that tomorrow's weather will be the same as today's. Most social science was in the same boat until recently.

The main (but not only) test of a theory is its predictive value[3]. To achieve a theory capable of prediction will always be a primary goal. However, one has to be careful, since even incorrect theories may have a surprising degree of predictive power and that is why prediction is not the final test of the validity (or truth) or any hypothesis. It could be argued that Newtonian Physics was false and Einsteinian correct, but this would be a spurious argument since the latter was a generalisation of the former. Newton was correct but lacked generality, and that is a matter we need also to watch for.

We use the word 'random' a great deal in statistics and call certain series of activities (like the roll of a fair die) random, but this must not be supposed to eliminate the possibility of a measure. The notion of "randomness" is a very complicated one that has concerned mathematicians and philosophers for a long time. Uncritical use of the word 'random' can lead to contradictions and apparant paradoxes. Furthermore it is apparently difficult for a human to produce a "truly random" sequence, say, of numbers. Many have believed this to be impossible given the psychological characteristics of a human being. This may account for the frequently found aversion shown by people when it is known that certain events do follow a random pattern where they would like to find some regularity of pattern. The answer is that in the end a pattern with a huge repetitive form can be distinguished from a random one. Still we have the measure of probability, and the theory of Random Walk states that future prices are knowable with certain probabilities, so by specifying a probability distribution over future prices, we can make predictions.

BUYING AND SELLING

Buyers of stock are confronted with new issues of stock or with old ("second hand") issues. Sellers, of course, may sell either new or old stock. The vast majority of transactions will normally consist of old shares changing hands. The holder of an old stock is not necessarily a seller at the market price; nor will he necessarily sell when the price goes up or down. He may buy more of the same stock when the price rises or falls. In the course of time the same stock may be both sold and bought repeatedly by the same person or institution. Sellers of new stock attempt to predict a price at which their entire offering will be absorbed. They would, for example, like to predict the highest price at which this will occur and which at least will be maintained by the market.

Buyers and sellers deal in a sense in titles to assets which are treated as "assets" in themselves. We need therefore to know something about assets. The concept of an "asset" is bound up with that of "value", since clearly something that has no "value" (either actual or expected) cannot be an asset. Hence it is clear that by an asset we mean something for which a demand exists. The value of an asset is clear either in the closed economy of an individual by virtue of the role the particular object plays in the individual's life, or in a bartering situation when by means of exchange or sale the occasion of a transformation of a given asset into another asset arises. In other words he either values it and keeps and uses it, or he values it for exchange purposes. The former would include razors, cookers, refrigerators and the latter cash, cheques, etc.

In a bartering (or exchange) economy the value of an asset other than cash must involve an actual or prospective transaction. In times of great price fluctuations even the value of a monetary asset is viewed in terms of its purchasing power which asks what its value is in terms of what it can buy. The well known truth is that assets are <u>worth</u> only what you can sell them for, and this is why we talked earlier about the liquidity of assets. Some can be bought and sold easily and some cannot. Value depends entirely on expectations, either of future use in a closed economy or of a future exchange in an exchange economy. This "future" may be imminent or it may be more distant, but the principle is exactly the same. A method proposed for determining the existence of the value of a stock is to observe that a share is a <u>claim</u> against the company and since the company has net assets these determine an inner value, possibly higher or lower than reflected in the market price of the stock.

This <u>claim</u> is a legal one. Similarly the value of a property may be reflected in the rental value it has on the market, as opposed to the more obvious value gained by an outright sale.

One thing we should like to do as an investor is to <u>value</u> the company whose stocks we purchase, and one way is often practised which is to multiply the share numbers by stock market price; but this is a poor guide. The liquidity of stocks can only be considered relative to the size of the transaction and the (random) variation of the stock market.

Indeed even liquidity can be uncertain, and as we have already observed in the case of arts such as are embodied in antiques and paintings, the market is variable enough to make any effort to show the intrinsic value of a company, a stock or any sort of asset, virtually impossible. We return again to the <u>operational</u> <u>definition</u> of value and say that the value of anything is what someone will pay for it. There are, as a result of these beliefs, no such thing as "certain assets" or assets with "certain values". All are risky even though their risk is in different degrees. Even the value of cash is subject to the variations in the price level, exchange rate and the like. An asset therefore has only, in terms of measure, a probabilistic value. As Granger and Morgenstern[4] rightly say:

> "Current accounting practices culminating in establishing balance sheets fail entirely to recognise this fact and are limited to a strictly deterministic viewpoint. This attitude is incongrous since we live in a stochastic world".

Bearing all these factors (and more to follow) each investor establishes a list of priorities from which arise the bids he is willing to make in order to acquire a given asset. Such bids are subject to several constraints such as the individual's available funds, his aim for greater income or capital, risk or security, his time preferences and discount ideas, etc. A distinction has to be made among investors, where here we are using the term "investor" in the sense of describing both buyers and sellers and recalling that the same people or institutions may appear in both acmps even for the same stock, even if at different times. The first class of investors will primarily be interested in expected capital gains over a period of time. Such capital-gains investors may even be averse to dividends paid out during the time the capital gains are expected to materialise, since expectations of the latter are a prime consideration for purchase of a given stock (particularly in the light of tax considerations); there is, of course, the second class of investor who is primarily concerned with income derived from dividends. They are, of course, not averse to captital gains made during the period in which the stock is held. The income-investor will obviously be influenced by a different set of factors from the capital-gains investor and he will, as a result, attribute different weights to the factors enetering into his decisions.

The next point for the capital-gains investor to consider is the extent of the price appreciation once it has begun. At what point is his aim achieved? This is basically a matter of opinion. The individual capital-gains investor's principal problem is to determine the point at which he should sell his stock and what part of it he should sell. This he should do on the basis of his theory, or theories, of the stock market. Among these, which we describe later, are the strong beliefs that the behaviour of the particular stock during the past (recent and long term) gives the best clue to the future of the market as a whole, to the particular industry and to the particular stock.

To summarise the whole matter at this point, we also have a mine if other information much of it of a "qualitative" nature (or subjective). The general economic news, available statistics, company reports, political news, opinions of all sorts are matters to be taken into consideration. From all this the investor somehow makes his decision and the whole purpose of this book is, step by step, to help make that decision. Since accurately described information combined with so many facts, allows a great variety of interpretations, it follws that investors, even those having access to exactly the same set of information, will differ widely in their ability to process it and aften arrive at different conclusions. This accounts for differences in portfolios and for the circumstances that, at the same time, the same stock is both sold and bought. If there were no such differences in evaluation (in willingness to both buy and sell) there would be few transactions and the stock market would become static. Our aim is to ensure we come to the correct conclusions.

INFORMATION ON THE STOCK EXCHANGE

Our next topic is the sources of information and the treatment of them by the investors. An effort is necessary to collect information of various kinds. Investors should not act without having gone through some search for the best ways of investing their money (that is the subject for later chapters) even though there are investors who act on little information, they are influenced by rumours, "inside information" or are presently attracted by companies dealing in some new and attractive field such as computers and the like. Sometimes investors have only a hazy notion (if any at all) about what the companies actually do whose shares they are purchasing. So we now outline sources of opinion and information on the London stock market.

MUI moderates its course

THE PAST few months have been traumatic for the Malaysian glamour stock company, Malayan United Industries, and its chief executive, Datuk Khoo Kay Peng.

After dazzling the imagination of thousands of Malaysian, Singaporean and Hong Kong speculators for 18 months with its spectacular share price climb, MUI was hit hard by the severe shakeout in the stock market which came in the wake of changes in the political leadership in Malaysia in June.

The collapse of the Malaysian and Singapore share markets undermined the ground on which the group had built a series of property acquisitions in Hong Kong and Singapore.

Datuk Khoo had many sleepless nights in July and August, he says, harrassed by abusive calls from investors who had been burned speculating in MUI shares.

Most financial analysts agree, however, that the worst is now over.

'It was crazy at one stage," recalls one stockbroker: "Imagine speculators grabbing MUI shares at 23 ringgit, 24 ringgit, when its net asset backing was no more than 5 ringgit, and it was giving net dividends of six cents per share."

MUI has emerged badly bruised, but, it is widely agreed, on firmer ground. The image of Datuk Khoo as a man with the Midas touch has been affected, but he is still a man of great substance by any standard. MUI remains one of Malaysia's largest 10 corporations, in terms of its market capitalisation of 1.23bn ringgit (US$545m).

The MUI saga began three years ago when it came under Datuk Khoo's control. Previously, it was a little known investment company operating from Penang Island.

Datuk Khoo, 43, began his career as a clerk with the Oversea Chinese Banking Corporation in 1955, rising to general manager of Bank Bumpitura in the early 1970s.

Tengku Razaleigh, the Malaysian Finance Minister, was then head of Bank Bumiputra and the two became close associates, a relationship which became important when Datuk Khoo embarked on MUI's expansion. In the expansion he followed a simple, and well-tried, system. Sensing that a share boom was about to begin, in 1979, he began a series of bold acquisitions, always using paper, together with a little cash, in exchange.

MUI's first major acquisition was the sugar refiner, Central Sugars, and through it, the cement producer, Pan Malayan Cement Works. At the time of each takeover, MUI paper was valued at a higher price than before.

MUI shares were worth three ringgit each for the acquisition of Central Sugars in January last year, but were valued at 10 ringgit six months later in the purchase of Southern Banking shares and at 15 ringgit when MUI began its series of property purchases in Hong Kong and Singapore last June.

An investor, who had put up, say, 20,000 ringgit for 10,000 MUI shares in 1979, and held them until the middle of this year would have made a capital gain of more than 700,000 ringgit.

Since the sharemarket shakeout, the Malaysian Government's Foreign Investment Committee (FIC) has rejected all the property deals of MUI in Hong Kong. These involved purchase of the East Ocean Centre and Advance building for U.S.$145m satisfied in shares, but underwritten by a cash option from Malaysian institutions.

The FIC felt the purchases would dilute MUI's earnings. Also, the FIC frowns on Malaysian concerns buying property overseas, as a matter of policy, particularly at a time when the country needs funds for its own economic growth.

Early this month, MUI cleared the last of its controversial property deals, when it announced an out of court settlement with the Goodwood Park group on a dispute over two Singapore hotels.

The settlement involved MUI gaining control over one hotel, Ming Court, on the earlier agreed terms of a share exchange, while dropping the bid to acquire the other, Hotel Malaysia.

The free-wheeling days have disappeared for Malaysia's business investors as the authorities, under the Prime Ministership of Dr Mahathir Bohamed, seek to enforce stricter rules, making it more difficult for acquisitions, mergers and takeovers.

An amendment Bill, giving wide powers to the authorities to control the stock exchange and corporate affairs, is expected to be tabled in Parliament early next year.

Although MUI has been humbled and has had its wings clipped, it is testimony of the market's confidence in the group that there is still active trading of its shares at around 12 ringgit. Basic investment guidelines suggest that current prices are still high but there is reason to think of the group enjoying healthy growth rates.

MUI has a diversified base, in banking, property development, hotels and manufacturing, and these are the growth sectors in the Malaysian economy.

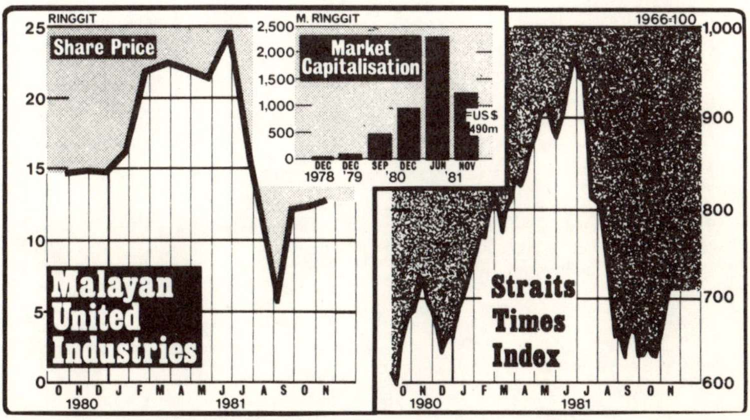

Next we look at Moodie's Investment Services Ltd. Investment Handbook.

REED INTERNATIONAL LTD.

EMPLOYEES 72, 000
REMUNERATION £102, 600, 000

CHAIRMAN S. T. Ryder.
REGISTERED OFFICE Reed House, 82, Pfccadilly, London, W1A 1EJ. Tel: 01-499-4020.
TRANSFER OFFICE Tudor Registrars Ltd., Bourne House, 34 Beckenham Road, Kent. BR3 4TU. Tel: 01-460-1116.

TO: 31st Mar.	SALES £m	TOTAL PROFITS £m	EARNED FOR. ORD. £m	BASED ON LATEST YRS. ORD. CAP. EARNED %	DIV. %	NET. ASS. PER SH. Pence	PRICE Pence HIGH	LOW	YIELD RATIO	ORD. CAP. £m	PROFIT Pre-tax & Int. £m	CAP. EMPLD. £m	PROFIT RATIO %	TAX %
1962	95.0	12.87	3.88	22.0	16.0	269	250	163	139	28.72	8.65	103.06	8.4	
1963	92.8	14.29	4.41	24.2	16.0	265	299	221	125	29.79	9.77	115.43	8.5	
1964	101.5	16.57	5.06	25.2	16.0	270	330	261	112	34.17	11.74	132.16	8.6	
1965	149.2	21.68	7.41	33.4y	17.0	280	301	232	99	37.26	15.95	160.16	10.9	
1966	226.1	32.51	11.43	21.2	17.0	277	336	201	95	53.89	24.51	270.00	9.1	37
1967	240.4	29.08	6.80	12.6	12.5	280	244	179	103	53.89	20.32	275.16	7.4	44
1968	249.5	30.59	6.85	12.7	12.5	285	220	172	129	53.89	20.88	281.44	7.4	46
1969	282.4	34.16	8.40	15.5	12.5	286	283	211	106	54.03	23.87	295.71	8.1	45
1970	314.4	39.92	10.01	18.6	12.5	294	279	160	102	55.27	28.33	320.38	8.8	43
1971	502.3	52.04	10.89	12.9	12.5	288	276	117	145	84.27	34.25	470.44	7.3	38

PRIORITY PERCENTAGES % OF EARNINGS TAKEN
DEBS & LOANS 0 - 23
PREFERENCE 23 - 24
ORDINARY 24 - 97

LATEST DIVIDENDS PER SH./STK(18.1) Z

YEAR	DIV.	PER CENT	Pence	DECLARED	PAYABLE	EX - DIV.
69/70	Int	5	5.00	28Oct'69	8Jan'70	10Nov'69
69/70	Fin	7.5	7.50	19May'70	7Aug'70	1Jun'70
70/71	Int	5	5.00	27Oct'70	8Jan'71	16Nov'70
70/71	Fin	7.5	7.50	18May'71	9Aug'71	28May'71
70/71	Int.	5	5.00	2Nov'71	10Jan'72	29Nov'71

NOTES (v) Est. 40% Corpn. Tax equiv. 22.7%.

MONTHLY SHARE PRICES (PENCE)

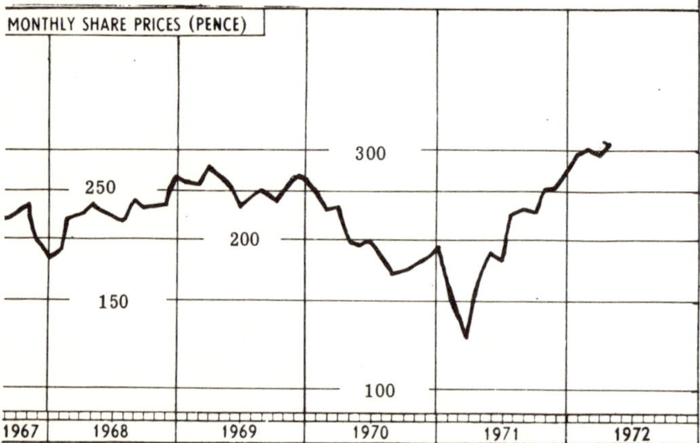

YIELD GUIDE

CAPITAL EMPLOYED - £m - 31Mar.-

SOURCES	1970	1971
EQUITY FUNDS		
ORD. CAP.	55.27	84.28
RESERVES	107.17	158.63
	162.44	242.91
PREF. CAP	4.07	4.07
LONG TERM DEBT.	95.51	142.51
DEFD. LIABS.	18.47	33.72
	280.49	423.21
USES		
CASH & SECS.	9.84	8.73
STOCKS & W. I. P.	70.98	92.64
OTHER CURR. ASS.	85.82	132.74
TOTAL CURR. ASS.	166.64	234.11
LESS CURR. LIABS.		
DUE BANKERS	39.88	47.23
OTHER CURR. LIABS.	59.81	98.34
NET CURR. ASS.	66.95	88.54
FIXED ASSETS (NET)	145.96	205.60
GOODWILL	67.58	129.07
	280.49	423.21
CAP. COMMITMENTS	5.84	9.02
NET CASH FLOW	15.60	16.04

CAPITAL & DEBENTURES
DEBS & LOANS £75, 519, 568
PREFERENCE £ 4, 068, 353
ORDINARY (£1) £84, 274, 790

GRADINGS PAST Id Gd FUTURE Ic Gc

BACKGROUND

Newspapers, publishing, paper and packaging make up the greater part of the turnover, with wallpaper, paint and building products the remainder. Subsidiaries include I. P. C., Spicers, and Wallpaper Manufacturers, and overseas interests are held in Europe, North America and the Commonwealth.

DEVELOPMENTS

9 mos. to 31st Dec.

£m's	1971	1970
External Sales	394.7	371.8
Pre-tax Profit	20.7	14.4
Tax	8.5	6.6
Minorities	0.9	0.9
Attrib. to Co.	11.3	6.9

In April, 1972 the Company announced it was acquiring for cash Van Meurs Golfcartonfabrieken N. V.

INDEX CLASSIFICATION INDUSTRIAL HOLDINGS

We give one further example from the Financial Times, and would mention here the Investor's Chronicle, The Economist and Money Which. From all these sources and the published accounts of each individual company, a picture (or model) of any company can be built up.

UK ECONOMIC INDICATORS

ECONOMIC ACTIVITY—Indices of industrial production, manufacturing output (1975=100); engineering orders (1975=100); retail sales volume (1976=100), retail sales value (1976=100); registered unemployment (excluding school leavers) and unfilled vacancies (000s). All seasonally adjusted.

	Indl. prod.	Mfg. output	Eng. order	Retail vol.	Retail value*	Unem-ployed	Vacs.
1980							
4th qtr.	100.7	89.7	79	109.0	205.2	2,020	98
1981							
1st qtr.	99.6	88.8	97	112.7	174.4	2,304	100
2nd qtr.	98.9	88.5	91	111.3	180.6	2,507	89
3rd qtr.	99.6	89.9		110.4	185.2	2,627	96
March	99.9	88.7	109	111.4	175.3	2,381	97
April	98.8	88.3	90	111.4	181.6	2,452	94
May	98.2	87.6	86	110.6	177.1	2,515	92
June	99.6	89.6	97	111.7	182.7	2,552	83
July	99.8	89.6	99	109.7	185.4	2,582	92
Aug	99.4	89.8	125	111.0	185.6	2,626	98
Sept	99.7	90.2		110.6	184.7	2,673	97
Oct				111.5		2,729	99
Nov						2,764	104

OUTPUT—By market sector; consumer goods, investment goods, intermediate goods (materials and fuels); engineering output, metal manufacture, textiles, leather and clothing (1975=100); housing starts (000s, monthly average).

	Consumer goods	Invst. goods	Intmd. goods	Eng. output	Metal mnfg.	Textile etc.	Housg. starts*
1980							
4th qtr.	94.1	91.0	117.0	86.1	70.6	76.9	10.1
1981							
1st qtr.	94.1	87.4	117.5	83.5	76.4	76.9	10.9
2nd qtr.	93.2	87.5	118.1	84.0	79.3	75.8	14.2
3rd qtr.	94.5	88.4	119.1	85.6	77.4	76.1	14.4
Feb	95.0	87.0	118.0	83.0	78.0	78.0	11.3
March	94.0	87.0	119.0	84.0	78.0	77.0	11.2
April	94.0	88.0	117.0	84.0	76.0	76.0	12.5
May	92.0	87.0	117.0	83.0	78.0	75.0	13.8
June	94.0	88.0	120.0	85.0	84.0	77.0	16.3
July	95.0	88.0	119.0	86.0	76.0	75.0	14.5
Aug	95.0	88.0	118.0	85.0	78.0	78.0	12.7
Sept	94.0	89.0	120.0	86.0	78.0	75.0	16.0

EXTERNAL TRADE—Indices of export and import volume (1975=100); visible balance; current balance (£m); oil balance (£m); terms of trade (1975=100); exchange reserves.

	Export volume	Import volume	Visible balance	Current balance	Oil balance	Terms trade	Resv. US$bn*
1980							
4th qtr.	126.6	111.8	+1,265	+2,110	+222	105.2	27.90
1981							
1st qtr.		107.0					28.34
2nd qtr.							26.73
3rd qtr.							24.26
Jan	123.9	101.3	+742	+1,178	+210	106.4	28.39
Feb	121.7	114.3	+314	+750	+231	105.2	28.43
March		105.5					28.21
April		106.2					28.07
May							26.49
June							25.63
July							24.57
Aug							24.51
Sept	130.2	135.3	+ 13	+147	+290	100.0	23.70
Oct	125.5	126.3	+116	+316	+ 89	98.9	23.32

Trade figures for March-August not available because of Civil Service dispute.

REFERENCES CHAPTER 3

1. C.W.J.Granger and O.Morgenstern, The Predictability of Stock Market Prices, Lexington Books,1970.

2. C.W.J.Granger and O.Morgenstern, Opus Citus.

3. Gordon T.Brand. The Industrial Buying Decision Wiley-Halstead, 1972.

4. C.W.J.Granger and O.Morgenstern, Opus Citus.

CHAPTER 4
THE SCIENCE OF INVESTMENT

FACTORS THAT INFLUENCE INVESTMENT

This chapter follows on directly from the last one in that we shall start our examination of some of the factors that influence our final choice of a portfolio. We are now beginning to concentrate on processing the data which we know where and how to collect. The fact that there are several different methods of making the choice of investment (a matter which we shall be discussing later in some detail) should not obscure the fact that they all have much in common. This means that in this chapter and the last, we shall be dealing in general terms with matters which most (but not all) investment methods include, whether explicitly or implicitly. There are, of course, huge differences in the approach to questions needed to be answered but a discussion of these difference can wait on the next few chapters.

It is clear that we are advocating the use of science, and no longer regarding investment purely as an art. There are some techniques that use some scientific ingredients within the general context of an art. The two main groups are called Technalists and Fundamentalists respectively;[1] and both come in this category of "a science within an art", so let me write a brief explanatory word on each.

First of all we see Technalism as a method of using (hypotheses) laws to make predictions. The basic variables (laws) are the history of the share price and the volume of trading, or the total numbers of shares traded in one day. The technique is usually one of curve-fitting (sometimes called "chartism") in the sense that the method is to look at the graph of the past and extrapolate from it to the future. Cohen and Zinburg[2] are among the best known Technalists, who themselves recognise some 15 different kinds of Technalism.

Fundamentalism is concerned with Technalism, but with the additional aspects of the economic state of the country and all available information on the company whose shares are under consideration. But at this point let us return to more general considerations which indeed include (to a great extent) both Technalism and Fundamentalism (but more obviously the latter).

If we recall Figure 1 of chapter 1, then Figure 1 (in this chapter) follows directly on; here it is:

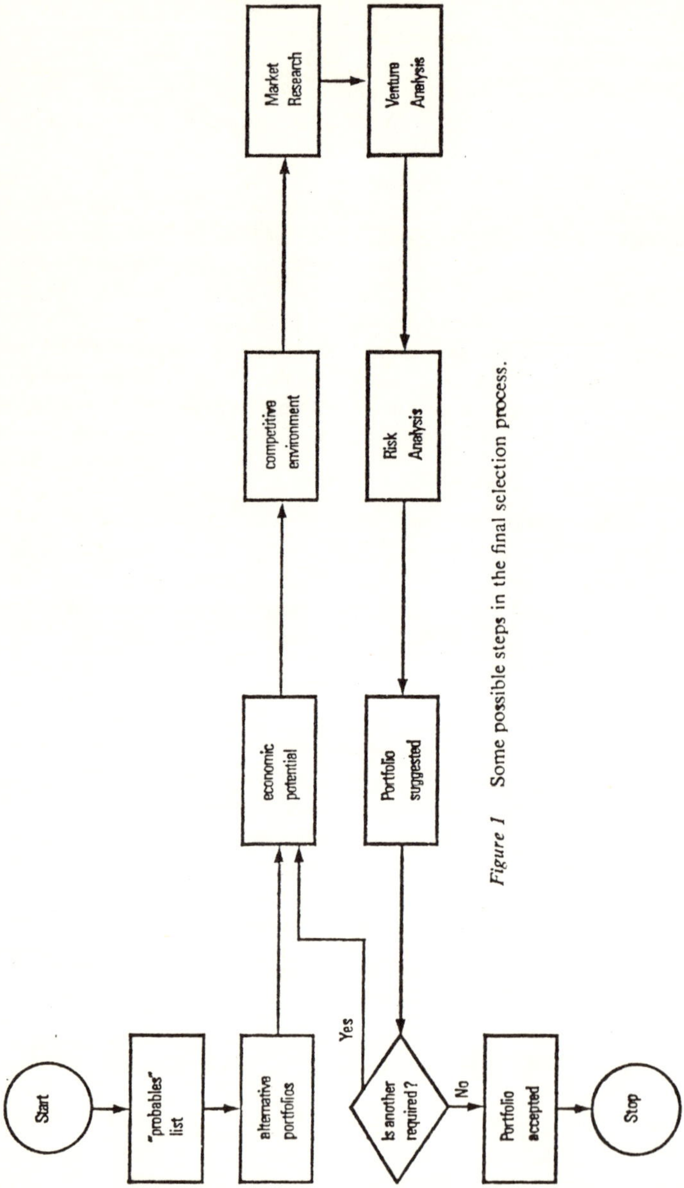

Figure 1 Some possible steps in the final selection process.

The obvious step is to follow up the "probables" (as we can now think of them) portfolio reached at the end of Figure 1 (chapter 1) and then submit it to a comparison with other "probably" acceptable portfolios and consider now the market state in terms of demand, market-share, the possibility of advertising and the like.

The economic potential of the shares depends largely on the nature of the business in which investment is to be made, while there are other shares, such as government bonds, which depend on such things as the economic state of the country and the rate of inflation, the import-export ratio, rate of exchange, etc. All these things reflect the confidence the potential buyer will have and this in turn is reflected in the share price.

Taking the main case of purchasing shares in a public company, we can see the obvious things to look for, apart from the forecasting of the continuing (increasing or decreasing) demand for their products, is the amount that has had to be invested to achieve their profits. We must therefore think in terms of Return on Trading Capital (RTC), or Return of Investment (ROI). Their market share and the nature of the competition are also very important. But more of this anon.

Market Research is something which concerns the company since by such means they assess demand and the need for advertising either to create or increase demand, but this information is usually only available to the company itself. Individual investors have been known to (and certainly can) do their own market research (or even some "espionage"), but usually the results needed are guided by the financial newspapers and journals.

Risk Analysis[3] we have already briefly explained, and Venture Analysis[4] is somewhat similar and it tells you the likely return on investment in terms of your competitiveness; this is at least how the individual can use it. He finishes up, in the light of his capital available for investment, and in the light of his goals, determining the degree of diversification he ought to indulge in. This also tells him (what is really part of Risk Analysis) the extent to which he will lose money if he invests wrongly and thus the sensitivity of the portfolio to the likely changing world economy, as well as all the other conditions that might influence the value of his shares. The OPEC oil prices are an obvious recent example of such a world influence.

We then can put our investigation through the steps of Figure 1 (chapter 1) and Figure 1 (this chapter) and repeat as necessary until we have what we would regard as a satisfactory portfolio. Let us now return to the question of looking at the data we shall need (however we use it) in rather more detail. It is not the Technalists or Fundamentalists (in their various forms) that we are thinking of particularly, since all methods use all the data we shall list, but most of it (if not all of it) is used by Investment Analysts collectively.

The selection rules are the strategies in the system and provide the logic for the selection of the required portfolio. The information on which the choice is made may be updated and strategies and constraints may change or be changed, so that the process may be adapted in precisely the same way as they need to be in other fields which are not static. In general, the four most important steps are to provide a list of "possibles", then a list of "probables", then to decide on an investment policy and finally to provide a portfolio for investment. The first of these steps is akin to choosing a football team or the like to represent, say, the country. You draw up a short list and play the probables against the possibles to choose the final team, which is then chosen with a view to the conditions under which the game will be played and the nature of the opposition. You may indeed have many trials and not just one before a decision is made. Much here depends upon the question of urgency.

The question of policy criteria is vital and involves confidence, as defined in terms of other buyers, the maximisation of either profit or growth or some sort of compromise between the two, and the minimisation of risk. It can therefore be assumed, as always, that some form of risk analysis is essential at some stage (or stages).

Our next problem is as to the data we need, or in terms of football, the height, weight, record, skills, etc. of all the available players. The attributes and values of shares we need are matters for some debate, but they will normally include those selected from the following list which is not, as yet, complete:

Return on trading capital
Return on investment
Cash flow per share
Sales
Earnings-profits
Debts
Loans
Subsidies
Working capital
Price-earnings ratio (P/E ratio)
Dividend-payout ratio

Prices
Dividend-per-share
Dividend yield
Price ratio with competitors

All of these can be thought of in terms of trends, both recent and longer term, as well as in terms of averages and even in terms of average rates of change. The most convenient way is to use the numerical scale to represent these capacities and the small number of classes are averaged out; this is the equivalent of a "batting average", and is the end product.

But the data now has to be evaluated and this can be done in several ways. There is what is called a Relative Performance Scale, an evaluative process which evaluates the average performance, the deviation of each company from the average (the extent to which a company is above or below average) and the deviation of each attribute from the average. These can all be readily calculated, and then the companies can be sub-divided into sub-groups in terms of an evaluation of their performance (first, second and third "division" shares). This procedure can be repeated for other variables such as relative value, relative prospects in terms of trends, current economic conditions, market state: these latter are rather more difficult to decide upon, but at a time when a product is in direct demand and short supply, then a large company with the bulk of the business should prosper.

When someone invests money on the stock exchange, and this applies especially to institutional investors such as multinational companies and government, he expects to make more money than the value of his original investment. The obvious need for resources to start an investment gave rise to the axiom that you need money to make money. The rise of the Unit Trusts means that for the cost of a holiday anyone can play the market, albeit one step removed from more direct forms of investment. Investment is an industry in itself, and whenever a large market is involved, new and improved methods are bound to arise.

METHODS OF INVESTMENT

Within recent years three particular research methods stand out from the rest in presenting new ideas; those of Markowitz[5] (Method I), Weaver and Hall[6] (Method II) and Clarkson[7] (Method III). The three examples of each method are not, of course, exhaustive. They are merely examples. They represent three widely differing approaches which are also fairly complicated, although we shall try to extract their essence in simple terms at this stage, but we shall examine them in more detail later.

Markowitz used mathematical techniques, which we will be describing. Weaver and Hall employed methods of traditional statistical analysis, in common use, and we shall discuss this shortly. Clarkson used simulation of the human investor's approach which is essentially 'heuristic', and which we discuss in detail in Chapter 9.

All three approaches however can be thought of as starting from a basic model of the investment process. Method I is the simplest and made so in order to fit his previous mathematical methods. Method II's model is more complex, although limited by the choice of statistical analysis which was that of correlation. This means essentially that there are statistical methods of measuring the similarity between two sets of data. Method III, however, concentrates on modelling the decision procedures which parallel the numerical techniques outlined above as much as the static model of investment similar to that of Methods I and II. By analogy with the other betting methods, Method III in essence. tries to find a good punter and then do exactly what he does.

Nearly all large investment is done in a portfolio of several individual investments. This only spreads risk over the whole of the portfolio (which could contain a hundred or more different securities) but in theory a higher return can be achieved over a long period of time by constantly changing the composition of the portfolio.

Method I attempts to answer the question "which securities should be invested in and how much of an investment should be made in each?" This is done by assuming that security return (increase or decrease in share price) is random and subject only to the "laws" of probability. The simple formulation of the problem led to one of maximising return, subject to various constraints, and Method I involved an algorithm (an automatic rule not unlike a certain strategy) to solve the resultant quadratic equations. A typical solution (i.e. to select 70 securities from a list of 500 takes less than 2 minutes on a computer).

The mathematical techniques are extremely elegant and highly efficient, but tend in some measure to obscure the issue, partly by giving a false impression of precision. The whole basis of the method is that probabilities have to be assigned to growth and yield forecasts and these are largely subjective or at least they are until an optimal method is devised for obtaining them. In other words, although accuracy is obtained in the selection process, the inadequacies of prediction and data collection methods are highlighted even more strongly. All this though is too technical to be of interest to us as yet, and I shall say no more about it in this chapter.

In may ways the Method III approach to investment is entirely contrary to that of Method I, since Method III is concerned primarily with reproducing the actual behaviour of a trust investment officer. This is done by observing the investor at work, extracting the basic procedures and simulating them (usually, but not necessarily, in a computer program). He succeeds in apparantly refuting several theories of investment current at this time. An interesting point here is that any theory of investment is also a theory of human problem solving and decision making and indeed of human gambling. The main conclusion in this area can be summed up in the founder's words:

> "It is our suggestion that the weighted decision functions and the maximising hypothesis of current theory be replaced by processes that can employ binary tests (yes or no answers) as the basis on which decisions are made and patterns recognised".

If a theory of investment is a copy of human investing behaviour, then we must ask about human investing behaviour. As far as investment analysis is concerned, Method II is interesting mainly in that it brings out some of the procedures actually used; however, it provides no direct answer to the question of an optimal portfolio. Presumably the investment officer learned his craft by trial-and-error over many years of practical experience and in this sense the portfolio produced is optimal, but is limited by the human processes outlined in the above quotation. Method III proceeds in part as we have done so far in this chapter and in chapter I, and we shall shortly spell this out in detail.

We must however add that Method III is inevitably - since it at least started as a simulation of a human investor - heuristic, and most of the measures used to set up the portfolio are inevitably to be included in any investment program. Such variables include current value (ten-year) average, recent changes ("how recent?" is of course the main question), average rate of change and P/E rates. Most of the rest refers to forecasting (which we will discuss in the next chapter) adapting quickly to change.

One of the principles of selection used in Method II is that:

> "A security is of investment quality <u>if and only if</u> it is being bought or being held by other leading trust institutions."

This should be regarded only as a general guide and should never, of course, be used instead of 'inside information' on an investment which, if sufficiently confirmed, will be overriding. We shall concentrate in the whole of Chapter 9, entirely on Method II, which we believe is the best bet. But in the meantime we should initiate our discussion of forecasting methods.

Investment analysis is a bit like Contract Bridge and a bit like Chess, and very much like the more characteristic business type activities known as forecasting, whether forecasting sales demand, supplies or anything else that necessarily has built-in uncertainties. A computer is obviously very helpful with this sort of forecasting used here for evaluation, both of an algorithmic and heuristic type. For the rest of this chapter, I will return to a brief discussion of theories of investment and say a little more about the relevant aspects of probability and statistics.

It would be wise, following Hartley[8] to distinguish between Theories of Investment and Investment Theories, however pedantic or silly this may sound. Investment theories are those which are partially scientific and are still partially (even largely in some cases) an art. While theories of investment attempt to be strictly rigorous and, if you like, completely scientific. We shall not as yet evaluate these two general approaches, which differ <u>in practice</u> in degree, rather than absolutely. But before the end of our discussions we shall have to say, as far as the records show and as far as seems logical, which is the most effective method (or combination of methods). On this matter we will finish by being absolutely clearcut in our opinion, which we will support with evidence.

The Technalists and Formalists are (variations on Method I) and with Method II, while wholly mathematical (statistical) are known as theories of investment. While Method III is strictly an investment theory.

The emotional aspects of investment play a vitally important part in choice of a portfolio and cannot be ignored. Nevertheless the Technalists have something to recommend their curve-fitting ("chartist") type of approach. The Fundamentalists view is that the share-price reflects the average share-holding opinion of the company's future earnings. These in turn depend upon certain fundamental variables and the question arises as to which these funamental variables are. Granger and Morgenstern's work on what statisticians call a <u>random walk</u>[9] are a particular whole multitude of such views.

A LITTLE MORE ON PROBABILITY AND STATISTICS

We now go on to consider a little more of probability theory, but very briefly. We will give some examples of some traditional techniques that you may want to use. But before doing so let us simply mention that probability theory is closely related to statistics. Statistics start from data collected from observations and then use measures and analyses to distinguish and compare data. Probability theory is concerned with the situation in terms of an a priori understanding of chance. This is done by assuming that coins, packs of cards, etc., behave according to the mathematical theory. If, for example, some dice were weighted, for cheating purposes, then they would not conform to probability theory, and we would need to collect statistics of its actual behaviour from which we could predict the probability of their behaviour. Now to some examples of calculating probabilities that are relevant, and some statistics that are even more relevant to what we have said.

The probability aspect we will pursue is simply that of estimating occurrences (what is sometimes called "subjective probability"). These subjective probabilities can be thought of as "numbers", as are usually used in Risk Analysis, but we could equally well look at the matter in what is, say 7-valued logic; we have already referred to this in Chapter I. This matter is important and bears some repetition.

This means we could say (and here we are repeating our table of Chapter 1 , but with intentionally different synonyms to remind the reader of the relevance of the semantic problems involved) of a forecast that it is:

1) (Almost) certain
2) Highly probable
3) Probable
4) 50-50 chance
5) Possibly
6) Unlikely
7) (Almost) certainly not

If we introduced four more categories, for example we could say that the subjective probabilities are associated with the 11 intervals ranging over the probabilities m/n which lie in the interval (0,1). Such four categories could be named "very high probables"(between 1 and 2) and "just better than 50-50" (between 3 and 4) and two equivalent on the lower scale, plus the removal of "almost" to make 7 into 7 and 8. All this is merely a matter of judgement, based (hopefully) on good evidence, and which we shall later show can be used in our assessments.

The statistical points which are relevant to this chapter are embodied in the simple notion of average and deviation from the average. The reader will remember that this applied particularly to the "performance" of each type of industry and each type of company. It can also be applied to prospects, trends, market states and the like.

The average and standard deviation will be familiar, and almost all the other statistical methods are based on them. This especially includes correlation (complete and partial) and the difference between means, and significance of a simple mean. The main non-parametric statistic is chi-squared, and we also may need stochastic methods, and analysis of variance.

REFERENCES CHAPTER 4

1. R.T. Hartley, Cybernetics Thinking and Share-Price Prediction, Brunel University, 1974.
2. B.J. Cohen and E.D. Zinbarg, Investment Analysis and Portfolio Management, Wiley, 1967.
3. R.E. Beard, T. Pentikainen and E. Pesonen, Risk Theory, Methuen, 1969.
4. F.H. George, The Foundations of Cybernetics, Gordon and Breach, 1977.
5. H. Markowitz, Portfolio Selection: efficient Diversification of Investments, Wiley, 1959
6. D. Weaver and M.G. Hall, 'Evaluation of Ordinary Shares Using a Computer'. J. of Institute of Actuaries, 1967.
7. G.P.E. Clarkson, 'Portfolio selection': A heuristic Approach. J. of finance, Die, 1960.
8. R.T. Hartley. Cybernetics Thinking and Share-Price Prediction, Brunel University, 1974.
9. C.W. J. Granger and O. Morgenstern, The Predictability of Stock Market Prices, Lexington Books, 1970

CHAPTER 5
FORECASTING

Our problem in investment is one of forecasting share prices and analysing other factors such as demand in terms of behaviour, both of people in the market place and other investors. But we need to prepare the way a little more before we can get to grips with our main subject. Demand itself, and indeed behaviour too, involves forecasting. Forecasting is bound up with the whole gamut of activities subsumed under the heading of planning. This includes decision making (and decision taking) and all that in turn implies various methods of problem solving. We shall not, of course, attempt anything like a comprehensive coverage of all these subjects, although we have already started to do so in the earlier chapters and we continue some of the more complex aspects in Appendix II. We must say something more about the background to our subject before we go any further, and we will distinguish decision making from decision taking (quite arbitrarily) by talking of the process of decision making as the actual process whereby you decide what to do. Decision taking we shall take to mean the actual implementation of the decisions made.

In talking of forecasting generally, one has to distinguish between short-term, medium-term and long-term forecasting. The words 'long-term', 'medium-term' and 'short-term' are obviously relative to each other in meaning. Short-term might mean anything from an hour to a day to a week to a year; medium-term could be anything between short-term and long-term, where long-term might mean anything from a couple of months to ten years or more. Broadly speaking, this means there are some things which come at the tactical level and should be capable of being forecast with some degree of accuracy and others which are longer term (strategic) and by the nature of things have a greater degree of uncertainty.

All forecasting should be adaptive or at least if not adaptive in the sense of anticipating change must be capable of reacting very quickly to change, then of course a long-term forecast can be modified in the light of short-term experience. Adaptive systems are always necessary when forecasting over "changeable" systems.

Forecasting, whether short, medium or long-term, is essentially (but not only) a process of extrapolation from the past. It is essentially, as we saw clearly in the last chapter, a process of curve fitting, saying in essence that in the past some variable has changed in a linear fashion, so in the future it is likely to go on changing in the same way. Such extrapolations from past experience are characteristic of all; or almost all (we must wait for our discussion of Random Walks) forecasting activities, and are always, of course, modified by particular knowledge of circumstances which might change. Entry into the European Common Market, or the knowledge of a forthcoming revolution or the knowledge that certain fundamental foodstuffs or raw materials (such as oil) are likely to become in short supply during the next year and other such factors, of course, modify the ordinary extrapolation from the past. It is precisely these weighting factors which are essential in forecasting activities, either in terms of events that have happened or events anticipated.

We should note that the extent to which forecasting is "not only" an extrapolation from the past, is the extent to which we do not merely depend upon repetitive cycles, but the extent to which we can predict by understanding causal relationships which are part of a theory (or explanation) which we have already referred to as "scientific" in the broadest sense.

It should be noticed in passing that the National Institute of Social and Economic Research, in the survey which is produced in their journal, has tables of reference to products of different countries which allows the forecasting of sales to be done when launching a new product with a fair degree of anticipation of likely results. Such tables could play a major part in marketing tactics.

In considering forecasting there are two important features to bear in mind. The first is that sometimes the results of a forecast are successful <u>to a degree</u>, whereas in other situations they may be of the succeed-or-fail variety. Investment in the stock exchange has its success gauged on what is virtually a continuously changing scale, whereas in forecasting football pools you either win a dividend or you do not. This distinction may become very important in a particular situation, since to be 'nearly successful' but still not to win is of no use, and the forecasting method (clearly better than chance) should be used in a circumstance where the scales of success are continuous rather than discrete.

Another important point about forecasting is that one can model a process by a statistical model, for example the Random Walk model has been used with investment and although the behaviour of the stock exchange may be random (there is some doubt about this), this does not necessarily wholly invalidate the possibility of prediction, nor is it, as we shall see in Chapter

Six, what the title Random Walk misleadingly implies. The main criterion in prediction needs to be spelt out carefully, since there are many cases where merely to predict about the level of chance occurrence is quite inadequate. There are other cases where to predict only marginally above chance is all that one needs for complete success: every case must be considered on its own merits; this matter is related to the point made above about continuous and discrete (success or failure) and continuous (successful to a degree).

Forecasting can be regarded as a commonsense process, as is obvious from the fact that we have to do it all the time in our everyday life (hence the connection we must seek with human behaviour). It is necessary to be able to recognise a certain number of features of the environment in order to make a good forecast. We can, of course, think of forecasting at many different levels, but although we shall be thinking mainly in general terms, we must particularise if we are concerned with business forecasting to the extent of looking at market research. Market research probes into the market place to find out what are the likely demands for the future, and this, of course, will affect the price of shares.

Various kinds of economic and econometric models (see Appendix I), tables of the cost of living, incomes and salary rates, etc of all the people in the market place are used. When employing motivational research (we shall call it motivational analysis), the main interest is to find out what underlines demands and what, in terms of changing circumstances, is likely to go on being in demand, this being a matter which can, of course, be influenced by advertising, for example. This is all rather like the corporate strategic point of view of trying to find out whether the forecast is sensitive or robust. In other words, there will still be a demand for food whatever happens, whereas there may not be a demand for private aircraft. To know whether demand is likely to survive economic crises and other upheavals, one can use motivational and market research as a basis for making the forecasting dependent in the sense that one can influence demand, and all of these things have to be understood. Indeed it is necessary, as we have already made clear, to know something about the statistical methods by which these factors or data are analysed, so that it may be decided what the market place situation is, or at least what it probably is.

Motivational analysis naturally links up with behavioural considerations, since it depends upon the extent and manner in which people, who necessarily show purposive behaviour, George and Johnson, Weir[2], are specifically motivated. This again leads to a consideration of how such motives (the platform on which demand depends) can be changed.

In forecasting, econometric models are central to our interest and these are interpreted for economic and business purposes. Market and motivational research are of special interest when trying to establish demand and possible ways of creating demand in the market place - this is, indeed, a part of the information needed for corporate strategic methods. The following factors briefly show what is required for good market forecasting:

1. Effective sampling (Quota or Random)
2. Effective interviewers
3. Effective questionnaires
4. Effective interpretation of the results (this is the behavioural issue)

First of all we look at sampling. We can forecast on a quota basis which biases the sample to specific types of people, or on a random basis which leaves everyone in the population equally likely to be questioned. What is important about sampling of any kind is to be sure that the sampling methods used are appropriate to the sort of information you need. For example, if I wish to discover national attitudes to a general election in the U.K, I do not confine my questioning to Hereford, I spread it over the whole country. It should be added that it sometimes can prove useful to take a typical (usually marginal) constituency, but such a method offers no basis for statistical analysis.

In sampling the population one may use the electoral register for names and addresses, but whatever is used as a data base must be unbiased. The same argument applies to sampling the data base.

In the second factor we come to interviewing. It too must be unbiased, without, by tone of voice, suggesting answers to questions. A good interviewer will also sound independent, unbiased and will never hurry the interviewee. The questionnaire itself must be carefully constructed. This is a matter requiring considerable skill and experience in the framing of questions. It is essential not to suggest the expected or desired answer. Furthermore the order in which the questions are asked is a matter of great importance. This is vital, since sometimes an early "key question" will bias the rest of the interview.

There are two types of question which play a major role in

market research. One is the 'factual' question about which products are actually purchased say, and the other is the 'attitudinal' question about attitudes to real or possible products. The asking of attitudinal questions calls for sophisticated indirect techniques which might require the completion of sentences, the selection of one or more from a number of alternative answers, and so on. This will often be supplemented by interviews, both in groups and for individuals, in depth.

Then there is the problem of interpreting the results of the market and motivational research. The relation between the results and their interpretation is much the same as the relationship between econometric models and their interpretation. This again is a specialised field, and whereas the marketing interpretation is primarily psychological. So much then for a brief general statement on market forecasting.

There are many kinds of methods which are used to carry out forecasting, and one that is important we shall look at next. They are what are called stochastic processes, or in particular a special version of them known as Markov nets[3] which we illustrate in more detail in the next chapter. If the sample is atypical then,of course, such probabilities will be misleading, but if there is no other available evidence, then this evidence must be used, and at the same time progress monitored, adjusting the probabilities as circumstances change, if indeed they do. Just to remind us we say that Markov nets are concerned with interrelated probabilities between successive events. So B occurs after A two thirds of the time and C occurs after B half the time. If A never follows A, and A and B are equally likely to follow B, and C is always followed by A, we have the following Markov table of probabilities:

$$\begin{array}{cc} & \begin{array}{ccc} A & B & C \end{array} \\ \begin{array}{c} A \\ B \\ C \end{array} & \begin{bmatrix} 0 & \frac{2}{3} & \frac{1}{3} \\ \frac{1}{4} & \frac{1}{4} & \frac{1}{2} \\ 1 & 0 & 0 \end{bmatrix} \end{array}$$

This provides a series such as:

ABCABACABBCAB

Forecasting now is the ability to draw up such tables for a series of events or single events over periods of time (short, medium or long), so that one can look at a series:

ABDABDADABCDEABABCABDAEAB

and so on, and from such a series discover sub-series (in a pattern) which are repeated regularly. If individual events can be unambiguously labelled, then all forecasting can be depicted by such a series. The table above is derived from the series and this is an example of learning or may derive the series from the table and this is teaching: the whole process (with series and tables) supplies the essence of the forecasting process. It goes without saying that for various reasons such methods cannot always be employed. The case mentioned already of Random Walks is just one sort of exception.

The step from the simple stochastic process with independent probabilities for each event, to the complex series of events, where one event may be contingent on a whole series of events - some of them themselves contingent on other events - may become exceedingly complex. Similarly it is possible to cater for the further complexity of simultaneous events which can be broken down into their component parts (the molecular to the atomic), so that ABC occurring together can be given the label F in the series. The logic is simple in principle, but the forecasting remain hazardous, and often complicated in practice.

An example of a Markov net application lies in the use of the English language. The whole of English (sentence-by-sentence) can be represented by a Markov net conditional probability table, where the most accurate basis is word-by-word, although ultimately a translation process is on at least a sentence-by-sentence basis.

Looked at on a word-by-word basis, the occurrence of any one word can only be followed (in general) by another word from a particular class of words. If the nature of the subject described is fixed (say behaviour or economics) then, of course, the probabilities are further weighted so that eventually every word in every sentence can be prescribed with increasing certainty. This brings out the point that the greater the sample of the past we take, the better the estimate of the future is likely to be for obvious reasons.

The Markov modelling procedure can be brought right down to a practical business problem. This could be for a production control system for any product whatever. Each step in the processing (for example, temperature, pressure, etc.) can be depicted as a step in a Markov net, and then the links between each step can be predicted and, as a result, controlled, and it is often possible to discover the optimum sequence for a particular final product. This is precisely where learning may play a vital part in an industrial process: where the optimum sequence is learned, of course, it is reproduced regularly unless (or until) some further learning is required, i.e. until the circumstances change.

A trend analysis program can now be used (also as, or part of, the adaptive program), and this searches for new patterns of demand behaviour. If such learning can take place, it can be undertaken off-line or on-line with the adaptive process available. Indeed, we expect learning to be used always in these situations in one form or another. A program (one of many such programs) called PATTERN (a form of spectral analysis which we discuss later) has been written precisely to be used in this context of looking for general trends in a sequential process, as well as patterns in sequences of events.

Estimates of demand can also be made to depend on subjective probabilities. Given a desirability matrix A, of hoped-for events, and a probability matrix B of expected events, one can then proceed to an element-by-element multiplication of the matrices A x B and then by adding rows of A x B we get vectors a,b, ..., n and the maximum of these vectors provides the best combination of 'desired' and 'expected'. Such characteristics taken together again clearly point in the direction of behavioural considerations.

In the so-called Venture Analysis method, we consider various alternative demands $d_1, d_2, \ldots, d_n$ and various alternative stock investment $s_1, s_2, \ldots, s_m$, say. The utility matrix U is then constructed in terms of net cash pay-off and this is a forecast which relates to sets d_1 and s_j.

From the utility matrix U one can then construct the regret matrix M, there the elements x_1 or M are constructed as follows:

$$\begin{bmatrix} x_{i1} = y_{1max} - y_{i1} \\ x_{i2} = y_{2max} - y_{i2} \\ ---- \\ x_{in} = y_{nmax} - y_{in} \end{bmatrix}$$

and select the minimum regret element which is the lowest maximum of a row. The aim is to estimate cost and look for the best combination of estimates of demand and investment. (See Appendix III for a more detailed description of these methods).

The confirmation methods, associated especially with the work of Carnap[2], are related to the notions of inductive logic and depend in essence on estimating the probability p associated with the confirmation c of hypothesis h by evidence e, which we write:-

$$p=c(h,e)$$

If a situation where:

$$e \longrightarrow h$$

then c automatically is maximum, where $\longrightarrow$ means "(logically) implies". Similarly:

$$e \longrightarrow Nh$$

where Nh = not-h, means c is a minimum. The practical cases all come in between these two limits and the problem is to assess the values of e, where e may be partitioned.

$$e = e_1, e_2, \ldots, e_m$$

and the probabilites $p_1, p_2, \ldots, p_m$ can be associated one-by-one with each e_j.

An example where the evidence (e) would be taken to be conclusively in favour of increased production is where demand was greatly in excess of supply, and the opposite is where supply greatly exceeds demand.

A number of different techniques and measures can be set out to estimate e and these are ways of trying to find the maximum likelihood of the estimate being correct in the light of all the available evidence. Once more the aim is to provide a method that allows good estimating of demand (or almost anything else) and quick and accurate processing of the estimates.

It should be noticed that all the mathematical models we have mentioned (and there are many more which we have not mentioned) depend on some sort of forecasting. The aim is to provide a quick and effective consequence of a forecast, with the usual combined use of trend analysis to pick up information which could then be used to improve the estimates (or evidence) used in the application of the model or models selected. This in turn is considered in terms of their behavioural implications.

This is perhaps a good moment to introduce the concept of a "normal distribution". It so happens that many key variables in the real world are normally distributed, hence we have built up a large number of statistical tests, such as correlation, which generally presupposes that the variables under consideration are normally distributed.[5] A normal distribution in graph form is bell-shaped, but with varying girths, etc.

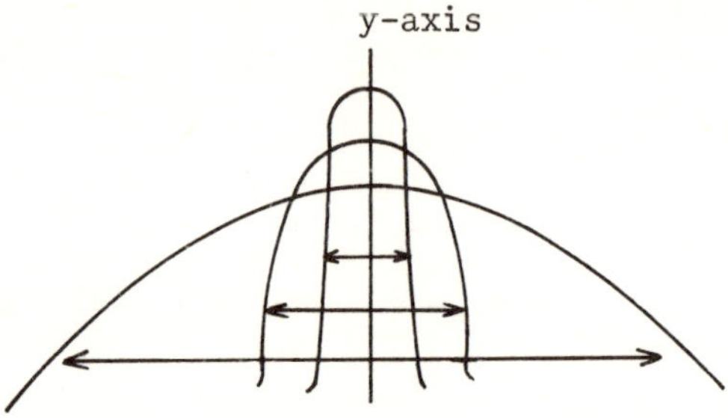

FIGURE 1

Thus to take them about the y-axis of a simple graph, we can see such normal distributions. They have, of course, a definite mathematical formula and each such distribution can be tested for its "normality". Most standard statistical tests can now be used provided the data is distributed at least "near-normally".

There are, of course, other distributions, e.g. Poisson (Figure 2):

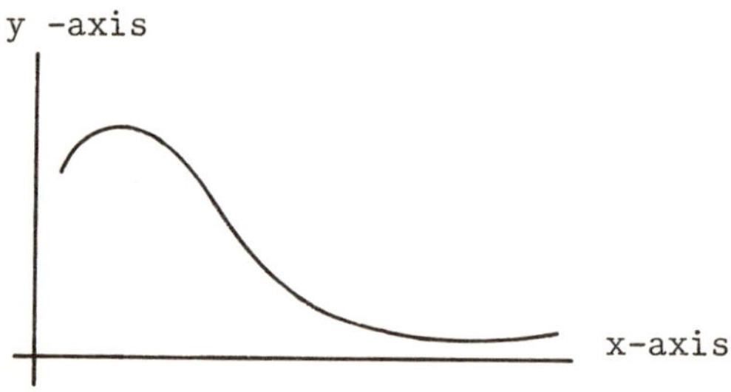

FIGURE 2

which refers to such features as your chances of winning the pools beyond some certain limit. If you consider Moroney's[6] example the number of times a team got a certain number of goals in a match, you get a Poisson type graph drawn here in the form known as a histogram (Figure 3):

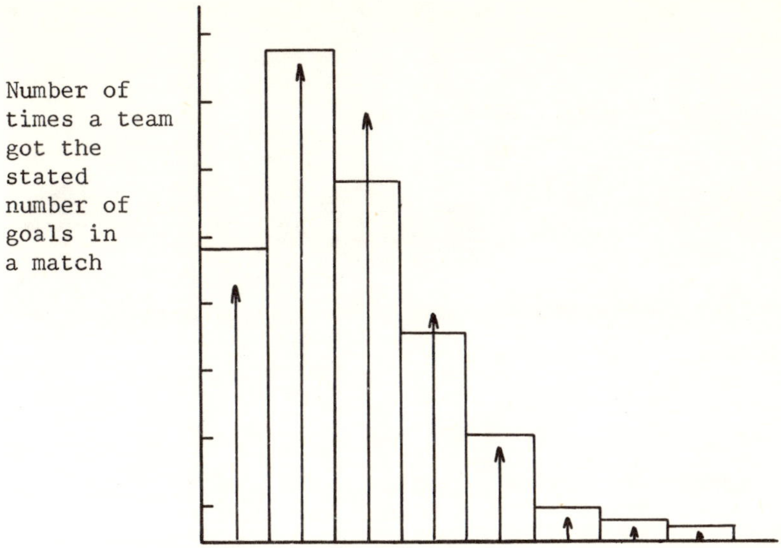

FIGURE 3

There are, of course, other distributions besides; but they occur less often.

To return to the normal distribution, it should be noticed that the arithmetic mean (often simply called the "mean") is the average, and in Figure 1 is shown by the y-axis and sigma (σ), the standard deviation by the lines showing average girth (s-lines). This brings out the point we have made about two distributions having the same mean and different standard deviations.

REFERENCES CHAPTER 5

1. M.J.C.Surrey, Analysis and Forecasting of the British Economy, Cambridge University Press. 1971.

2. F.H.George and L.Johnson (Eds.) An Introduction to Purposive Behaviour, Gordon and Breach (to be published).
M.Weir Teleological Systems, Gordon and Breach (to be published).

3. J.G.Kemeny and J.L.Snell, Finite Markov Chains van Nostrand, 1960.

4. A.Ghosal, Applied Cybernetics: Its Relevence to Operations Research, Gordon and Breach, 1978.

5. R.Carnap, Truth and Confirmation In Readings on Philosophical Analysis (Eds. H. Feigl and W. Sellars) Appleton - Century - Crofts, 1949.

6. C.E.Weatherburn, Mathematical Statistics, Cambridge University Press, 1946.

7. M.J.Moroney, Facts from Figures, Penguin Books, 1956.

CHAPTER 6
SCIENTIFIC FORECASTING METHODS

We have already seen that accurate forecasting is quite basic to investment of any kind, so we step aside from a direct discussion of the problem of investment in particular in this chapter and look at forecasting in some measure of isolation, but we shall always have forecasting in the context of investment in mind.

You have, to make a "guess" or some systematic estimate, or some more serious scientific forecast at how many copies of a magazine or brands of tobacco a shop will sell (and therefore you buy from the wholesaler) if you run a shop. The same applies even more obviously to large stores, chains of stores, manufacturers and government departments, and of course any sort of gambling, especially that involved in the Stock Exchange. These latter cases demand the serious and best possible methods of forecasting in order to leave as little as possible to chance.

Many of the same methods can be used by all concerned, but whereas the shopkeeper can do it with paper and pencil or a calculator, the big store will need at least a microprocessor (Apple, Pet, etc.,) and in the very large organisations a main frame computer, probably using satellite microprocessors, VDU's, etc. All this comes under the heading of forecasting and this is what this chapter intends to follow up from its introduction in the last chapter.

There are certain techniques known as DELPHI, Scenario Writing and the like, which are mainly appropriate to governments and the very large companies, but the investor should know of their existence, and be aware of the methods used and results obtained. The above are both methods of assessing or forecasting the future, the first (DELPHI) is done by getting a consensus of opinions fron various independent experts or a small group (syndicate) of knowledgable people, the second (Scenario Writing) is achieved by formulating a set of assumptions (hypotheses, guesses) and seeing where they are likely to lead you. These methods are used for short-and-long-term-forecasting, and follow exactly from scientific method (or science). We intend short-term here to mean primarily the search for a capital gain and long-term primarily the search for income, or an eventual pension or "lump sum" payoff. Let us look a little more closely at these techniques, since the scientific approach to investment implies a thorough knowledge of their use.

"QUALITATIVE FORECASTING METHODS"

It was E.H. Carr[1] who said:

"Modern history begins when history becomes concerned with the future as well as with the past".

This reminds us of the well known attack on historicism by Popper[2] which has been widely misunderstood as an attack on the ability to make a scientific study of history, whereas he was much more concerned with holistic explanations and Utopian despotism in the form of Fascism and Communism. Our interest is in planners and forecasting, which does though stem in part from history.

In fact historicism is not, as many writers have thought, that forecasting trends should be confused with the establishment of permanent laws of (social) behaviour. The use of the word 'permanent' indeed is a curious usage here and reminds one of von Bertalanffy's[3] comment that the distinction is not a radical one between "structures" (slow process of long duration) and "functions" (fast processes of short duration). In the light of this it might be thought that the "laws" of the physical sciences only differ from the "laws" of history in degree and not, as it were, in kind.

Chandler[4] has made it clear that the apparent differences between the repeatable events of physical science and the apparently "one-off" events of history are not quite what they seem from either side: much of science is not entirely repeatable and some of history is. In any event, science is as much concerned with (causal) explanation as it is with periodic or quasi-periodic occurrences. Finally, if history is made up of complex events determined by people and events that are themselves subject to economics, sociology and psychology at the very least, then it is doubtful if anyone would deny that these are at least potential sciences.

We certainly take the view that history is the main guide to the future and thus must, in principle, be a handmaiden to forecasting and planning, however difficult it may be to carry through the application. It is, a science, an essential back cloth to the mathematical methods which we discuss later in this chapter. It will also be admitted that much forecasting has turned out to be wrong, even worthless at times, but this should in no way deter us from our pilgrimage; it should merely make us extremely careful. Mario Bunge[5] has made a very relevant point in saying that forecasting should not rely solely on experts and their views, but should involve research. This raises the question though of what form the research should take.

Experiments are difficult (although perhaps not impossible) to carry out in history. Research though, rather as in the undoubted science of astronomy, can still be carried out by the construction of models of a whole range (mathematical, logical, physical, pictorial, etc) with or without quantification. In investment, experiment is clearly possible, but in a limited way. The obvious use of "paper investments" (trials without money) suggests itself immediately.

We shall later, after a more detailed study of forecasting techniques, discuss the main purpose of forecasting, which is to make and take decisions. Decision making and taking (certainly when sufficiently abstract) are the same as planning and problem solving.[5] This makes for an enormous potential range of investigation; we shall, of course, only be looking at selected aspects of the problem - especially investment - bearing in mind our goals. Let us now look at the now traditional methods of forecasting which are largely preliminary to the mathematical methods we have already mentioned, and some more besides that come later.

The aims and purposes of forecasting are precisely those of science itself and indeed of all intelligent behaviour. We often say that science is concerned with prediction (as well as understanding and control) and certainly we can only learn and behave intelligently if we can predict successfully. The goals of society we should remember are more difficult to define, and they go beyond the merely scientific and depend upon something much more fragile and ill-defined. They indeed may involve survival and other things besides, but at least we can be sure that we do not all agree on what they are.

Prediction (forecasting), when generalised to all sorts of situations, leads to understanding. By understanding we mean a degree of awareness of a range of predictions based on a theory (or model) which allows predictions (forecasting) from that theory or model.

Now to the DELPHI model. It was developed by Olaf Helmer[6] at the RAND Corporation. It avoids, as we mentioned, the difficulties of confrontation between experts in different disciplines who so often, when exchanging opinions, become more concerned with making debating points and "winning over opposition" rather than making more objective estimates and guesses. The Delphi Model avoids this problem of confrontation by using questionnaires which are dealt with by individuals in a series of "rounds".

The various experts invited to join the group are first asked (as an example - one of many) what technological breakthroughs they may expect in the next so many years. The answer is to be in the form of a statement such as "the use of drugs to increase the levels of human intelligence" or "mining the ocean beds of the world", and written against each of these forecasts are dates such as "in ten years" or "between ten and fifteen years hence".

We now sort through the range of forecasts and pick, say, the thirty most frequently predicted and set them out in a list which shows their average expected breakthrough point. This new list is then re-cycled to the experts and their view sought as to the most probable of these forecasts and a re-assessment of the lead time. This re-cycling can proceed further and may involve the use of a new team of experts, but whatever variations are offered the result is a sort of concensus chart.

It is well known that the Delphi method has serious limitations:

1. It creates a false impression of fact rather than a forecast.
2. It is extremely difficult, semantically, to know whether different people's forecasts (worded slightly differently) amount to the same thing or not.
3. Forecasts often mask each other so that the actual occurrence of forecast A rules out the likelihood of forecast B.
4. Questionnaires when used are often vague and semantically untrustworthy.
5. The selection of the Delphi panel may (even unconsciously) be biased.
6. The results achieved, where they have been testable, show conservatism and some unreliability.

All this in no way means that Delphi should not be used, rather it should not be depended upon in isolation. It should be regarded as one of a family of methods.

A second method used is that of Trend Extrapolation. This involves a more sophisticated look at growth curves, a careful analysis of what might be called precursive events and what is in fact, in some cases, called "envelope curve extrapolation". Envelope curve extrapolation is a method with tremendous potential, but has enough uncertainty and difficulty involved in the necessary interpretation to make it daunting for the uninitiated to use. The use of any extrapolating activity needs, of course, re-modelling in the light of new experience - much as Bayes' Rule does when applied in the light of new evidence (see Appendix III).

The principles of association and continuity underly Trend Extrapolation in whatever form it takes. The basic assumption is that any relationship that exists between two parameters in the past will hold, at least for the immediate future. It is a use of history, in the form of some sort of mathematical forecasting. It is, by its very nature, mainly used for short term forecasting, and is often used as a precursor for other methods (such as scenario writing) for middle and long-term forecasting.

Now to our second main "qualitative method" which is Scenario Writing. This is now widely practised, and is especially associated with Herman Kahn and the Hudson Institute. The aim is to show all the logical possibilities that follow from the present (or any other) state of affairs. It is not only a means of making predictions, indeed it is more a matter of showing all the contingencies that follow from the given starting conditions. Herman Kahn himself regards his problem as discerning long-term trends.

Such work on Scenario Writing led to the prediction that the existing material developments will continue and that presently underdeveloped countries will acquire modern technologies quickly. It also predicts a world-wide zoning to deal with weaponry, pollution, trade and technology, and it sees an increased self-questioning in more developed countries regarding our purposes and goals.

The principal difficulties which are encountered in writing scenarios are the presence of subjective selections in lines of approach, the use of value judgements, which are inevitable, and the usual assumptions that today's relationships and our perception of them are necessarily going to lead into relationships that are uncontaminated by <u>other</u> "unforseen" factors, besides those expected ("forseen"). Perhaps most important of all in practice has been the concentration on the relationships <u>between</u> nations as opposed to <u>within</u> nations. One can see that many of these difficulties are the same as confront all forecasters, and they need not stop us attempting to forecast but should make us aware of the liability to error in depending on any one approach in isolation.

Systems Analysis[8] is another technique which has been widely used especially by the Rand & Systems Development

Corporation, and in the McNamara era in the defence headquarters at Washington. Systems Analysis has been used to analyse integrated techniques, cost effectiveness, feedback features and the way the whole of an abstracted system (like a model or theory in science) can be used as the basis for what we would call an executive information system. This is usually computerised and allows the use of interrogation - eventually by natural language - of a video terminal backed by a vast computer system.

The last method we shall mention here is that of cross-impact matrices. It was developed by Olaf Helmer and T.J. Gordon[9]. The essential principle is that of considering the interrelationship between forecast events (as perhaps its name implies). It was a criticism of the Delphi technique that it failed to do this, although it seems in many ways an unfair criticism, since an interpretation of Delphi studies could certainly do so.

Matrices are used to classify the cross-impacts (interactions) between events, so for ten events forecasted, there are clearly 100 possible interactions (of first order) between them. This implies a 10 x 10 matrix. We then investigate the strength of the cross-impact and apply simulation techniques and subjective probabilities (with their attendant and inevitable uncertainty) to them. It is usually made to depend upon Delphi studies and is regarded by many as therefore having an unreliable basis. But this need not be the case, since the method can be imposed on other methods of forecasting. It can also be used analytically as in the case of Morphological Research. But of course, here too, as in the case of Morphological Research itself, criticisms are possible, since either way the imagination may not be sufficiently engaged, concepts may be missed and so on.

All this merely serves to remind us once more that these methods of forecasting should not be used in isolation, nor should they be independent of human imaginative skills, this has been called the "logic of discovery" by Reichenbach[10]. Such methods though do serve to provide a basis for forecasting and could, in many circumstances, provide a context for the use of the mathematical techniques of time series and the like, which we are to discuss at some length, especially in the form of regression analysis.

The investor will rely mainly, as we have suggested on publications (The Financial Times, etc) for his information, but he should try and acquire as many Delphi studies as possible, because these studies act as an important guide to the future sources of investment. Let me briefly outline one Delphi study, before we return to our build-up towards regression analysis.

A DELPHI STUDY

The seventies was expected to bring about simple and cheap fertility control, but there is still a problem of educating people in their use, however cheap and however effective the methods. To some extent, religious barriers have been lifted against such controls as exemplified by the new view of the Irish, but even so there remains a lot to be done.

Another prediction was the use of ultra-light synthetic materials for construction purposes - this has been investigated from various viewpoints and will be implemented indefinitely into the future.

Automated language translators do now exist but the problem has been surprisingly difficult to deal with. This has mainly resulted from the fact that language translation has been tackled algorithmically whereas, because of the contextual nature of semantics, it should have been tackled heuristically.

The next thought is one that has certainly been given a great deal of publicity. It is that of transplanting organs in the human body. This has already been done for many internal organs and more especially has been achieved, with some measures of success, even for the heart which is rather obviously among the more important organs, and involves rather more critical skill in the transplantation operation. We may expect further developments in the future where artificial equivalents are used rather than transplantation of existing organic equivalents. The replacement of limbs in this manner has already occurred and we have for a long time had means (deaf aids, spectacles, etc) of amplifying inadequate existing systems.

Another idea was that of reliable weather forecasting. This was thought (in 1960) to become a reality in the 1974 - 1978 period. There is, of course, a vagueness over the use of the word 'reliable' which makes a confirmation of the start of such developments difficult to determine. It is certainly the case that more widespread data is now collected and more methodical - mostly computerised - techniques are now being used.

It may well turn out that our ability to control weather by artificial means will outstrip our ability to predict it in natural cases.

Should this be so, our original need for reliability in forecasting will be greatly lessened. This is an example where the full gamut of understanding - ideally demanded by science - can be overcome by changing the nature of the problem.

A whole number of computer advances have been predicted: Chemical storage systems, the use of laser beams, the use of heuristic methods - both on and off-line for speeding search and problem solving procedures, and so on and so forth.

The widely accepted use of non-narcotic (or indeed narcotic) drugs for changing personality characteristics was favoured to occur between 1980 and the turn of the century. This again is under way already in limited fashion and supplied us with some of our fears about information pollution, specialisation and the ultimate control - even enslavement - of human beings. We can carry on this list for many pages, but let us select just a few more especially important examples.

1. Psychiatry will come of age and with the aid of physical and chemical methods will cure ten times as many psychotics. (1984-2016).
2. Genetic engineering will be developed sufficiently to control hereditary defects (1990-2010).
3. Economic ocean farming to produce 20 per cent - 30 per cent of world food (2000-2015).
4. Drugs used to increase intelligence (1984-2024).
5. Chemical control of ageing to expand expectation of life by 50 or more years (1995-2025)
6. Breeding intelligent animals as workers (2000 on).
7. Direct input to brain (rather than through speech and special senses) to increase education (1985 on).

This last, of course, is reminiscent in effect of Brave New World but very different in that it is by direct contact (as by use of implanted electrodes) on the brain. This again encourages our fears of misuse and the element of specialised control over people that would occur.

More generally, what we see is that there are a vast number - far more than the few examples listed - of possible innovations (involving discoveries and inventions) that will occur since also it is predicted that the lead time (and gestation time) for such break-throughs is diminishing fast, even though it is still fairly long. One may guess now that most of the above predictions derived by Helmer are fairly conservative in the light of our knowledge of 1983.

A problem now looms up; this is an economic one. It is well illustrated by space-travel. We have the technical know-how, or could certainly quite quickly attain it, to launch a colonisation of space. But can we afford it? The amount of the investment is (and no pun is intended) quite "astronomical".

At this point we have to ask ourselves whether there is any point in exploring outer space. It seems likely that the very same question was asked by people prior to the colonisation of the earth. But the Phoenicians, the Spaniards, the Portuguese and all the other early seafaring and exploring nations carried on and eventually succeeded.

The question still remains. Might not Britain or Spain have been happier and more sensible to have kept within their own frontiers. It is a philosopher's chestnut to ask what would have happened had you done something other than that which you actually did. You cannot answer questions based on the contra-factual conditional except in terms of guesses and suppositions. But it does look as if such an inward-looking parochialism would have been absolutely fatal to the development of the modern world with the outstanding success of medical science, better living conditions and increased knowledge. But the joke is obvious enough: you cannot have (apparently) the advantages without the disadvantages. Perhaps then it would have been better (one should notice the inadequacy of the words like 'happier', 'better', 'sensible', etc we use in evaluating our activities) had the Phoenicians stayed at home.

The plain fact is that human beings are insatiably curious. Curiosity is a basic drive which is essential to our survival. It is no more possible for us not to investigate new ideas and new worlds than if it would be for us not to listen to people who tell us of new ideas. How difficult we find it not to answer the telephone when we have been expressly told not to. Let us nowreturn to more immediate problems of forecasting for investment in the present state of affairs.

FORECASTING AND SCIENTIFIC METHOD

The important point is that as an investor, when forecasting you must, like everyone else, take the present and the past as a guide to the future. We are said to extrapolate from the past to the future, and there are many methods for doing this and more are made available almost every year. It is all rather similar to the scientist at work making predictions, and this emphasises again the need for an understanding of scientific method which overlaps common sense. We shall now give a slightly more detailed description of scientific method. The use of an hypothesis or hypotheses is vital to forecasting and science. The only difference is that scientists usually use the word 'prediction' instead of 'forecasting'; the meaning though is identical in the two cases.

Science is often thought of as the collecting of facts. It is certainly true that fact-collecting plays an important part in science, but it is by no means enough. To invest efficiently you certainly need to know a great many facts as has already been made clear in the earlier chapters. Just as important though as fact-collecting is the setting up of theories, theoretical structures, models, etc which allow the use of both deductive (which we will discuss) and inductive logic (which we will also discuss). What we must now do is to outline each of the various steps involved in the total scientific process in more detail.

Scientific procedures can be thought of in terms of two principal operations which can occur in either order and therefore we will arbitrarily select the deductive procedure first for discussion. Given a set of assumptions, whether these be set out explicitly as postulates in a formal system such as Euclidean Geometry, or whether they are implicit and merely stated in ordinary language, or indeed whether they be in some sort of special symbolic form as in organic chemistry, they can represent the starting point for the making of deductive inferences. A deductive inference is based on the language which is used to describe that part of the system we are interested in (here it is the Stock Exchange and investment), it being obvious that science is partitioned into various sub-departments all of which are part of the totality of human knowledge, but nevertheless are somewhat <u>specialised</u>, and we are concerned with science (sometimes called disciplines) of economics and business "science".

The process of deduction is one of drawing logical inferences from assumptions. From these inferences further statements are generated which are the consequences, although sometimes called theorems in a formal system, which apply to the system being described. Deduction (at least as deductive logic) itself is a symbolic process and refers to the conclusions that follow from the assumptions. Some deductive inferences are sometimes made in very complex circumstances and can involve statistical and probability methods of inference as well as logical ones, and indeed the logical can be fuzzy or uncertain. Since the results of a statistical analysis, for example, is an inference with some degree of uncertainty attached to it, e.g. share X has just "bottomed out" and has started to climb and the economic environment seems appropriate, so the inference you may make is "it is <u>probably</u> a good time to buy". None of the argument is guilty of <u>deduction</u> in science so justly criticised by Rom Harre[11].

One has to be careful about using formal arguments for factual information which do not have the same structure as the formal structure. Equally, in any sort of factual discussion one has to be careful about fallacious arguments (paradoxes). Thus we find examples like "If the (cleanshaven) barber in the village shaves everyone except those who shave themselves", if we ask who shaves the barber, the answer cannot sensibly be given because the argument has been stated paradoxically, which suggests that he both shaves and does not shave himself at the same time. Russell's famous paradox [12] is exemplified by the cretan who says "all Cretans are liars".

Stage two of scientific method starts from observation and goes through the process of induction, which is sometimes characterised by the name inductive logic, and what Sherlock Holmes frequently referred to erroneously as deduction. The aim is to arrive at generalisations which are the hypotheses which are broken down into assumptions which are the starting point for deduction.

The process of induction is that of generalising on the particular and is therefore in some sense the opposite of deduction which is particularising from the general. Like deduction, it is dependent on language since knowledge can hardly be thought of as knowledge unless it is communicable and therefore capable of being stated in some sort of language, whether symbolic or otherwise, and has hopefully the added ingredient, in the case of induction, of being "factual". An inductive argument would be one of the form "I have seen one crow and it is black, I have seen two crows and they are both black, I shall assume therefore that all crows are black". We are very careful to say, in making the inductive generalisation, that a crow is defined independently of its colour, otherwise it would be logically true to say crows are black, and anything that was in every other way a crow, but some other colour than black would be regarded as not-a-crow.

We, of course, need evidence to justify our hypotheses, which we even call 'laws' if we regard the evidence as being very strong. Now let us look at an "everyday" equivalent (anecdote) of science, which admittedly has probably never actually taken place.

Let us suppose we do not know of the existence of train timetables (or understandably in the world of 1983 we do not believe in them). Our job then is to find out when trains run and to make our problem slightly more tractable we limit our study to someone living in Hungerford (the subsequent analysis is even more fictitious than the contents of the train timetables). Let us talk now in the first person.

I arrive at Hungerford station and take a chair on the platform. I wish the station staff "good morning" but do not ask about the trains. The reason is that a scientist in general (psychiatrists, psychologists and one or two others have no alternative) does not ask questions of the things he observes: atoms, pottassium chlorate, biological and botanical specimens are not conversationalists. Even where conversation is a possibility for the scientist he can never be sure he is being told the truth.

So I sit and note that at 9.30 a train stops and carries on eastwards (the sign on the train says Reading), the next train is going west and does not stop, but I notice it says on its side "Taunton, Exeter and Plymouth". Another train going east with "Taunton, Reading and Paddington" on the side, goes through quickly. These two fast moving trains pass through at 11.00 and 11.30 hours respectively.

The next train stops at 12.00 and goes on west, and the sign on the front says Westbury. At the end of the day and the night (I use a flashlight through the night which mostly picks up freight trains) the next morning I see the train from Reading which comes in this time at 9.34.

I sit back and draw up my model (or scheme) which shows twelve stopping trains - six going west and six going east - fourteen non-stopping trains, again equally divided between east and west. I recorded times at Hungerford for all twenty-six trains. I have also recorded four freight trains - three going east and one west - so far so good.

I can now, while I sit and wait, make only one inductive inference and this is to the effect that it will be the same every day. The game is clear now. We are looking for repetition if not on a daily basis, at least on some sort of repetitive basis.

If my deduction is correct then I can deduce that today (Tuesday did I but know it) will be like Monday was. So I sit and wait, observing and noting down trains and times. Tuesday is the same as Monday, except for fairly small variations in time. This observation confirms[13] the correctness of my model and the theory about train behaviour which I have based upon it. This increases my confidence for my Wednesday observations.

After an evening in Hungerford that night and a night's

sleep, I check Wednesday and again Thursday and they all "fit the facts" perfectly with only minor differences over time.

My growing confidence receives a shock on Saturday and again on Sunday, since these days are somewhat different from what has happened so far, and also they are different from each other.

I am worried about my observational powers, since we know that errors creep into observations, so I decide to watch the trains as frequently as possible and keep sleep to a minimum.

What the next few weeks showed was that there was a sort of pattern discernible, and this was what I was searching for, and it meant breaking up my model (a "timetable"), into Monday-to-Friday trains, Saturday trains and most different of all, Sunday trains. I average my times so that I can tell pretty well when I need to get to the station if I want to travel either east or west, and I can even tell approximately when the non-stop trains go through. I am a little clever now and I can make a deductive inference that allows me to tell which train to board to get to Reading in order to catch the fast train at Reading to get to Paddington.

This last inference I can try out in practice (experiment) by estimating the time both the slow trains and the fast trains take to get to Reading. In fact I might find other trains at Reading (going to London) coming from other sources. This could cut down my wait there.

My model has a "set back" when I get to my first Bank Holiday, I find excursion trains are put on, and after a few years at Hungerford I see that summer services are not quite the same as winter services. I can set up a 365-day timetable but even this is not quite correct if, as they seem to, modifications in time occur occasionally, and one or two trains seem to have ceased to run altogether, and less frequently new ones are introduced.

My job is complete though, I can do some part of what science required. I can give a fairly accurate prediction of what occurs at Hungerford station and by acquiring a railway map, I can hazard some reasonable guesses as to how you could get to other places besides London, Reading, Taunton, Exeter, Plymouth and so on. I should need to do some more experiments to make these guesses more precise, and I would have to accept the fact that my timetable would not be quite as good as that acquired from British Rail. But even if I acquired the official timetable, it would still not be wholly accurate; trains are late and sometimes break down and are sometimes taken off due to strikes and other causes.

But the scientist's aim of prediction and understanding are being satisfied as far as is humanly possible. If you live in Hungerford and want to go to London by train you will have a better chance (assuming you cannot get a timetable) by consulting me rather than going to the station on the off-chance.

You should notice that prediction and understanding are not quite the same thing. As a general practitioner I can predict, from experience, that blue medicine will take away the pain in your arm, but I may have no idea why it does so. If I analyse chemically the blue medicine and consider its pharmacological effect on your nervous system or muscles, and see what effect the medicine has on other states, I can generalise my prediction to a theory and this causes me to say "I understand why that happens".

Let us step back now to look at the four nodal points in our scientific model. We will start at the opposite node this time. I formulate a hypothesis: "that all bodies when dropped gravitate towards the earth's centre" I can add a number of other hypotheses and to draw the deductive consequences most conveniently I may formalise my hypotheses as a set of axioms or postulates, as in Euclidean Geometry, and after that is done I make my inference "If I drop this box it will fall to the ground", and when (and one should say "if") it does I have added some confirmatory evidence to my hypothesis. This does not require an induction to amend my assumptions.

If however looking at the whole of my theory of physics, I find an instance that does not behave in the predicted way, I have to make some new inductive generalisations or amend existing ones. This involves the well known Popperian[13] notion of falsification.

A classical example of this sort of thing occurred in physics when it was discovered that the perihelion of the planet Mercury did not behave as was predicted by Newtonian physics. Einstein reformulated (generalised) Newtonian physics by introducing new concepts regarding the finite velocity of light, the simultaneity of events, the fact that events and velocities are relative to a frame of reference, and that in the physical world there are no preferred frames of reference. This was the birth of the theory of Relativity and Einsteinian physics.

We can now see clearly another problem. If you study only the trains at Hungerford, say, and even they vary to some extent, you cannot necessarily apply the same rules to the rest of British trains. The same details do not help at all when applied to America or France, or most other European countries, but the principles by which we discover the timetable do.

Statisticians come in here and say that you can only talk sensibly (scientifically) and make predictions (forecasts) about the domains you have actually sampled. The trouble is that we have, by necessity, only sampled, and we use average times or some such statistical measure of the times of trains passing through Hungerford. Another trouble is that we cannot be sure the whole system will not suddenly change, and in any case we know our model (timetable in this case) is what scientists sometimes call a theory, is not 100 per cent accurate because of public holidays and special extensions at holiday times which are not always the same.

If you can forecast events you may also be able to control them. If you can control events you are in a very powerful position. It is precisely the increase in that control wherein lies the dramatic power of science. We shall say more about this later, but the likelihood of exercising control in investment is about as good as the meteorologist controlling the weather.

So we are arguing that intelligent day-by-day behaviour and scientific method are different only in degree of precision and forecasting is the highlight of both. Neither science nor common sense though depends upon events being repetitive, you can still explain (at least you can sometimes explain) the occurrence of events by their causes (the principle of cause and effect) and their frequency of occurrence,even if not regular (or near-regular) like the trains at Hungerford. This will eventually lead us to what is called a statistical model of forecasting, which is really concerned with analysing sequences and the frequency of occurrence of elements in that sequence, but before doing so let us look briefly at a very simple sort of Trend Analysis (a part of a forecasting method called Time Series). We shall need this as "chartists" (Method I of investment forecasting).

FIRST STEPS IN MATHEMATICAL FORECASTING

The methods involved are, in part and at first, those of Trend Analysis such as are depicted by Time Series (which will be the subject of later and slightly more detailed discussion), but we shall be looking at other methods besides. Our method is that of looking for the simplest case of trade cycles and seasonal fluctuations, exactly as a scientist uses the cycle of events to detect repetitions. We want to know if share prices fluctuate according to certain conditions, and whether such changes are indicative of a steady increase or a mere perturbation.

There are some well-known examples of such "trade cycles" and the classical one is that of ice-cream sales; they are minimal in January and maximal in August. There is also the longer-term question as to whether the ice-cream cycle is diminishing or increasing over successive years. We can fit a trend line to a time series by means of the well-known method of least squares. There is perhaps no need to emphasise that such methods do not suit every situation and sometimes a real trend can be disguised by outward appearances, or mere perturbation confused with a permanent change. We shall now outline what is involved. Let us start with a very simple example.

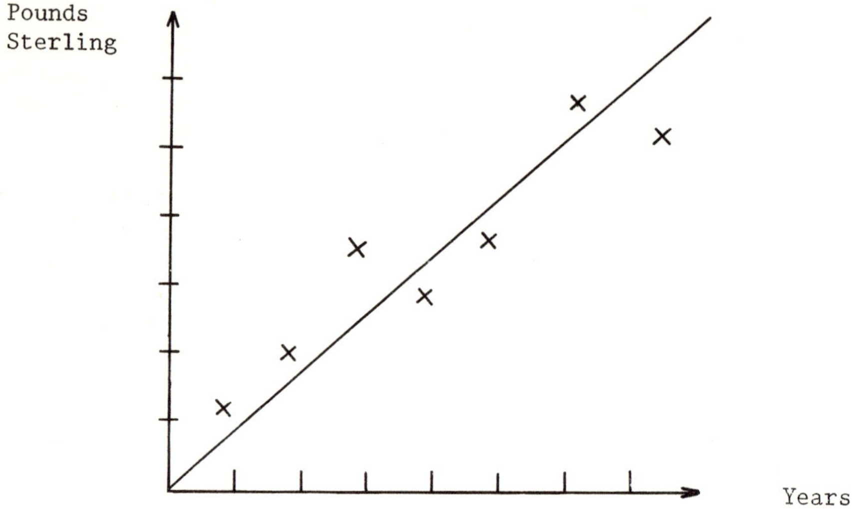

Figure 1

This shows the price (in pence) of ice-cream graphed against time (in years). (see figure 5)

The problem is to graph price against time, and the readings show a steady (linear) increase of price with time. We have to decide what the nearest sort of "curve" is to the readings of price (of share) for each successive seven years. The points seem to suggest a straight line as a sort of "average" development, so that (on the average) the share prices go up about 20p per annum.

We shall next look at a particular method (the method of least squares) that has been designed to deal with just this sort of situation.

If a distribution of the values of a dependent variable y is linear with respect to the values of an independent variable x, it can be plotted on a straight (regression) line. The ordinary algebraic equation $y = a + bx$ is used here. We gather as many pairs of values (x,y) as possible and add such equations together (call this A) and then multiply each of the equations so built up by its respective values of x (call this B). We then solve the simultaneous equations A and B to obtain values of a and b.

Let us spell this out carefully. The reader who is already familiar with this simple mathematical approach can move on to Figures 5 and 6.

$$y = a + bx$$

is the equation of a straight line, where b tells us the gradient and a the distance from zero on the y-axis that the line crosses the y-axis, e.g.:

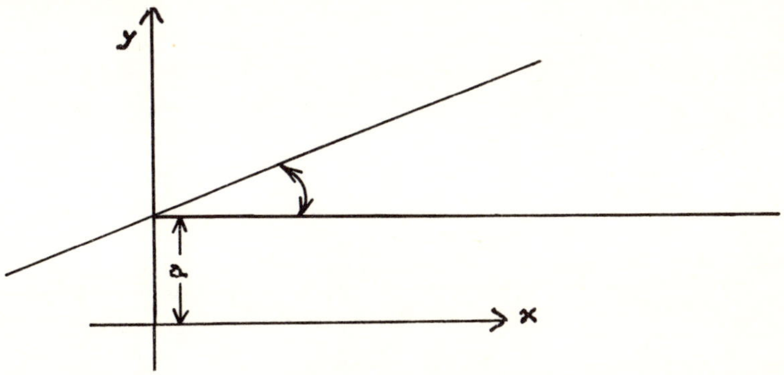

Figure 2

This shows the straight line and the significance of a and b in its equation.

For those unfamiliar with algebra, let us give a few simple examples.

Any point R, say, can be represented by 2 cartesian co-ordinates which is their distance from x(x_1) and from y(y_1), so R is (4,3) say. Any point on the plain can be described, where S can be defined as (-4,-3),so that x goes from + to - and y the same.

Now we say a straight line x given is by the equation: y = a + bx. So consider the lines d,e,c,g,h and i in Figure 4.

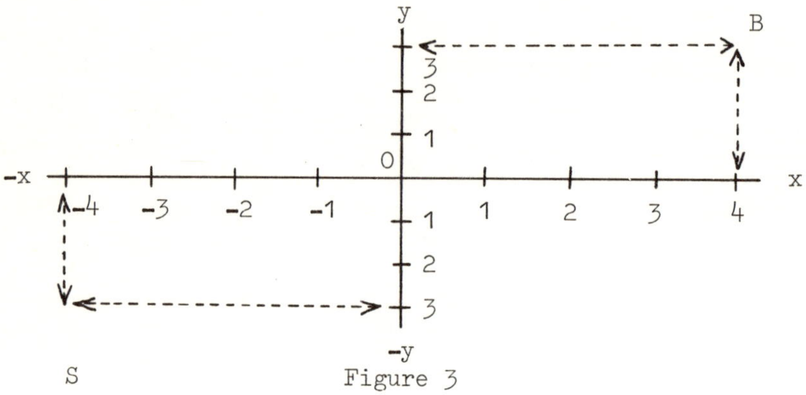

Figure 3

could be represented by:

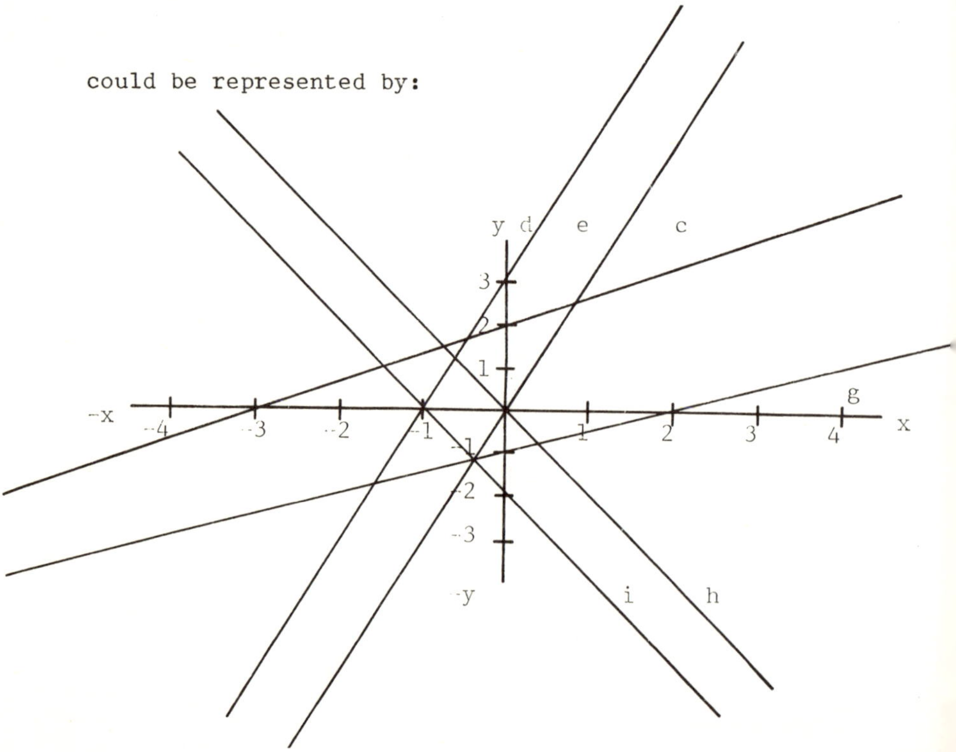

Figure 4

d is such that a = 0 since it goes through the origin (0,0) and b say = 60° which is 2/3 of 90°.

So d is $y = \frac{2}{3} x$

e has the same slope as d but cuts the y-axis at -3, so a = -3 and

so e is $y = -3 + \frac{2}{3} x$

For c and g we will say b = 30°, therefore is $\frac{1}{3}$ of 90°.

$$y = -2 + \frac{1}{3} x \qquad \text{--- (g)}$$

and $$y = 1 + \frac{1}{3} x \qquad \text{--- (c)}$$

Since the lines cut the y-axis at -2 and 1 respectively. Finally, h and i have negative slope say of 45° i.e. ½.

Therefore $y = 2 - \frac{1}{2} x$ --- (h)

and $y = -\frac{1}{2} x$ --- (i)

This makes clear how algebra is connected with geometry in the simple case of the straight line. The two axes y and x have the equations x = 0 and y = 0 respectively.

Now given a number of linear equations ....

So far say 4 values of x and y, we get, say:

x = 1,2,3,4 and y = 2,4,5,7

This gives us:

$$2 = a + b$$
$$3 = a + 2b$$
$$5 = a + 3b$$
$$7 = a + 4b$$

$$A = 17 = 4a + 10b$$

and then: $xy = x(a + bx)$ gives:

$$2 = a + b$$
$$8 = 2a + 4b$$
$$15 = 3a + 9b$$
$$28 = 4a + 16b$$

$$B = 53 = 10a + 30b$$

This gives for the simultaneous equations A and B:

$$4a + 10b = 17 \qquad \text{--- (1)}$$
$$10a + 3b = 53 \qquad \text{--- (2)}$$

Multiply (1) by 5 and (2) by 2 gives:

$$20a + 50b = 85 \qquad \text{--- (3)}$$
$$20a + 6b = 106 \qquad \text{--- (4)}$$

Subtract (4) from (3) gives:

$$44b = -21$$
$$\text{therefore } b = \frac{-21}{44} = -0.46$$

And now we substitute b in (1) which gives:

$$4a + 10(-0.46) = 17$$
$$\text{i.e. } 4a - 4.6 = 17$$
$$\text{i.e. } 4a = 12.4$$
$$\text{i.e. } a = 3.1$$

Let us illustrate Regression Analysis in practice by an economic example. We presume a relationship of a linear (represented by a straight line) kind between income and expenditure on consumables, where the expenditure (y) depends upon (in a linear fashion we think) income (x).

So the ordinary algebraic equation of a straight line $y = a \div bx$ is used to represent it. (Note: if we used more complex equations such as $y = a + bx^2$, then we should be involved in multiple regression and non-linear equations. We shall not consider such equations here).

Because $y = a + bx$ does not exactly fit the facts, since there will be differences in age, number of children, etc., we add an error component (ε) to our equation and write:

$$y = a + bx + \varepsilon$$

for the individual and

$$y_g = a + bx$$

in general; the suffix g reminds us that this is the general equation. If we assume a = 1,000 and b = 0.8, then:

$$y_g = 1{,}000 + 0.8x$$

So we would "expect" in general an individual with income of £7,000 or $7,000 to spend $6,600 or £6,600.

Yet we may find a particular individual spends $6,300 and therefore in our individual equation is -300 and y = a + bx + is

$$1{,}000 \div 0.8(7{,}000)-300 = 6{,}300$$

So we can go on picking up minor deviations from the general and what we need to know is whether they even out as they did in Figure 1.

Thus, if we have a table of readings for x (income) and y(expenditure) in £'s or $'s, then all we do is write out the set of equations for each pair of x and y as above and find values of a and b and therefore arrive at our regression line as we did before. This will show that the errors (or the squares of those errors) do approximately cancel each other out, so we can say that expenditure is (approximately) a linear function of income.

So the equation for the (regression) line is:

$$y = 3.1 - 0.46x$$

which is the best approximation to the points in the 2-dimensional set of points of a figure like Figure 1. It is a problem of fitting the best "curve" (in this case a straight line) to a series of actual observations.

The important point here is that you really need to understand the process involved, or at least have a hypothesis with high predictive value. But what we are saying is that a straight line is a good guide to the average fluctuations above and below that line (in fact this is the method of least squares).

Figure 5 shows the takings total of ice-cream sales (Moroney, 1956) predicted by reference to a regression analysis based on a regression of sales (the y-axis) on times for a period of 16 months (the x-axis).

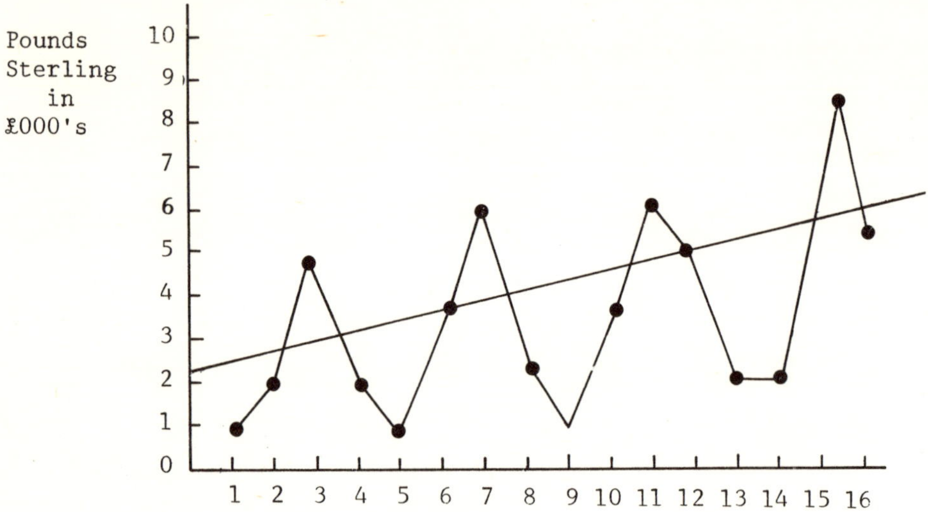

Figure 5

Ice-cream sales in £000's graphed by quarters over 4 years. The x and y-axis are in actual values, rather than coded as in our example.

Now lacking any additional information (much needed) which allows us to give some causal picture, we become what we have called "Chartists" in investment forecasting. We simply assume that the same pattern will continue.

So the following table shows the date on which figure 5 was based:

Quarter Year	1	2	3	4
1	1	2	5	2
2	1	3	6	2
3	1	3	6	4
4	2	2	8	4

The figures in the table show takings in thousands of £'s.

Let T = table and Q = quarter, and the we now code the data (purely for ease of computation).

$$q = Q-8, \quad t = T-3$$

and then to fit the regression line we need the following table, and subsequent computation:

Q	T	q	t	q^2	t^2	qt	t'	(T-T')= (t-t')	T'	$\frac{(T-T')}{(T')}$ 100
1	1	-7	-2	49	4	14	-1.22	-0.78	1.78	-44%
2	2	-6	-1	36	1	6	-1.04	+0.04	1.96	+ 2%
3	5	-5	2	25	4	-10	-0.87	+2.87	2.13	+134%
4	2	-4	-1	16	1	4	-0.70	-0.30	2.30	-13%
5	1	-3	-2	9	4	6	-0.52	-1.48	2.48	-60%
6	3	-2	0	4	0	0	-0.35	+0.35	2.65	+13%
7	6	-1	3	1	9	-3	-0.17	+3.17	2.83	+112%
8	2	0	-1	0	1	0	0.00	-1.00	3.00	-33%
9	1	1	-2	1	4	-2	0.17	-2.17	3.17	-67%
10	3	2	0	4	0	0	0.25	-0.35	3.35	-10%
11	6	3	3	9	9	9	0.52	+2.48	3.52	+70%
12	4	4	1	16	1	4	0.70	+0.30	3.70	+8%
13	2	5	-1	25	1	-5	0.87	-1.87	3.87	-48%
14	2	6	-1	36	1	-6	1.04	-2.04	4.04	-51%
15	8	7	5	49	25	35	1.22	+3.78	4.22	+90%
16	4	8	1	64	1	8	1.40	-0.40	4.40	-9%
Totals		8	4	344	66	60	for n = 16 quarters			

We shall refer the reader interested in detail now to Moroney[13]. But we mention here that our current search is for a long term forecast and we use:

$$\bar{t} = \frac{\Sigma t}{n} = \frac{4}{16} = 0.25 \text{ and } \bar{q} = \frac{\Sigma q}{n} = \frac{8}{16} = 0.5$$

t and q being simply the totals of columns t and q in the table. This gives the regression equation:

$$b = \frac{\Sigma qt - \frac{\Sigma q \Sigma t}{n}}{\Sigma q^2 - \frac{(\Sigma q)^2}{n}} = \frac{60 - \frac{8x4}{16}}{344 \text{ x } \frac{8x8}{16}} = \frac{58}{340} = 0.17$$

and in our case all this heavy but simple arithmetic leads to b = 0.17 and because we use q = Q-8, we add our 8 back on giving 8.5 instead of 0.5. Similarly t comes to 1.6. This leads to a trend equation T' = 0.17Q + 1.80. We now insert the trend values from column 8 of our table. Column 10 shows T', the trend, in actual units and column 11 (the final colum) shows the difference between trend and actual takings as a percentage of the trend value. Figure 6 shows this trend graphically.

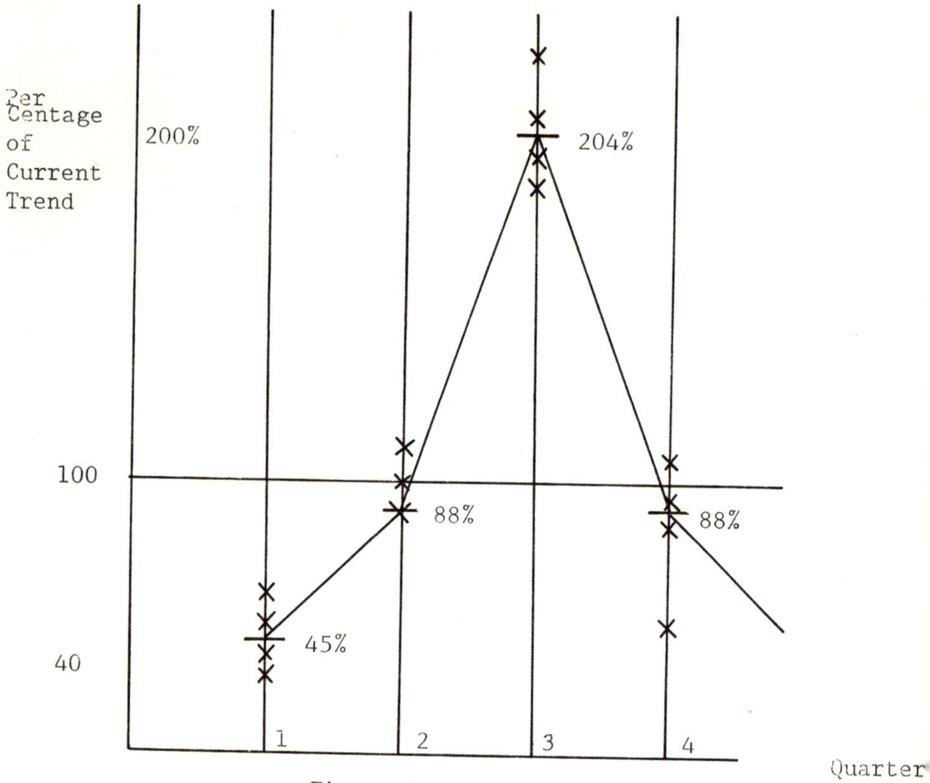

Figure 6

Takings on a quarterly basis within the year as a percentage of the current trend value.

This takes care of our long term trend. If we now look at each of the quarters in turn, taking each quarter in turn and using the last column of our table, we get Quarter 1 for the four years is -44%, -60%, -67%, -48% and do the same for each quarter, we find quarterly totals and averages as follows:

	Q1	Q2	Q3	Q4
Total	-219	-46	+416	-47
Quarterly Averages	-55%	-12%	+104%	-12%

The first quarterly average is 55% below trend and is therefore considered as 45% of trend value. Similarly the other quarters show 88%, 204% and 88%.

Figure 6 shows the seasonal effect in terms of these percentages, and we can produce a forecast based on seasonal effect and long term trend, provided of course nothing in the future changes. This forecast is for the next year and is illustrated by Figure 7 for months 17,18,19 and 20.

This was derived from the regression equation:

$$T' = 0.17Q + 1.80$$

and substituting the Q values in turn gives:

$$T' - 4.69,\ 4.86,\ 5.03 \text{ and } 5.20$$

The uncertainty is measured by 50% of trend, so we have firm predictions with upper and lower limits of uncertainty; so we could be quite a bit out. The prediction is based on a Moving Total, which is much the same as what we call Moving Average. Let me give a word of explanation.

A Moving Average is simply the average of the last n observations divided by n. So if we deal in the quarterly sales of ice-cream, we add up the four quarters and divide by 4. This allows us to extrapolate and make a prediction.

We should add that a normal Moving Average has the disadvantage of giving equal weight to all quarters. So to offset this we add progressively increasing weights. This technique is called Exponential Smoothing. To achieve this we need a smoothing constant A, say, which also lies between 0 and 1, and we simply use the formula:

$$\text{Latest MA} = \text{Latest actual figure} \times A \div \text{Previous MA} \times (1-A)$$

A lies near 0 with no fluctuation and near 1 with heavy fluctuation.
MA = Moving Average, and latest actual figure is the actual score derived from the data. To illustrate simply consider an output with four quarters 800, 1000, 1200, 1400, 1600 and then this gives:

(1000 x 0.4) ÷ (800 x (1-0.4)) = 880
(1200 x 0.4) ÷ (1000 x(1-0.4)) = 1080
(1400 x 0.4) ÷ (1200 x(1-0.4)) = 1280
(1600 x 0.4) ÷ (1400 x(1-0.4)) = 1480

On the right we have the exponentially smoothed totals.

So much then for our digression into regression analysis. Textbooks on statistics are required if the method is to be used systematically. But the reader should be encouraged at this stage to think of these methods as part of a whole battery of methods waiting ready on his shelf. But remember to use Time Series methods (these include trend analysis techniques such as regression analysis) out of the context of scientific method, i.e. of some causal understanding of the process makes it something of a lottery. For a more detailed account of these methods see Appendix II.

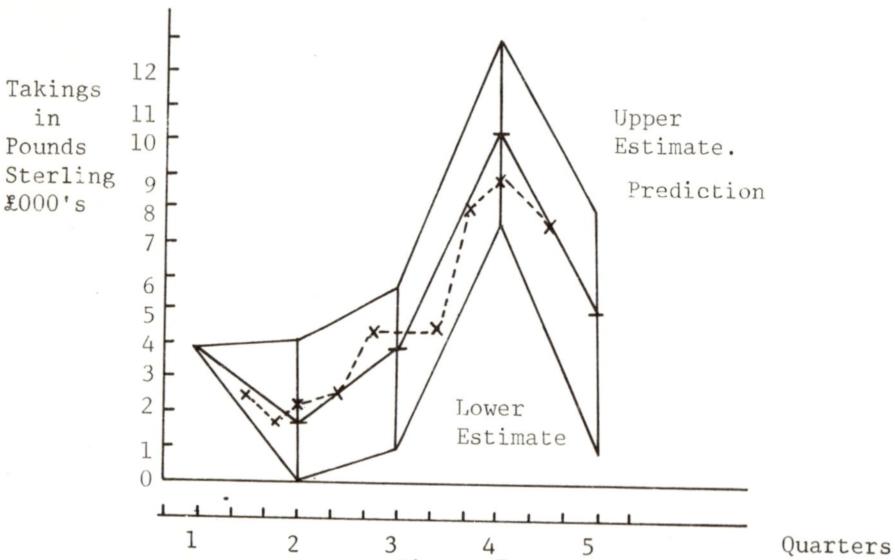

Figure 7
Three monthly moving takings totals and the assessment of confidence "belt" (possible error).

The whole idea of a change of a periodic kind is obviously of great importance and usually involves the well-known method of moving averages, much as we saw in Figure 7.

We shall now show in Figure 8 methods for building, identifying, fitting and checking models for time series.

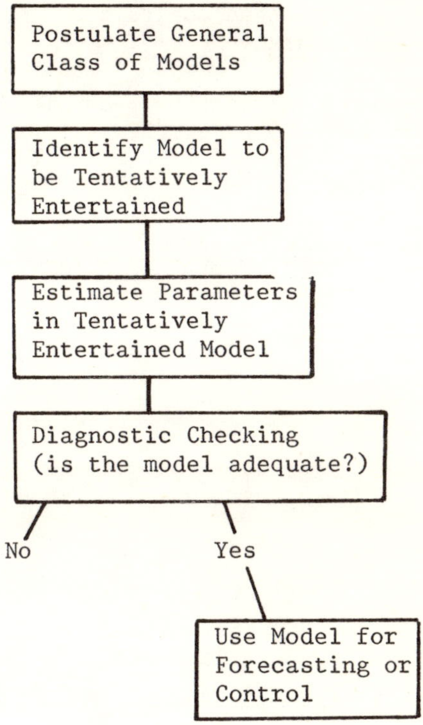

Figure 8

Building, identifying, fitting and checking, forecasting models.

In general terms we consider the forecasting of future values of a time series, given current and past values, and if the system is controllable, we control it. But as investors we can virtually never control it. The word 'virtually' is used here in case you are a huge investor who puts an enormous sum into a particular share, etc., such acts could provide some sort of control.

What we are now doing is attempting to get ever more precise estimates of likely changes in share prices. Can we recognise situations where share x has fallen before, or share Y risen? What is the causal relation between the two (or more) events? This leads us to Trend Analysis which is a sort of Regression Analysis, and is one of the simplest of the Time Series methods and can be run on a standard program in many of the more advanced calculators, let alone a computer, and can be done with paper and pencil. But now to Trend Analysis or to a very special case of it in the form of Markov Nets[14].

We considered only Markov Nets of length 2 in the last chapter. You can now, of course, extend the length of your Markov Net and have:

	aaa	aab	etc
aaa			
aab			
aac			
aad			
abc			
etc			

or

	a	b	c
aaa			
aab			
etc.			

or	aaa	aab	etc.
a			
b			
c			

to any length at all.

One application the present author has made of this method is to predict football results, e.g. as percentages over a sample of several successive pairs of home matches. (George)[15].

	W	D	L
W	45%	32%	23%
D	46%	25%	29%
L	45%	24%	31%

And for two successive away matches:

	W	D	L
W	44%	20%	36%
D	9%	31%	60%
L	20%	23%	57%

And for a match between Arsenal and Liverpool, say, you put these two tables together, as you would for a match between any two teams. But you must weigh the percentages according to the class of the two teams (e.g. by league position): so strictly speaking you need to have a series of tables; if you divide the teams in each league into A,B and C, this requires six tables and nine combinations.

It all becomes more complicated if you take 3 successive home and aways, and rather more still if you insist on 3 successive matches, whether home or away, which might be home-away-home, away-away-home, etc.

To return to the investor we can say, in general terms, that all he now has to do is keep a chart of events referring to purchases and sales, frequency of resulting profit and loss, etc. for any period of time (say on a weekly basis or a monthly basis) and he can see at a glance the trend, and will recognise that if a occurs (more and more of a particular industry's shares fall) then b is sure to follow (i.e. he loses money if he does not sell in time); or if c occurs b will not follow, but d will and he knows he should buy those shares and make money, if he sells at the right time. Although you cannot control the system you can, accurately forecast its behaviour.

REFERENCES CHAPTER 6

1. E.H. Carr, *What is History?* Macmillan, 1961; Solomon Encel, P.K. Marstrand and W. Page, *The Art of Anticipation*, Martin Robertson, 1975.

2. K.R. Popper, *The Logic of Scientific Discovery*, Hutchinson, 1972.

3. L. von Bertalanffy, *Problems of Life - An Evolution of Modern Biological Thought*, Wiley, 1952.

4. W.J. Chandler, *History as a Science*, Brunel University, 1978.

5. F.H. George, *Problem Solving*, Duckworth, 1980.

6. O. Helmer, B. Brown and T. Gordon, *Social Technology*, Basic Books.

7. John Chandler and Paul Cockle, *The Techniques of Scenario Planning*, McGraw-Hill, 1982.

8. C. de Hoghton, W. Page and G. Streatfield, *And Now The Future*, PEP, Broadsheet, 37, No. 529.

9. E. Encel, P.K. Marstrand and W. Page, *The Art of Anticipation*, Martin Robertson, 1975.

10. H. Reichenbach, *Experience and Prediction*, University of Chicago Press, 1938.

11. R. Harre, *The Principles of Scientific Thinking*, MacMillan, 1970.

12. B. Russell, *An Inquiry into Meaning and Truth*, Allen and Unwin, 1940.

13. R. Carnap, *The Unity of Science*, Kegan Paul, 1938.

14. Kemeny and Snell

15. F.H.George, *A Better Bet*, Topaz, 1967.

CHAPTER 7
BUSINESS & INFORMATION SCIENCE

In this chapter we now switch our point of emphasis from forecasting (and investment) as such, to look at it in its total business context. The same principles are involved as are involved in scientific method, and indeed this is the main unifying principle that underlies this whole monograph. As a human being, it does not matter whether he is acting as scientist investor or business man, his problems are basically the same. They hinge on prediction and forecasting which are, as we have said more or less, the same.

The planners are the people who, in a business house or a government department co-ordinate the activities of all the members of whatever system in which they are involved, and in doing so, need to look carefully at business itself.

A business is concerned with profitability and the management is responsible to its shareholders, customers and its employees. They need to be concerned with long term and short term profits and weight one against the other. Government departments (and we shall not be mentioning them as separate from business houses from here on) are concerned with supplying an efficient service and doing it economically. Their methods are the same as a business house, even if their goals are different.

Frequently a business will have a production line where raw materials and components (often subcontracted parts) represent the input, and require storage space. The production line may take various forms, which may require careful planning, and the output is the finished article. This finished article may be itself a component for some other production line. But this is of no consequence to us except perhaps to recognise that it may, when we are investing in a business in some way, influence our judgement of the success of a finished product. We can judge the success of something such as a motor car or aircraft more easily than we can judge the success of the companies that contribute their components such as batteries, plugs, etc.

There are, of course, wholly different kinds of business houses, such as those that deal in information (e.g. marketing, consultancy companies, actuarial companies) or provide a service (legal, accountancy, etc.). These two groups obviously overlap and are more in line with government departments. The fact that they are not in the production field should not obscure the similarity of their organisation and planning problems.

When we think specifically of investment, especially in public companies (but also in private) we need to know, as we have emphasised, a good deal about their organisation, history and prospects, and this implies seeing Annual Reports, Profit and Loss Accounts and Balance Sheet at the very least. But at this stage I wish to return to the general organisational and planning problems that are universal to business. It is necessary that the investor knows something about these matters if he is to achieve successful investments, especially as a scientist. He is taking a "systems approach" and must necessarily cast his net widely.

We need now to look at the roles that groups (or individuals) adopt in business; such as Marketing, Operational Research, Finance, Personnel, etc., and identify their activities in terms of scientific method. The marketing man (aided by statistical surveys, Motivational Research, (analysis) and the like) is part of the step of the observation process (cf. science) and is concerned with observation of the market place, and more particularly with what motivates the need for demand; this we have already discussed sufficiently. When discussing scientific method we did not say that it was sometimes motivated by ignorance of some important fact or facts. This though is precisely what leads the way to problem solving and all that follows from it with respect to any system. The Operational Research man is using scientific method when working off-the-cuff, and otherwise uses the recognition process in order to work off-the-shelf.

Financial decisions and personnel decisions should also involve scientific method but, in the case of the former, are sometimes derived from such factors as company philosophy. All these matters though are (or should be) adaptive even if carried out over varying time spans. In other words, company philosophy will be slow changing but demand for a particular product may be fast changing.

The personnel man's "scientific approach" can identify his four steps as:

1. A need for change of (new) personnel, selection and re-training, etc.[1]
2. Deducing the consequences of the need, seeing how it could best be achieved.
3. Doing it, and as a result
4. Finding out the results and modifying his step 2 in the light of new demand at step 1. The process necessarily involves feedback and adaptation.

The ordinary behavioural factors are as follows:

1. Beliefs, ideas, etc. held by individuals.
2. Inferred consequences of step 1 in the light of goals, motives, needs, etc. (a state of expectancy).
3. The behaviour itself, change of belief or action or both.
4. Modification of beliefs (increase in knowledge) as a result of 3 (experience).

Motivation operates in all applications of scientific method (however informally) since the scientist is motivated to find the "truth" or the particular facts or an explanation of them, the personnel officer is motivated to find the right people, the finance officer to make the best investment, and so on (at least this is (or should be) generally true).

A BUSINESS AS A SYSTEM

Business houses fall into a number of different categories and the particular methods applied to different business depend upon the nature of their goals and their methods. This is akin to the problem facing the psychologist who, in dealing with different people, has the problem of recognising their differences as well as their similarities. This is sometimes called the problem of individual differences. In other words Don is not exactly like Harry and not at all like Bill. So it is with firms which seem to be similar but may also differ, and sometimes differ very considerably from each other.

The kind of companies which are being generalised upon range from very small to vast, and they are companies with various goals. They may also be private, public or they may be nationalised industries or multi-national conglomerates, or even government departments - certainly some of the same principles apply to this latter group.

It should be said again that businesses are systems and capable of having scientific method applied to them. This, indeed, is what this monograph is about. It has to acquire a view here designed to sharpened our ability to make successful investments, and the only surprising feature about the relationship between science and business is that business has not become scientific before. It seems now, in spite of all their complexities, and whether they are public or private, that business houses are just as much a source of activity for scientific organisation and control as the worlds of physics, chemistry and biology.

The models of business are similar to the models of science, much as depicted by Braithwaite[2] and others[3]. They are concerned with structures and functions, in that they are concerned with the structures of business organisations - and this literally means a block diagram and flow chart operation - and the nature of their goals and methods. At the model level, this means that finally there is a very abstract picture of the bare bones of a business system, but then one must know how to put flesh on the skeleton. The putting of flesh on the skeleton entails interpreting the models in terms which are realistic from a business point of view. Goals are identified as profit - whether short or long term - and the movement of items are identified as part of a production line or a matter of transportation.

It is important now to mention two particular sciences which are closely related to the problem we are describing and constitute the bulk of business science, and constitute a large part of the "systems approach". They are Operational Research and Cybernetics. Operational Research is precisely concerned with statistical techniques and models by which decisions can be taken as to how much stock of a product to hold, or how much time is likely to be wasted in queueing for a raw material. Cybernetics emphasises the more dynamic features of systems, and the goals that are being sought. Such systems include especially those with feedback of information and which are, as a result, adaptive.

It is difficult to provide precise definitions of Operational Research and Cybernetics, but both are bridge activities in relating science to systems (in this case business systems) by using modelling techniques. They are both closely related to the systems analysts' job in providing models for computing purposes. Operational Research and Cybernetics overlap very considerably, but it is perhaps true to say that the former is narrower in its range of statistical and probabilistic methods than the latter, and perhaps there is a tendency for the latter to be more concerned with higher level longer term decision making - although the distinction here is rather arbitrary.

Operational Research and Cybernetics are both very relevant subjects to anyone who is interested in running a business, since they place great emphasis on precisely those aspects of the methodology which are being discussed in this book. They are sciences directly related to one of the principal topics of forecasting, and also to the other main related topics of planning and decision making. Most important of all, their methods are vital to investment.

The aims of this chapter are to provide a suitable guide to investment methods (and Investors) at all levels and of all kinds - and perhaps especially to understand the management and executive levels of business - whereby the problems of business systems can be analysed openly and objectively and allow the investor to judge its worth and potential. It is in the light of this that the planning and organising of a business, with the emphasis on forecasting - and thus anticipating changes of demand - can be improved, and investments well made.

One last point about business systems of whatever kind is that they are clearly subject to economic considerations. There is a sense in which this is a primary fact of business life and is also one that has been widely recognised, though it is the case that large companies will always maintain economists, accountants, and solicitors who will pay attention to the relationship of the company to its customers and shareholders, well aware of the need to relate the economy's activities to certain aspects of systems which are at least quasi-scientific. It is now suggested that this is only going halfway along the line; there is now a need to introduce information scientists in particular (and information technology with them), who are capable of making business wholly scientific.

As far as the economic background is concerned, much data can be found in the Economic Review and a whole host of other journals on marketing, statistics and business science. If a new product is to be introduced, as in the well known case of the American typewriter company[5], then a knowledge of wage levels, import and export capacity, prices, etc. in other countries - where it is hoped to export or use a producer - is quite vital to decision making. Where should a pilot study be made? Are business conditions there typical of the overall market as contemplated? Could it provide its own production centres? And there are only some of the questions that must be asked. Not only the Economic Review is relevant here, but reports by the National Economical Development Council, Le Centre de Recherches Mathematique pour la Planification[6], and a large number of other sources of factual data and forecasts throughout the world.

COMPUTERISED INFORMATION SYSTEMS

A whole range of models and methods have been prepared for the computer, in order to provide relevant and reliable information quickly to senior management and other people, to aid their planning and decision taking. Essentially the same principles are involved in other information systems, but we shall concentrate primarily in this section on what we have called "Management Information Systems".

The idea is to model some aspect of a business such as cash flow or information flow and then to extract relevant data from the models. The model is usually a computer data base which carries the information relevant to that particular business and which is important to the taking of a decision.

A Management Information System will generally provide more than data retrieval, since a very important consideration is to test one's plans, or proposed solutions to problems, and above all, proposed investments before carrying them out. We want to know the implications of such decisions and plans, and the likelihood of success of such investments. This requires the appropriate simulation of the future state of affairs in the light of both the plan and likely, or feasible, changes in the environment.

One may, for example, wish to test a plan for its robustness. Is it very sensitive to a change in the bank rate, or to a credit squeeze, or some political change, such as may be involved in a change of government? If it is sensitive to these changes, you may prefer to reconstruct the plan to make it more robust (or choose an alternative), and therefore less liable to fall foul of likely occurrences which would spoil the plan. Where comparisons are being made, the less sensitive plan - everything else being equal - would be chosen.

You can, by such simulation methods, provide projected balance sheets, profit and loss accounts etc., in the light of any plan working in any possible environment.

Risk Analysis, Venture Analysis, Bayesian Analysis[7], Markov Nets and other such techniques[8] can also be employed to test decisions and plans, assess their payoff and assess the risk entailed in taking one course of action rather than another.

Natural language programming[9] (the use of ordinary or near-ordinary English for computer programming), in one of various forms such as that of Winograd[10] or Simmons [11], can also be used in our Management Information System, so that questions can be asked of the computer in simple terms, literally approximating to ordinary English. You can, for example, simply type out "How much did we spend on X in 1931?" or "How much will Y cost us next year if we follow plan Z?" and get an immediate answer. This naturally entails appropriate special computer languages and appropriately organised data-base and data-base interface. This form of questioning helps to ensure that only strictly relevant information is collected from the information system.

Today all this is open to be done by the individual with his home-based microprocessor or mini-computer; the PET, SHARP or APPLE, among many others, can do a great deal for the investor. Such (computerised) systems deal with investment, expansion, acquisition and diversification in the company context, as examples of processes which come up in most corporate planning contexts, and almost all other methods from mathematics, statistics, probability and logic are available in the context of the information system.

The context supplies the essential novelty, since this depends upon adaptive heuristic methods which are necessarily goal-determined. Heuristic methods are essentially ad hoc rules of thumb, hypotheses. They are contrasted with algorithms, and the contrast is very similar to that between inductive and deductive logic.

In what follows we supply two block diagrams showing some of the stages in the corporate planning type of information system.

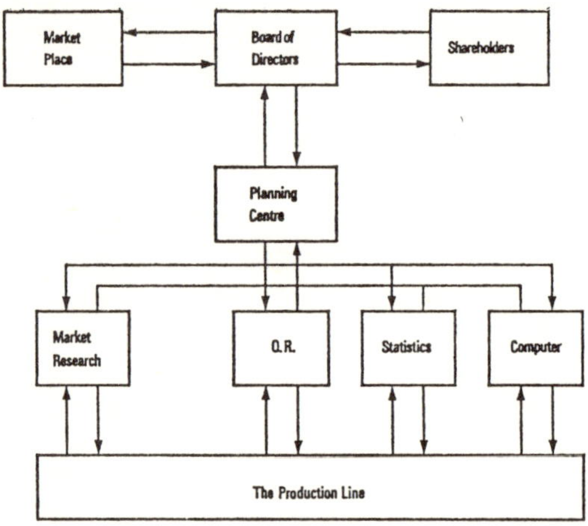

Figure 1

This figure shows a very generalised representation of an idealised factory.

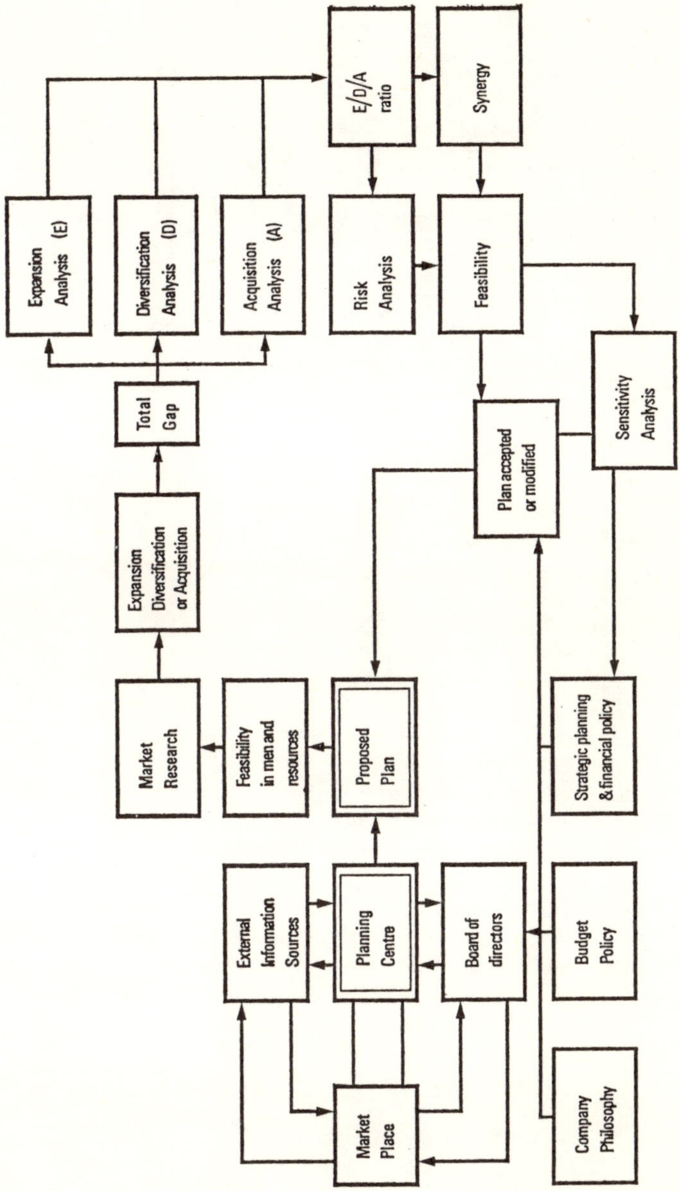

Figure 2
A very broadly depicted horizontal slice of the company with respect to the analysis of plans in terms of cash-flow.

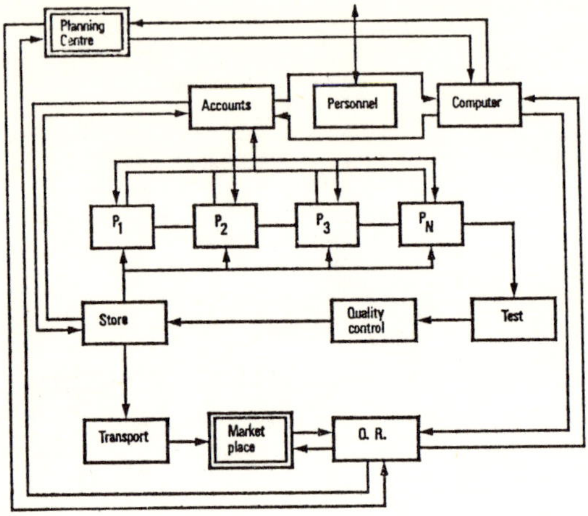

Figure 3

A general picture of the production level of the company.

This figure and the following figure taken with figures 1 and 2, give a very abstract picture of the typical business house and its activities, and particularly represents the problems of corporate strategy and is thinking largely of terms of expansion, acquisitions and diversification.

There are naturally variations between different industries and even more between different types of industry, but in general the commonality is greater than the differences.

In figure 4 we have summarised that part of business which deals with innovating and is concerned primarily with research, development, management know-how and resources.

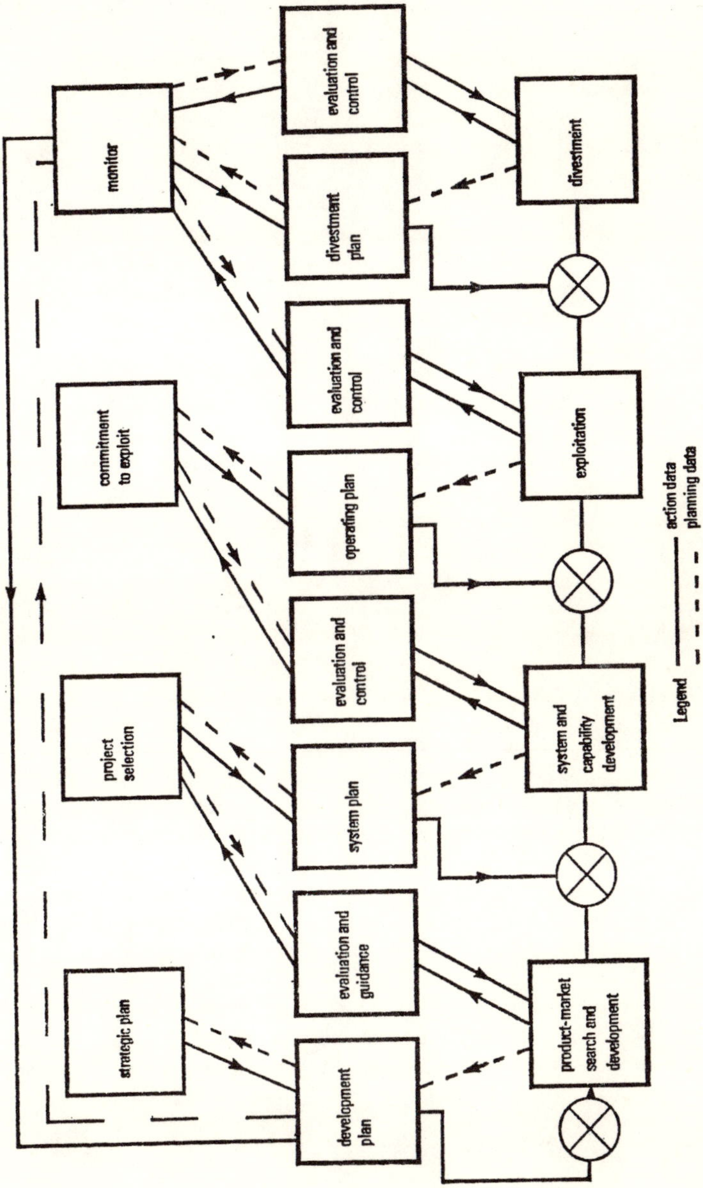
strategic plan
development plan
evaluation and guidance
product-market search and development
project selection
system plan
evaluation and control
system and capability development
commitment to exploit
operating plan
evaluation and control
exploitation
monitor
evaluation and control
divestment plan
evaluation and control
divestment
Legend
action data
planning data

Figure 4

Management Information Systems (MIS) Operating Under Conditions of Urgency. When an M.I.S. is used in conditions of urgency we have usually to omit all the techniques (e.g. Venture Analysis, Bayesian Analysis (see Appendix III, etc.) which are possible in ordinary more relaxed conditions. Risk Analysis is still maintained in abbreviated (heuristic) form - but the operations to be performed are normally pre-planned (algorithmic) or in some cases require the use of a heuristic optimisation technique. We have (or should have) contingency or conditional plans available, at least for those more obvious and foreseen emergencies.

In emergency cases it is external physical sensors which are radically different (high speed and accurate), but accumulated experience, which makes the algorithm adaptive, is also vital. Examples of such systems are: Early Warning Systems, Ambulance, Fire Brigade, Police, emergency, etc.

COMPROMISE INFORMATION SYSTEMS

This as the title suggest, is a compromise system (still a form of M.I.S.) between the urgent and the non-urgent. In fact we have to compromise between urgency and precision. The input now is often human information collected and "typed in" to the computer data-base. Examples of this are Computer Fault Finding, Medical Diagnosis, Routing problems, and some military decision making.

These three types of Information Systems are taken as representative, but a whole range of "mixes" can be arranged to create a tailor-made system for a user. The "modules" available are much the same and the mixture is obtainable by variation in the arrangement and choice of modules. In general, as investors, our interest will be in the ordinary, relative leisure use of M.I.S.'s and have some contingency plans for a sudden drop in share prices (in the limit signs of a "Wall Street Crash"). We shall always hope to anticipate the need for their use, rather than show the quick reaction to the event having actually occurred.

The purpose of these information systems in all cases is to achieve speed and accuracy to facilitate the human decision maker.

SPECIALIST MODELS AND SYSTEMS

Here we could include, for example, econometric models as one of many examples which are specific to economic forecasting. The trouble with econometric models is their rather complex mathematical form, so we shall relegate (if this is the right word) our example to an appendix, so only those who really want to know will delve that far (Appendix I).

We shall take another path (but briefly) which leads us via <u>corporate strategy</u> to expansion, acquisition and diversification.

We have discussed business so far in general terms and we have distinguished between different types of business houses in a very general way. It is essential in considering strategies and plans for business houses that these differences should be looked at, since manifestly they are going to affect the type of decision which would seem to be best in any particular set of circumstances. This is the process of looking at different industries (and understanding their differences) in making an investment.

In real life one has to make decisions about any sort of activity (but especially we are thinking of investment) in the light of ill-defined goals and incomplete information. Furthermore decisions are usually made in the light of particularly selected constraints. These particular constraints may reflect the special interest and knowledge of the decision maker or planner himself, or they may, for example, reflect the urgent requirements of the particular business house. It will be remembered that the business house's investment is not basically different from the individual.

We accept the fact that the overall goal or objective of a firm is profit, and the same applies to the individual. But our individual is looking in on the business house and this he does largely with a view to investment in it. To make a judgement he must understand how business operates. Whether the firm is prepared to sacrifice short term profit in the interest of greater long term profit by various possible strategic decisions is a question which must be answered by the decision maker. He must make the decision along these lines in the light of the circumstances in which the firm is operating. It is for this reason that the sub-goals such as the activities that should motivate the particular decision maker, perhaps within the structured context of a complete firm, are so important. He should always bear in mind the overall constraints and objects of the firm in making his particular decisions or sub-decisions.

Whatever the total range of decision making, even if made in terms of sub-goals which bear only an indirect relationship to the overall goals of the company, the fact remains that methods have to be adopted to ensure that the decision made is likely to implement the relevant goal. This focuses our attention on the actual decision making process which occurs in the corporate strategic context and also in particular the problem solving activity which is relevant to achieving such goals. The implication is, of course, that all decision taking (making) is the result of (or is) problem solving. Planning in turn is also a form of problem solving, which forms a bridge with forecasting to all corporate strategy, business control and, our main interest, investment.

We shall not discuss problem solving[12] as such, since that would take us one step too far away from our goal. The reader will remember that we have only introduced this chapter on business and business methods in order to make clear to the investor what makes (in a very general way) business "tick" and the insight that might be derived from their forecasting and investment methods.

One further concept we must mention briefly before we discuss business investment by expansion, acquisition and diversification, is that of synergy. Synergy is something that is very important to the business problem solver, and we make some mention of it here. Synergy implies a "similarity" between systems. This might be a method, strategy or solution to a problem which works well in one system will work well in another which is sufficiently similar. Systems which have commonality or a resemblance to each other, or are susceptible to the same sort of treatments and skills on the part of the personnel working in the relevant departments are synergic. This allows one to carry over easily from one to another. It is the presence of synergy which is essential to diversification. To be able to do one thing and then diversify to do something else is best done where maximum synergy exists.

There are a number of different aspects to synergy. One is sales synergy, and occurs when products use common distribution channels, common sales techniques, common sales administration and organisation, common warehousing and so on; also any opportunity for linking products together in this way, such as in the case of having a salesman who can reasonably carry a whole range of products that pre-supposes there is some sales synergy between them. Common advertising and common sales promotion are characteristic of this situation.

Operating synergy is the result of high utilisation of facilities and personnel, the spreading of overheads and the advantage of common production situations. This also perhaps involves large-scale purchasing of raw materials or sub-products which are common to a whole range of production systems. This does not mean that conglomerates (a business with many different aspects) cannot exist, only that then they have to be very different and virtually independent businesses under one ultimate control.

The investor, who is investigating closely the business in which he is planning a possible investment, will look carefully at that company's acquisitions, its diversity, etc. as a safeguard to his investment.

EXPANSION, ACQUISITION AND DIVERSIFICATION

Finally in our brief business survey we come, as promised, to a brief summary of a company's treatment of expansion, which might also involve the need to acquire other companies and possibly, either by acquisition or not, to diversify. We have already mentioned this concept at work with shares, where we diversify to avoid "putting all our eggs in one basket".

As far as expansion, acquisition and diversification are concerned, they are all forms of investment and therefore are subject to exactly the same conditions which apply to investment analysis. Expansion is obviously part of investment, because as we get more capital we expand our portfolio. The acquisition process also applies, of course, because this is merely acquiring the stocks in the first place. We are now thinking though not of a portfolio and stocks and shares, but we are thinking of actual business.

When considering an actual business, whether it is a manufacturing one, a service one or whatever, there are certain problems that are involved, all of which are closely linked with corporate strategy. In fact, it is important to bear in mind all that was said about corporate strategy, which includes a brief comment on expansion, acquisition and diversification, and the notion of synergy. In other words the corporate planning department has to decide how much to put into expanding existing products, as opposed to how much should be put into products in other fields. It is evident that if you are on a declining market in your own main fields, then the diversification may need to be great, whereas if you are on an expanding market it is the expansion that is likely to be of most importance.

Satisfactory investment depends a great deal upon synergy. There must be some similarity of activity or some similarity of purpose (or both) between the activity currently being carried out and the activity considered for the future. In the case of expansion, complete synergy exists, at least as far as the product is concerned because you are simply expanding existing activities. The is no problem here of finding out whether you have synergy, at least in the narrow sense, or not. There is clearly the possibility of a problem with size, since it may well be that the principles and methods used by a small company do not apply in anything like the same way in a large company; economies of scale occur but cannot be taken for granted. You may have, for example, need to go from a simple manual production line to a highly automated production line. Thus something which is easy at one size is not necessarily easy on a larger size, if only because of different production methods and increasingly the need for computer control. You might also have to provide far greater marketing effort and perhaps involve yourself in advertising and suchlike activities which very much change the nature of the business. Such changes then obscure the "obvious synergy" available.

In considering acquisition you may be acquiring something in the same line as (have immediate synergy with) your present business. It may be part of an expansion procedure or it may be part of a diversification plan; acquisition can be either. But whichever it is, acquisition also has its own particular problems since problems, especially psychological problems, always arise especially where one is going in to a field involving new people, new factories, possibly new products, all of which you need to have some knowledge of. This problem of new products and new people, of course, always arises in diversification, since now you are taking over a new type of activity which you hope will have some sufficient synergy with your present activity, otherwise the problem of buying arises and that, if your existing company does not understand the issues involved, can be very tricky.

The main symptoms for the need for expansion are very much more clearcut in the sense that if the demand is greatly in excess of the supply in your particular factory then of course expansion is absolutely necessary, and the problem may be purely a matter of raising the capital; this is what is sometimes called the debt-equity ratio.

Forecasting is, as usual, essential, because you must know the market penetration of future products, since even within your own field you are going to introduce new products from time to time, you must know what their marketing potential is, but expansion is a relatively straightforward activity and the main question at issue is the extent that you are prepared (or able) to lay out capital for the expansion activity, and the rate of expansion.

In many ways acquisition is more important than diversification. Acquisition can imply both diversification and expansion and is a particularly difficult problem, since when you acquire new organisations you acquire the ethos, the background and the actual personnel of another company; they often prove difficult to assimilate.

Expansion without acquisition raises special problems. The answer to the doubt is partly circumstantial; sometimes you cannot expand other than by acquiring other companies. You automatically acquire them as a matter of acquisition policy. Again it is a circumstantial thing; have you the necessary expertise? Can you take on the necessary people directly and sufficiently rather than acquire *en bloc* a complete new team? The answer is that if the demand is great and the need to satisfy is urgent, then acquisition almost certainly replaces expansion.

In conditions of change certain demands decrease, others increase, and the demand for certain things vanishes completely. The demand for new products is always great and usually increasing, thanks to science and technology. Our talk of forecasting makes clear that the market place is always open to new products, even if the potential customers have not demanded them because they have not thought of them. Even old products can be resuscitated through advertising, say.

All these matters discussed (and more) determine how you actually plan your strategies for the future in terms of investment capital. This is usually in terms of diversification, expansion or acquisition and depends on a few fairly simple and straightforward principles. You diversify if you have to, because you are on a declining market; usually you expand because you want to increase your profit because you are on an expanding market. You can afford to expand your existing business by further capital investment or you acquire new businesses.

You forecast certain trends by extrapolating from the past, and you then meet those trends and the demands they imply by adequately reading the symptoms and planning your strategies and tactics accordingly. While you do this you always bear in mind that in the end you are dealing with human beings. These human beings provide the main single problem of assimilation and understanding.

DECISION TABLES

This is the moment to bring in a new technique which has been used with considerable success in decision making and forecasting. It starts with decision tables which are specialised flow charts and go on to testrolog (George)[13] which were developed by Stavros Foundos[14]. I will indicate their method of construction and then an example of their use in the context of acquisition which directly relates to the contents of this chapter.

There are a number of types of decision tree. One well known one is a decision table, e.g.

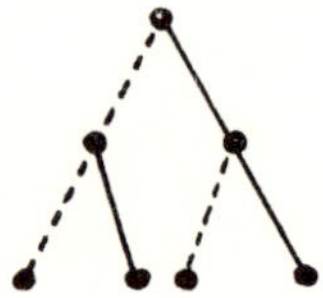

Y = ----
N = ____

A decision tree may be made up of more than binary choices, e.g.

Uncertain = - -
(say)

These trees can be drawn up in advance (explicit) or generated and terminated as required (implicit). Some of the best known methods of search are heuristic; this is a short cut method made necessary by the enormous complexity of some problems, e.g. chess playing (a complete explicit tree for chess has some 10^{120} nodes).

The method of search is usually a combination of search-in-depth and search-in-breadth, or these two combined, they may be both backward or forward or both.

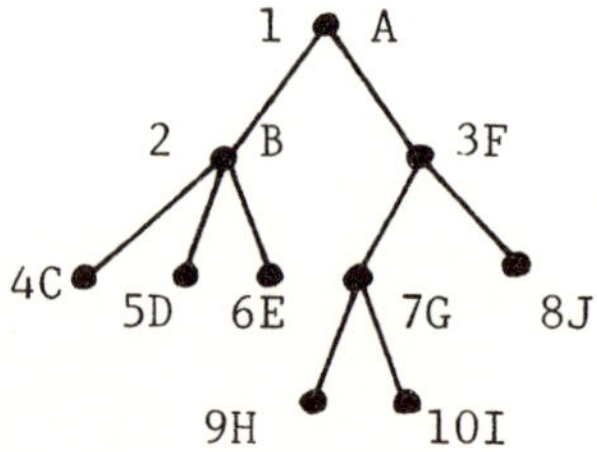

Breadth (numbers)
Depth (letters)

All such trees (sometimes called graphs) have nodes and connecting lines, with a starting node, and branches moving downwards like a family tree. A simple decision table (binary tree) with n levels will have 2^n final outputs (terminal nodes) and the problem is when n is large, 2^n is very large. If $n = 4, 2^n = 16$; $n = 10$, $2^n = 1{,}024$ and for $n - 16$, $2^n = 82{,}792$, and so on. So a tree has enormous girth and the details are quite impossible to follow. The testrolog tree slims this down to handleable proportions, mainly by elimating irrelevant branches and mapping the tree onto a few chosen relevant outputs. It also slims it (where necessary) by partitioning so that a human eye can see each step in the whole procedure, both backwards and forwards. This allows whatever modification is desired or needed in output to be made, since the relevant lines can be easily seen. It is also true that problems of the order (especially of the questions) and their semantic properties are easily spotted.

If you need to know why a decision has been made and how it can be modified then the testrolog tree is ideal, since you see the whole argument (set of decisions) from start to finish, and indeed backwards from finish to start. There is no form of planning, decision making and the like that cannot be performed in such a manner. All problems can (and usually are) dealt with by sequential analysis.

Testrolog trees can be used to solve virtually any problem, and in most cases make problem solving a great deal easier, while in some cases provide virtually the only method of solution. They can be searched in breadth or depth or both and should they be developed as implicit trees they could involve backward pruning (i.e. the goal, or goal-priority) would be used to develop the tree. As an example of the application of a testrolog tree, let us look at acquisition, where one (parent) company is considering acquiring a satellite company. We shall need a whole set of testrologs $T_1, T_2, \ldots$ and we shall show the detailed networks for the first three only.

ACQUISITION AND TESTROLOG

The following seven testrolog programs are intended to cover the field of acquisition and conform to the criteria adopted by an imaginary firm we shall call XYZ.

The testrolog programs are provided in linked fashion so that the cumulative weighting is carried forward from one testrolog (filter) to the next. They need not however be used in such a limited fashion, and each output can be noted and the whole pattern or profile inspected. For example the set A-A-A-A-A-A-A cannot be bettered on all scores and C-D-D-D-D-D-D could not be worse, except by elimination, en route or at the end. In between we get a profile such as A-B-B-C-B-A-A which looks good and perhaps especially so, as although it falls down a little on "immediately generated income" (C) on T4, it must be at least capable of adding the mandatory 5% to XYZ's trading profits because of the A on T1, and this is in accord with A's on T6 and T7. This can all be seen at a glance at the profile and this may for some persons prove a better way of using the testrolog set for acquisition. Care should be taken to consult the notes and it should be remembered that some questions that arise from such a testrolog analysis may need a deeper analysis at some point by use of methods such as regression analysis and other forms of Time Series or by more market research before the testrolog question can be satisfactorily answered.

Now we show T1 - T7 with questions, programs, and linked cumulative outputs and attendant notes.

Q1: Is it a new product?

Q2 Does it add 5% or more to XYZ's trading profits?

Q3: Could it be made to add 5% or more in "reasonable time"?

Q4: Will XYZ have 100% ownership?

Q5: Will XYZ acquire 100% ownership within 5 years?

Q6: Is management of "sufficient ability" still available with takeover?

Q7: Can management of "sufficent ability" be acquired?

Q8: Is "know-how" available within XYZ?

Q9: Can it be acquired in XYZ?

Q10: Does a "general synergy" exist between the acquisition and some existing section of XYZ?

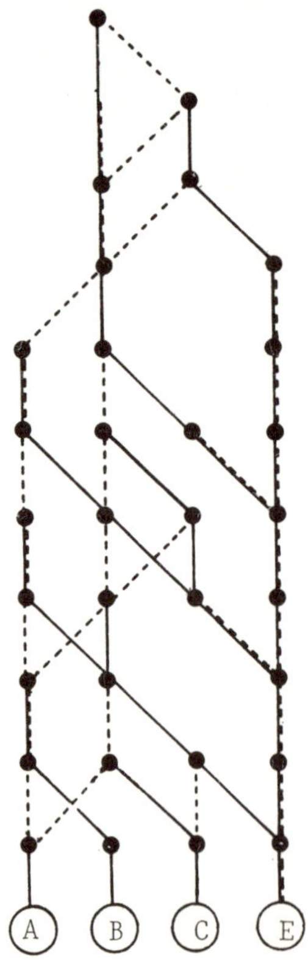

A = Excellent so far
B = Very good so far
C = Fairly good
E = Reject (not good enough)

T1 NOTES

1. "Sufficient ability" must be a subjective judgement.

2. "Know-how" involved people with knowledge of, or experience in, a field and must be to some extent a subjective estimate, certainly this may be so in certain cases.

3. "General synergy" implies a similar sort of product to make and sell. It implies:

   1. Market synergy?
   2. Labour synergy?
   3. Production synergy?

It should have "yes" as an answer to at least one of these.

T2: MONETARY VALUE OF ACQUISITION

Q1: Are sales very high?

Q2. Are sales sufficiently high?

Q3: Is turnover very high?

Q4: Is turnover sufficiently high?

Q5: Is profitability very high?

Q6: Is profitability sufficiently high?

Q7: Is ROTC very high?

Q8: Is ROTC sufficiently high?

Q9: Is P/E sufficiently high?

Q10: Is P/E sufficiently high?

Q11: Is market share very high?

Q12: Is market share sufficiently high?

A start from T1

B start from T1

C start from T1

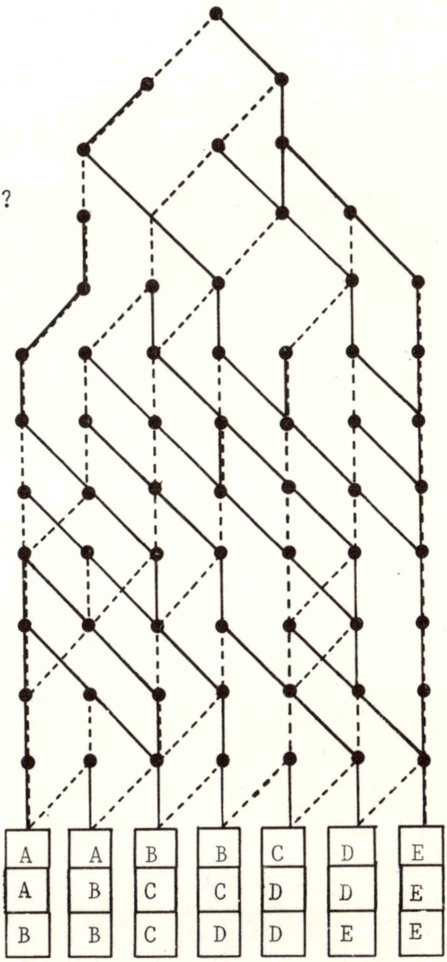

A = Very good acquisition in terms of income.
B = Good acquisition in terms of income.
C = Fairly good acquisition in terms of income.
D = Poor acquisition in terms of income.

T2 NOTES

1. High sales and poor profitability implies low profit margins per item.

2. If in 1 above turnover is low then price is low.

3. If profits are high and market share is low, then the question of trend becomes important. If trend is important and it nearly always is put test through T2A before T3.

   N.B. P/E could also involve 2 questions in T2.

We add notes next in advance for the third testrolog of the series. This is the last for which the network will be supplied.

T3 NOTES

1. The Trend Analysis implied is fairly evident.

2. Any doubts can be resolved by Regression Analysis where possible and if needed.

T3: TRENDS

Q1: Have sales increased in last 3 years?
Q2: Did sales increase last year?
Q3: Has turnover increased in last 3 years?
Q4: Did turnover increase last year?
Q5: Has profitability increased in last 3 years?
Q6: Did profitability increase last year?
Q7: Has ROTC increased in the last 3 years?
Q8: Did ROTC increase last year?
Q9: Has market share increased in the last 3 years?
Q10: Did market share increase last year?

A start from T2

B start from T2

C start from T2

D start from T2

A = A very dood acquisition in terms of trends.

B = A good acquisition in terms of trends.

C = A fairly good acquisition in terms of trends.

E = A poor acquisition in terms of trends.

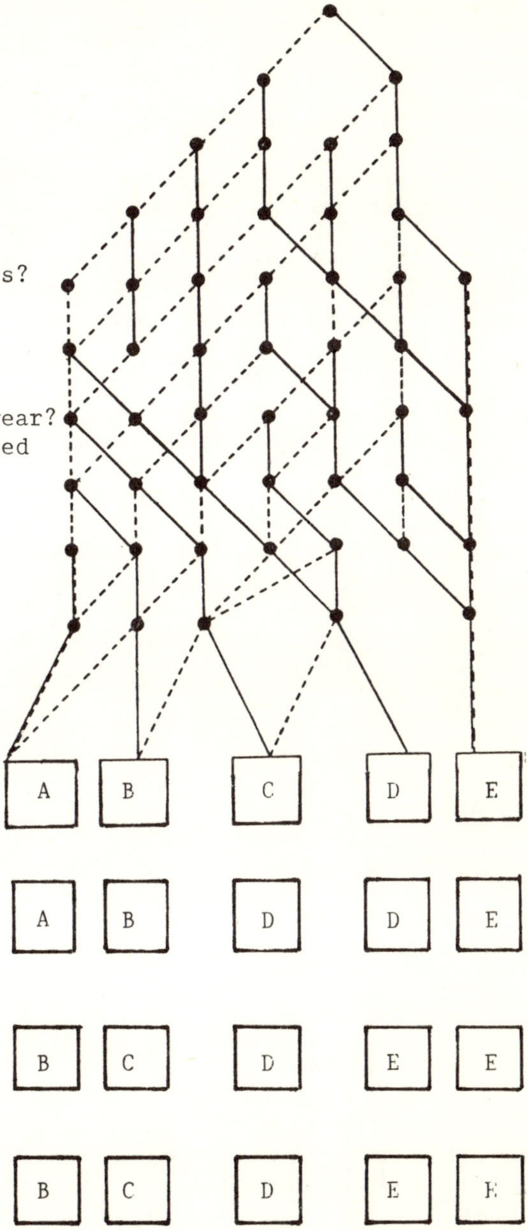

We now continue with T4 - T7 questions but do not show the net which the reader could now draw for himself in the light of his own opinions.

T4 FINANCING

Q1: Is working capital available?

Q2: Is working capital obtainable without too much increase in debt/equity ratio?

Q3: Is net "worth" acceptable?

Q4: Is net "worth" borderline?

Q5: Is cost acceptable in light of Q1-Q4?

Q6: Is cost borderline in light of Q1-Q4?

Q7: Are available buildings as new?

Q8: Are available buildings in adequate condition?

Q9: Is machinery/equipment as new?

Q10: Is machinery/equipment in adequate condition?

A = Very good acquisition financially.
B = Good acquisition financially
C = Fair acquisition financially.
D = Not a good acquisition financially
E = Reject on financial gounds.

T4 NOTES

1. "Worth" means value for money in circumstances.

2. "Cost" means adequacy of price in light of worth and available money for purchase.

3. "Borderline" and "acceptable" are terms for which XYZ should decide a value (of 5% and 100% in T1).

T5 : STABILITY OF MARKET

Q1: Do sales fluctuate very little?

Q2: Do sales fluctuate quite a lot?

Q3: Do earnings fluctuate very little?

Q4: Do earnings fluctuate quite a lot?

Q5: Does P/E fluctuate very little?

Q6: Does P/E fluctuate quite a lot?

Q7: Is proposed acquisition in highly diverse business?

Q8: Is proposed acquisition in highly diverse technology?

Q9: Is there a wide diversity of demand?

Q10: Is the range of demand synergic with purchaser?

T5 NOTES

1. Purchaser will decide as in T1 and T3 what limits should be applied to give meaning to "very little" and "quite a lot" and in qualitative terms how to apply the words "highly diverse".

2. The question of the significance of fluctuations must also be decided. In general an even sales and earnings is desirable, but with ice-cream as we saw earlier this is not possible. This means that you will have good synergy with a fluctating takeover if you yourself fluctuate, otherwise not.

T6: FORECASTS FOR PROPOSED ACQUISITIONS

Q1: Are forecast sales very high?

Q2: Are forecast sales sufficiently high?

Q3: Is forecast profitability very high?

Q4: Is forecast profitability sufficiently high?

Q5: Is forecast ROTC very high?

Q6: Is forecast ROTC sufficiently high?

Q7: Is forecast growth very high?

Q8: Is forecast growth sufficiently high?

Q9: Is increase of M/S very high?

Q10: Is increase of M/S sufficiently high?

T6 NOTES

These forecasts are partly an extrapolation from the past (including especially trends) and partly subjective estimate.

It will be clear that we have moved in the sequence of Testrologs from matters of fact (more or less) to matters of prediction and forecasting and this inevitably leads to a measure of greater uncertainty.

T7: RISK ANALYSIS - applied only to those proposed acquisitions that are regarded as "possible" after T1 to T6.

Q1: Is probability of success very high?

Q2: Is probability of success high?

Q3: Is probability of success good?

Q4: Is probability of success average?

Q5: Is probability of success no worse than poor?

Q6: Is probability of success no worse than bad?

Q7: Is probability of success no worse than very bad?

Q8: Do you stand to lose 20% or less if you are wrong?

Q9: Do you stand to lose 40% or less if you are wrong?

Q10: Do you stand to lose 60% or less if you are wrong?

Q11: Do you stand to lose 80% or less if you are wrong?

Q12: Do you stand to lose 100% or less if you are wrong?

We can now summarise the various stages of the testrolog approach by saying that T1 is general and each user, apart from making his own decisions about criteria, must decide whether such basic criteria are both complete and, as always in such analyses, consistent.

T2 and T3 clearly go together and deal with the very heart of the matter, where the only differences between them is the difference between an "absolute assessment" where the average, the current state, the last complete year or some combination of these might be used; while T3 deals with the trends.

The analysis of T2 and T3 deserves some more detailed consideration, since it is probably the most important part of the whole exercise. The reason for this is that T1 is inclined towards a do-or-die consideration which asks in effect whether the whole analysis is even worth starting. There still remain three acceptable categories of success mainly concerned with questions on personnel (Q6-Q9).

In the event of getting through the filter of T2 and T3 (and many will fail) then we return to the practical question "It is within the compass of company philosophy and policy and looks a good prospect, but now can we afford it, and if we can, is it good value?"

This leads to T5 the important, but not necessarily critical, matter of markets and their fluctuation; then on to forecasts for the future in the same terms as in T2 and T3. This acts as confirmation of the sufficiently good results necessarily already achieved.

It should be made clear that the actual testrolog filter is not meant to be used without an understanding of the whole matter, much as regression analysis should not ideally be used in forecasting without some understanding of the causal relationships involved; this implies a theory that applies to the situation. It is quite clear, for example, that all sorts of extenuating circumstances may apply. This sort of explanation based on suitable evidence, could greatly change the result of an unthinking application of the methods.

One of the most important features that this analysis demonstrates is that the setting up of the testrolog analysis forces the analyst to understand the problem and the values and the criteria to be adopted. It also enables the setting up of suitable forms which can be used to record the relevant information in the correct order. Now given that criteria are all available, then a person relatively untutored could (we are not necessarily advising it) go through the analysis without difficulty.

Before we look more closely at the programs (especially T2 and T3) we must make it clear that the testrolog programs can be worked either way - from beginning to end or from end to beginning.

This means that if you need a first class acquisition, then you need to track back from the three A's at the end of T6, say (leaving out risk analysis at this point) and find out what conditions have to be satisfied to achieve this end.

Looking back through T6 from the A-ending and asking what are the minimum requirements for success, then they are that a B-start can be acceptable (but nothing less), and then the minimal route is:

Q10(y)-Q9(Y/N)-Q8(Y)-Q7(N)-Q6(Y)-Q5(N)-Q4(Y)-Q3(N)-Q2(N)-Q1(N)

So even if the forecast sales are not sufficiently high, success is still possible provided all the other factors of profitability ROTC, growth and market share as forecast,are sufficiently high. The argument is such a case already based on two considerations:

1. Getting through T1-T5 and coming out no less than B, and
2. That even if the forecast sales are not sufficiently high (i.e. as high as one would choose and that over the next year or two only - the criteria become vital here) the whole thing is acceptable if all the rest is right.
3. It should be noted in the example we have just quoted that the obvious plan is to stimulate demand and increase market share.

Such an analysis is possible (even desirable) for all routes through the testrolog. Even an "acquisition" which is eliminated could be recovered if we are prepared (e.g. for some reason which is not included in the analysis) to see what requirement is, say, minimal. In the case of T6, if elimination comes from Q10 (the lack of sufficient market share M/S) then the acquisition can be saved if we are prepared to make an extra effort to increase M/S over and above what is demanded by the criteria used in Q9 and Q10. This then can (reading backwards) be achieved by the minimal sequence (Q9-Q1):

Q9(N)-Q8(N)-Q7(Y)-Q6(N)-Q5(N)-Q4(Y)-Q3(N)-Q2(N)-Q1(N)

This means that with "poor" forecast sales and profitability, if forecast ROTC is high and growth is sufficient we can still believe in the worthwhileness of the investment. This though would only happen in a special case and could occur, say, if in a "sufficiently" growing market, the increased market share in that market is attainable, and you may have evidence to believe it has longer term potential.

So it is that whole sets of combinations can be analysed, either forwards or backwards. This whole matter can now be conveniently placed in a formal notation the meaning of which is fairly clear in the case of M and D ("rising" and "falling" respectively) but less so in the case of M, where the symbol means increasing ("appreciably") greater than and G, its opposiste. E will mean "could be rising or falling or constant", and the symbol is the logical connective 'implies'.

Now let us use the following letters

S = Sales
T = Turnover

P = Profit
RI = Return on (investment) TC.
M/S = Market Share
Prs = Prices
C(s) = Costs
D^1= Demand
Pr = Productivity

1. SU.TU.PU.RIU.M/SU → PrE Costs E Pr M Costs
2. SU.TD.PU.RIU.M/SU → PrD Costs D
3. SU.TU.PD.RIU.M/SU → PrE Costs U Costs M Pr.
4. SU.TD.PD.RIU.M.SU → PrD Costs U.
5. SD.TU.PU.RIU.M.SU → PrU Costs D.
6. SD.TD.PU.RIU.M/SU → PrU Costs D.
7. SD.TU.PD.RIU.M/SU → PrU Costs E.
8. SD.TD.PD.RIU.M/SU. → PrE Costs U.
9. SU.TU.PU.RID.M/SU. → PrU.Costs U.
10. SU.TD.PU.RID.M/SU → PrD.Costs U or Costs M Pr.
11. SU.TD.PD.RID.M/SU. → Pr is too low or costs too high.
12. SU.TD.PD.RID.M/SU. → Pr is too low or costs too high.
13. SD.TU.PU.RID.M/SU. → PrU . D^{1}D
14. SD.TD.PU.RID.M/SU. → PrU . D^{1}D
15. SD.TU.PD.RID.M/SU. → PrU .D^{1}D (Pr 15 G Pr 13)
16. SD.TD.PD.RID.M/SU. → D^{1}D. . (D 16 G D 15)

Now all these 16 equations are repeated for M/SD, but we shall not repeat them here, except for the very first as an example, the rest will be obvious:

17. S .T . P . RI . M/S D → DU.

It is clear that all these statements are, as it were, part of a kind of probability logic, since other factors may occur in practice and therefore could causally account for the changes given on the right hand side of the sign →. We are thus reading from effect to minimal cause. This is basic but can clearly be extended.

The whole process of writing decision tables can, of course, easily be computerised, and with that thought we shall bring this chapter to a close.

REFERENCES CHAPTER 7

1. Cliff Saunders, Selection and Training in the Third World. To be published.
2. R.B. Braithwaite, Scientific Explanation, Cambridge University Press, 1953.
3. R.M. Harre, The Ideals of Science, Hamish Hamilton, 1970.
4. K.R. Popper Objective Knowledge, The Clarendon Press, 1972.
5. F.H. George, Anatomy of Business, Associated Business Programmes, Wiley Halstead, 1974.
6. C.M. Berners-Lee, Models for Decision, English University Press, 1965.
7. Bertrand Russell, Human Knowledge: Its scope and Limits, Allen and Unwin, 1948.
8. D.J. White, Decision Theory, Allen & Unwin, 1969;
   D.J. White, Finite Dynamic Programming, Wiley, 1978.
9. R.F. Simmons, 'Answering English Questions by Computer - A Survey', A.C.M.J, of computing, 1965.
10. T. Winograd, Five lectures on Artifical Intelligence, A.I.M. - 246, 1974.
11. R.F. Simmons, Opus Citus, Stanford Artifical Intelligence Memo.
12. F.H. George, Problem Solving, Duckworth, 1980.
13. F.H. George, A manual for Testrolog, BIS. 1980.
14. S. Foundos, Communications on Testrolog. Various.

CHAPTER 8
THEORIES OF INVESTMENT

The chapter title of "Theories of Investment" means to refer to the methods which are partly a science and partly still an art, and we cited Markowitz[1] as one example of a Technalist, but we shall say a few words about Technalism generally before we go on to consider the more complex model of Weaver and Hall[2] who employed traditional statistical analysis to the problem.

Markowitz's model is the simplest and is constrained to fit his precise mathematical methods. Weaver and Hall's model is more complex, although limited by the choice of statistical analysis (linear regression). Clarkson however (Chapter 9), concentrates on modelling the decision procedures which parallel numerical techniques as much as the statistical model of investment similar to that of Markowitz on the one hand and Weaver and Hall on the other.

In other words the investment process can, from one point of view, be split into two parts. The first is static and states the factors on which share-prices depend as well as their relationship. This function can be manipulated in a number of ways to yield valid predictions of future share-prices. The techniques employed by the three authors mentioned are three ways of manipulating the function, but many others exist and some are still untried.

The problem of Technicalism will be treated quite generally however, and not refer to any one person's interpretation of it. Cohen and Zinbarg[3], two Technalist investment analysts, said the following about Technalism:

> "It is the influence of ... rumours, facts and statistics that causes men to buy and sell their stocks. It is their actions that build the familiar chart patterns. You are not interested in <u>why</u> they are doing what they are doing. So far as your trading is concerned you are interested only in the results of their actions. The habits and evaluative methods of people are deeply ingrained. The same kinds of events produce the same kinds of emotional responses, and hence the same kinds of action".

The search is for precision and rigour, but independent of the investor's behaviour. The thinking by some Technalists is sometimes described as "Chartism", and is essentially a curve-fitting activity. Fundamentalism, with its use of Regression Analysis is also though a curve-fitting activity but placed in a slightly different context.

The idea behind Chartism has something to recommend it, in that, as we can see with some approaches to commodity trading, predictions can be made by observing cycles and anticipating trends. This indeed as we have already seen, is implicit in scientific method. But it assumes that the changes that occur in share prices are not random and this is the presupposition we are making. A presupposition not necessarily denied by what is called the Random Walk model. We shall say a little about this later.

To return briefly to Markowitz's model, it should be said that his was the first (historically) to provide highly sophisticated statistical techniques involving capital asset values, the idea of an optimum portfolio, capital budgets and the analysis of risk. In particular Markowitz made the important point that investment risk could be reduced by spreading the investment over a number of shares (diversification).

In his approach to making up the optimum portfolio by considering the return on each share, he defined "optimum portfolio" as the closing price for the year (P_{t-1}) plus the dividend for the year (D_t). He divided this by the closing price for the previous year, i.e.:

$$\text{Return (R)} = \frac{P_t - P_{t-1} + D_t}{P_{t-1}}$$

The prices are taken at the end of each year, and then risk the estimated in term of the (expected) return from the whole set of shares (portfolio) in which the investment took place.

All this depends upon predicting future dividends and price changes, and this proves in practice to be difficult. Dividends can sometimes be predicted, although with some considerable difficulty, but price changes are nearly impossible to predict, where the prediction depends only upon previous price changes. Dividend and earnings at least are needed in the forecast, and even then we have difficulties. What is still missing is something we have already seen in the use of any forecasting method (e.g. Regression Analysis). If you do not have knowledge (well founded hypotheses about the system, i.e. evidence) then forecasting becomes very unreliable. This implies in the case of investment, considerable knowledge of the industry and of any particular firms in the industry.

As has been said, the task is not to estimate individual returns, but to estimate returns relative to the stock market. In many ways this is similar to the need to know a company's change of market share, and not just its change in earnings. This is because an increase in earnings (in isolation a good thing) seems much less satisfying when coupled to a steep decline in market share. The implication is that demand has increased, but that the firm in particular is still losing ground.

More sophisticated studies of relative price changes have been given by:

Current Price
Average of current price and the preceding 26 prices.
Average of current price and the subsequent 26 prices.
Current Price.

The same two ratios were also considered for 4 prices looking both backward and forward.

It is suggested that the private investor generally gains very little more security by diversifying over more than 10 different shares, although for the large investor (Trust Investment and mutual funds, Pension Schemes, etc) the problem is somewhat more complicated. We also have always to consider the trade-off between expected risk and expected return, and this is where the particular method of risk analysis arises.

In all these issues Markowitz's model depended to a great extent on the investor's beliefs, although his methods do not take care of the interrelatedness of these beliefs which is something which is carefully considered by Clarkson (see the next chapter) in his investment model. Although I believe that Markowitz's model is too simple, and simple Chartism, based on a belief in cycles (often 50 month cycles) is also too simple, both have something to recommend them and the private investor should know of such methods. They have influenced people in their own thinking; but such people have normally tried to extend the ideas as in the case of the use of relative price change, cited above, which was the work of R.A. Levy.[4]

We next look at Fundamentalism and illustrate it by the model of Weaver and Hall. They, unlike most of the others we have and will consider, use British (rather than American) data. They constructed a regression equation for dividend yield based on past earnings growth rates (and their variability) and forecasts and dividend growth rates.

There is some evidence of success for these methods (as indeed there is for the Technalists), especially regarding price changes. It is also the case that it sometimes reveals undervalued shares, which is obviously of great importance.

One of the assumptions which Weaver and Hall, and indeed most investment analysts (and by implication their methods) make is that there is a strong resemblance between the behaviour of companies in the same industry, but that industries themselves vary greatly from each other. This has been a matter, and indeed remains a matter, for considerable debate. It therefore cannot be taken for granted.

To be a shade more precise about Weaver and Hall let me say that they look for their relationship between share prices and share data, and to this end they use the traditional method of multiple regression analysis. The predicted variable is the dividend yield of the share and the dependent variables (the 'predictor' variables as they call them) are:

1. dividend payout ratio
2. forecast earnings growth rate - short term
3. forecast dividend growth rate - long term
4. historical earnings variability
5 historical earnings growth rate.

It can be seen straight away that variables 2 and 3, being themselves forecasts, have to be obtained subjectively whereas the others can be obtained directly from past and present figures. The exact formulae used for calculating these factors have been carefully chosen over a long period of time and are not based on any strict theory of the stock market beyond that of the regression model. However, they are, according,to Weaver and Hall, probably the main ones uppermost in the investors minds when ordinary shares are evaluated.

This is of vital importance since a statistical technique, such as regression, used in much similar work, mathematically satisfying as they are,relies heavily on having well-organised, well thought-out data to provide meaningful results. Many erroneous conclusions have been reached based on false statistical arguments. This is, of course, a very familiar state of affairs to which I have already drawn attention.

The computer programs derived from Weaver and Halls' method have been operating successfully in a stockbroking environment for a number of years and are the most sophisticated of their kind in the United Kingdom, if only because of the amount of work put into the whole project. According to their published results, the computer analysis out-performs other much-used investment analysis procedures and is consistently much better than the average, as embodied in the Financial Times index.

We must next consider two other models of investment forecasting which have been described by Granger and Morgenstern[5], and both of these people have made major constributions to the use of the investment methods. The first is called the Random Walk model, and it has been somewhat misunderstood, perhaps because of its name, as suggesting that a portfolio can be just as easily set up by random methods as by using all available data and making a forecast. It does not mean that at all. All that it asserts is what cannot be done is that future prices can be accurately forecast by studying past prices alone. It is necessary if you are to extrapolate from the past to use many more variables such as earnings dividends and the usual questions of confidence and expectations, forecasts (necessarily "subjective" in some sense), where the forecast is likely to be more accurate when it is embedded in an understanding of the changing financial climate. We have already made this point emphatically: we can explain and understand the situation best when we know the causal chain linking the past to the future, at least with a high probability; unexpected things will, of course, sometimes occur.

One Random Walk model is simply stated:

Price P at time t = Price at time t-1 + Residual (E) at time t

i.e. $$P_t = P_{t-1} + E_t$$

The reader with a statistical background, who wants to know the mathematical details of Random Walk models should read Granger and Morgenstern (Chapter 3).

The point about the model is its conceptual simplicity, since it asserts that the future price depends on the present (not the past) price. It is the residual (E) in the above formula that is the subject of careful scrutiny. It is often the case that the residuals of the past are uncorrelated but not independent. The past here may be anything from 1 day to a month, but not normally longer. This type of Random Walk model seems to provide an excellent approximation to "whatever is the true generating process for stock price series". For the average investor who wants only the minimum burden of statistical methods, the Random Walk model may be unappealing. But for those with such knowledge, and it is, it should be emphasised, very simple to use, that statistical knowledge is minimal and the method extremely good as far as it goes. Bearing in mind it deals with absolute (not relative) price changes, and it does not purport to be a unique model of the market.

Lastly we shall briefly mention Spectral Analysis. This involves a study of ordered sequences, and we are concerned with samples of such sequences. The price of share is just such an ordered sequence, where we may consider daily, weekly or even monthly closing prices (or averages of them, especially when taken over a longer period). The fact that the stock exchange is open only 5 days a week creates an obvious problem, and raises a doubt about the time alone as being the correct yardstick.

In general, however complicated the problem, the search is for correlations between different time series. The results obtained by Spectral Analysis confirm that the Random Walk model's results, except at high and low frequency regions of the spectrum, are correct.

In Random Walk either the prices themselves or the logarithm of the prices can be used. Here the log of the prices and first differences are always used in the data analysis. So the difference d is given by:

$$dx_1 = \log P_{t+1} - \log P_t$$

i.e. if $P_{t+1} = 100$ and $P_t = 80$ $dx_1 = 20$ or, in fact, the log of 100 - the log of 80.

The basic data transformed in this way are merely nearly "normal distributions" in statistical terms and more stable over time. One commonly used transformation is the use of the average of the high and low over some period of time and this approximates closely the simple moving average which we discussed earlier.

One point of interest mentioned by Granger and Morgenstern in talking of Spectral Analysis (Chapter 4 of their book) is that the stock market is almost as active when officially closed as when open.

We will conclude this brief chapter by saying that the investor will (or should) make himself familiar with Chartism, Technicalist and Fundamentalist models, and also with the Random Walk and Spectral Analysis if he can bring himself to do the necessary (but simple) study of statistics. Later we shall suggest methods, which although they demand more data collection than the Random Walk, say, are simpler to operate.

We now look further into general principles of investment, and first we quote Fairweather[6]:

> "An investor who buys a security at one price and finds that soon afterwards he could have bought it at a lower price without anything having happened, so far as he can discover, to affect the quality of the security is bound to feel that he has bought unwisely or that he has been cheated and would be less than human if he did not want to know why. As we have attempted to show, he has not been cheated, but he has bought unwisely because he took insufficient account of the general economic situation at the time. In this he was not alone. Many other investors did the same. But there were also other investors who did not make his mistake. In future he must try to be one of these other investors".

Fairweather goes on to advise that one should never give up the fight and resign oneself to the fact (which it is not) that investing is always a random process and prediction is impossible; that way lies "the end of the road". He makes a further comment which is very much to the point:

> "Those who make opinion and lead opinion are in a much better position to 'get in' and 'get out' of over-priced investments than the ordinary investor who has only his knowledge and common sense to guide him".

Last of all in this chapter we mover over to consider the opinions of two experts in the field: Richard West and Seh Tinic[7]. They point out that stock prices vary largely because of investor's reaction to new information. They also quote a well known expert, E Fama[8], who says:

> "Independence of successive price changes for a given security may simply reflect a price mechanism which is totally unrelated to real world economic and political events. That is, stock price may be just the accumulation of many bits of randomly generated noise, where by noise in this case we mean psychological and

other factors peculiar to different individuals which determine the types of "bets" they are willing to place on different companies".

And furthermore:

"Even random walk theorists, however, would find such a view of the market unappealing. Although some people may be primarily motivated by whim, there are many individuals and institutions that seem to base their actions in the market on an evaluation (usually extremely painstaking) of economic and political circumstances".

One conclusion is that there is another approach to rationalising randomness and this is due to the high communality of information coming to investors. This, many people feel, automatically leads to stocks taking a random walk over time. West and Tinic say:

"Indeed, it is the probability that there will be divergences among the investors' discounting of news that makes the stock market a "horse race".

The idea, or analogy, of a horse race is not as bad as the authors might think, since horses at least have form, which is really more than can be said, at least in quite such a definite way, of stocks and shares. This matter we have drawn to the reader's attention.

The point at issue is a very important one. West and Tinic put it this way:

"For example, if new information reaches investors with varying lags, is it not reasonable to expect that stock prices would exhibit short term trends? Similarly, is it not logical, as investors revise their probabilities over time in response to new information, for the growing recognition of the information's "true" significance to cause nonrandom elements to creep into the series of price changes?"

This in turn leads to a clear expression of the view we believe is relevant, and expressed by J. Lintner[9] although we quote from West and Tinic:

"Lintner describes some traders might become "opinion leaders", in the sense that their actions cause others to revise their expectations. And, if so, would this not represent still another force working toward the creation of dependencies? The point, of course, is that even if the answers to the questions just posed are in the affirmative, the inherent tendency towards nonrandom behaviour might still be overcome by the actions of other traders. Fama suggests that certain "sophisticated traders", for example, might be able to offset the development of nonrandom behaviour. He identifies two types of sophisticated traders: (1) those who are "better at predicting the appearance of new information and estimating its effects on intrinsic (stock) values than others", and (2) those who are "better at doing statistical analysis of price behaviour". He comments that the two types might be "roughly thought of as (respectively) superior intrinsic value analysts and superior chart readers"."

This means that the "intrinsic value analysts" would approach the matter differently from the Chartists. The first would eliminate dependencies by recognising the influence of the less sophisticated trade investors. The (superior) Chartists would not depend upon recognising lags and assessments in the less sophisticated, but would recognise the same trend in their charts and eliminate the dependency - generating process.

The point here is rather like that of the tipster in horse racing; he lowers the odds with respect to a single horse by the very fact of tipping it. So the advantage that can be gained on the stock exchange is to a great extent bound up with stock market attitudes and their correct reading. This is a matter we shall bear in mind in our final assessment of the best methods of investing (Chapter 11).

It should be borne in mind here all theories of investment and investment theories (Chapter 9) consider the economy, industries and companies as well as the client's requirements (Boxes 1-6, of Figure 1, Chapter 1); this <u>must</u> be true of any approach to investment, even if, after so doing, you merely look at the graphs (charts) of the shares under consideration and perform some rough and ready estimates of their trends.

But so, in the next Chapter, we look at Method III.

REFERENCES CHAPTER 8

1. H. Markowitz. Portfolio Selection, Efficient Diversification of Investments, Wiley, 1959.
2. D. Weaver and M.G. Hall, Evaluation of Ordinary Shares Using a Computer. Journal of Institute of Actuaries, 1967.
3. J.B. Cohen and E.D. Zinbarg, Investment Analysis and Portfolio Management, Wiley, 1967.
4. R.A. Levy see C.W.J. Granger and O.Morgenstern Opus Citus.
5. C.W.J. Granger and O. Morgenstern, The Predictability of Stock Market Prices, 1970.
6. W.L.B. Fairweather, Investment, English Universities Press, 1960.
7. R. West and S. Tinic, The Economics of the Stock Market. 1971.
8. E. Fama, Random Walks in Stock Market Prices, Investment Analyst, 1965.
9. J. Lintner, see R. West and S. Tinic. Opus Citus.

CHAPTER 9
INVESTMENT THEORIES

This is (or these are, as we will cite two examples; the second only briefly) the method which is different in that it is "wholly scientific" and heuristic and is carried out, at least in the first case, by simulation of the "best" trust investment officer. We have referred to it as Method III.

The process is one of taking decisions under conditions of uncertainty, which is like most business decisions, and like all gambling - horses, football, dogs, roulette, etc. Since it comes very near to what is now regarded as the best way of making money on the stock exchange. It will be described in some detail, especially that version developed by Clarkson.[1]

Heuristics[2] are ad hoc methods, or hypotheses, (which it will be remembered are part of scientific method and are really essential to the methods such as regression analysis). They are contrasted with the precise algorithmic methods which are applied by Technicalists and Fundamentalists. It is not that the outcome is "certain" in their case, it is rather that the application of the statistical methods are certain. It is rather like saying that when I toss a coin I am certain it will be heads or tails, but I am quite uncertain which it will be. Let me turn now to Clarkson's heuristic (as opposed to Technicalist's and Fundamentalist's) methods.

Method III (the heuristic method) then is illustrated by Clarkson's model of investment, and the study is based on the investment of trust funds held by banks in the United States. The purpose of the model is to simulate the trust officers who make the decision regarding the portfolio. There is a vast amount of information on the operation of firms and the market valuation of their stocks. and published reports make predictions about the future state of the general economy and stock market, while constraints such as legal restrictions and the desires of the client must be borne in mind. As usual, the question of whether he wants capital or income, for example, or some combination of the two?

The investment process is indeed clearly a problem in decision making under uncertainty. The Clarkson model is written as a computer program and simulates the procedures used in choosing investment policies for particular accounts. In evaluating the alternatives presented by the market, and in selecting the required portfolios.

The basic assumptions made by Clarkson for the analysis of the investment decision process are:

1. That we have a data base that contains a list of industries each of which has a list of companies. The memory also contains information associated with the general economy, industries and individual companies.

2. There are also search and selection procedures that involve a search through the lists of information stored, selecting those bits that have the required attributes, according to the principles we have yet to describe. This information is then processed in a manner similar to that of a clerk who prepares lists of stocks suitable for current investment.

3. A set of rules or criteria that guide the decision making process that produce the final portfolio.

We go through the repeated processes of selecting "possible" and "probable" until the final portfolio is decided upon. The program stores the final portfolio for possible future use.

As a result, as the same problem reoccurs, the entire process need not be repeated or the program re-written. The list may be judged by present criteria, accepted, adapted to meet new conditions, or rejected. In the latter event the program would renew its search and selection activity until such a time as a new list had been formed.

The trust investment process can be divided into three parts: (a) the analysis and selection of a list of stocks suitable for current investment - what Clarkson calls the "A" list (the "possibles"); (b) the formulation of an investment policy, and (c) the selection of a portfolio (the actual team to play). Each of these sections can be also broken down into a number of sub-sections as in Figure 1, which is almost identical to figure 1, Chapter 1, which was indeed based on Clarkson's model.

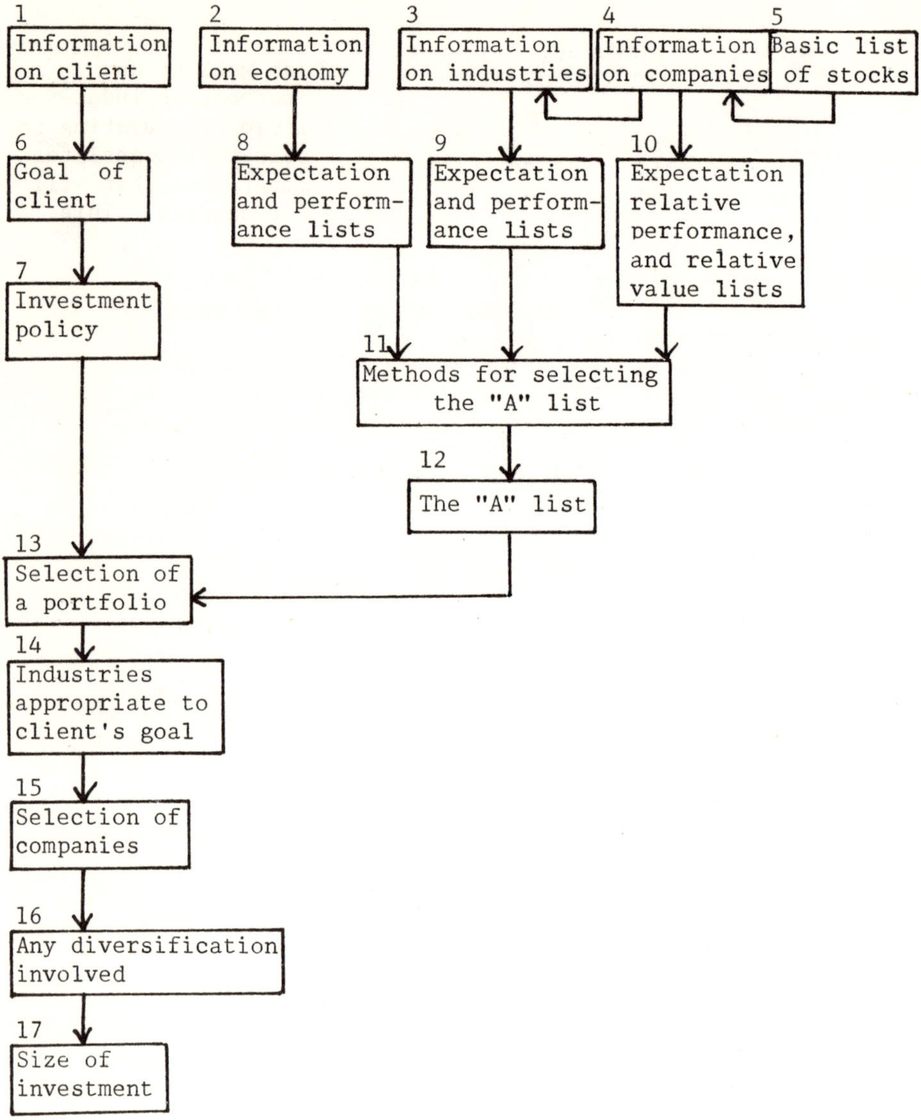

Figure 1
"THE DECISION PROCESS"

Clarkson's procedures are fairly characteristic for all investment procedures, except in the choice of expectation and performance.

A process of selecting a current list of stocks (step (1)) entails an analysis of individual companies as well as an appreciation of the factors affecting their respective industries and the economy in general. The problem of formulating an investment policy (step (2)) involves a process that translates the information on the client into an investment goal that will yield the desired combination of income and/or capital. This process requires the investor to consider such things as the effect of taxes on the income generated by the portfolio as well as the stability of that stream. The actual selection of a portfolio (step (3)) follows directly from steps (1) and (2). The selection procedure contains rules of diversification. In presenting this model of trust investment behaviour, we shall follow up in detail the processes given in Figure 1. For all practical purposes the basic criterion, although it sounds circular, is: a security is of investment quality if and only if it is being bought or is being held by other leading trust institutions or investors. This is, of course, only a guidline as the second principle; investors avoid taking losses, i.e. selling stocks whose prices have fallen below the purchase price, allows an even stronger prediction to be made. The basic list of stocks (Clarkson calls this the "B" list) that are considered to be suitable for trust investment will remain reasonably stable over time, any changes being in the form of additions. Therefore, for any given trust investor, the basic list of stocks from which he can choose is given to him by the "probables" records. At any particular point in time an investor selects stocks (the "probables") from a subject of his basic list (the "possibles"). This subject of the "B" list is defined by the concept of "relative value". As expectations, prices yields, and other measures change with time so does the "A" list.

It is not to be supposed that Clarkson's methods are the final word in portfolio selection. He himself did not think so. They should be regarded as a "jumping off" point for improvement through experience (learning).

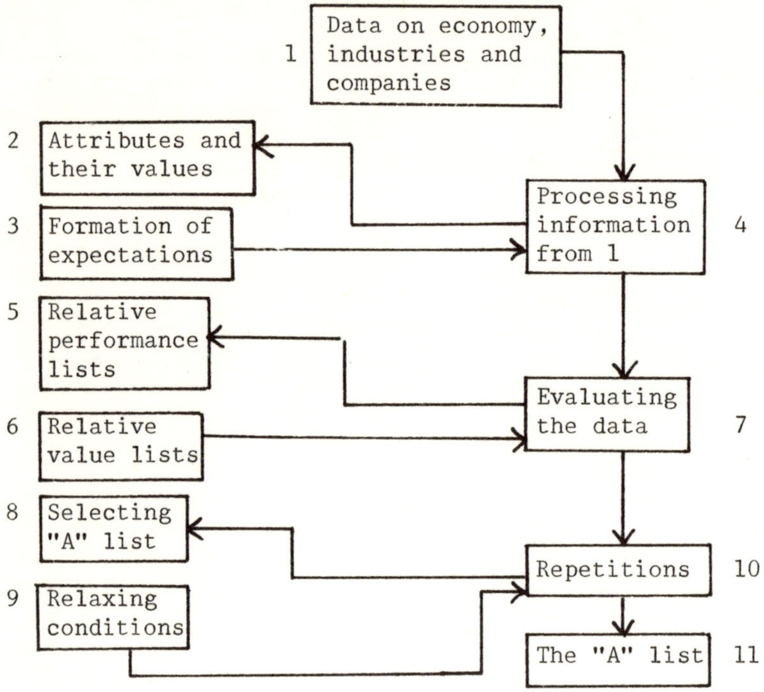

FIGURE 2
Selecting the "A" List

It is here that Clarkson's methods can be seen to be different from method I and II.

PROCESSING THE BASIC INFORMATION

Although the information used to derive the current list of stocks is classified into three main categories, which are: the general economy, industry and company, the processes by which the information is handled are much the same. Differences occur in the material content of the information processed and the manner in which interrelations are formed, but the basic structure of the sorting and evaluating processes remains the same.

This means that for each category there is a set of attributes that correspond to the important variables in that category. For example, for all companies the set of attributes consists of:

Sales
Earnings
Cash flow per share
Profit margin
Working capital
Price earnings ratio
Dividend payout ratio
Dividends per share
Dividend yield
Prices

The values of these attributes are their numerical values, and these are determined by the information which is fed into the model. Since the values will reflect the changes that occur in the economy, industry and company variables those that change frequently are readily distinguished from those that do not. Those that change infrequently with time reflect the general trend of the economy, industry or company, while the others indicate those attributes that are most sensitive to short-run fluctuations.

DETERMINATION OF ATTRIBUTES AND THEIR VALUES

All information, except that dealing with economy or industry forecasts is fed into the model numerically. The data consists of the historical values of each attribute in the system for the last ten years. The data is entered in the form of lists, and from these basic lists the model generates, for each attribute, three additional lists:

(a) Trend. The list contains the last annual values of each attribute arranged in chronological order, so that the most recent is at the head of the list.

(b) Average Form. We take a ten-year average each time a new value is added in (a) a new average of ten values is placed on this list. Thus, this list contains a ten year moving average of the values in (a).

(c) Recent Form. This list contains the rate of increase (or decrease) of each value in the Trend List over the value immediately below it. Thus, if the values of the Trend List are called x_1, where i = 1, 2, ..., 10, then the Recent Form List will have nine entries whose values will equal:

$$\frac{x_i - x_i{-1}}{x_n + 1} \qquad \text{where } i = 1,2, \ldots, 9$$

(d) Another Average. This is the average rate of change. This list contains the average rate of change of the values of list (a) for the entire ten-year period. Like list (b) this is revised every time there is a new entry on the Trend List.

THE FORMATION OF EXPECTATIONS

Information on forecasts is fed into the model in two different forms. Forecasts for economy and industry attributes are converted for input into a three-valued scale "above" (A) "below" (B) or "equal to" (E). The entry is based on the published predictions that the value for a given attribute is going to rise, fall or stay the same over the next interval of time.

All forecasts attributes have the current forecasts as their only (numerical) value. Previous forecasts are not kept and the model takes each forecast at face value without making any attempt to judge its "goodness" or "record of success".

EXPECTATION LISTS

(a) Economy and Industry Expectation Lists. For each attribute in both of these categories the Expectation Lists contain two entries. The first is the forecast value for that attribute converted into the input form of "above", "below" and "equal to". The second is the first value on the Recent Change List - namely the rate of change of that attribute for last year - converted into the same three-valued scale. Hence Economy and

Industry Expectation Lists contain pairs of "aboves" "belows" or "equals to" which under two possible sets of conditions will form a pattern of only "aboves" or "belows".

(b) Company Expectation Lists. Expectation Lists exist for five of the ten company attributes:

Sales
Earnings per share
Cash flow per share
Profit margin
Dividends per share

These Expectation Lists contain one or two entries all of which are in numerical form. These entries are derived from the twelve-month and three-to-five-year forecasts recorded in the model for these attributes. The first entry is on all Expectation Lists and is obtained by converting the twelve-month forecast into an expected rate of change. The second entry exists only for sales and earnings per share, and Clarkson then derives his Expectation Lists converting the three-to-five-year forecast into an expected average rate of change.

THE RELATIVE PERFORMANCE LIST

In order to determine the relative performance of each company within its given industry a list is made for each attribute of the mean for that attribute for each company. Hence, for each attribute there is now a list of means each of which belongs to a particular company within a given industry. The average of this list of means is taken so that we now have a distribution of means for a given attribute, plus the mean of that distribution. The deviation of each mean from the distribution mean is calculated as a percentage deviation and is then converted into the three-valued scale "above", "below" or "equal to". These per cent deviations from the distribution mean are recorded on the Relative Performance List of each attribute.

Clarkson uses a matrix method for calculating the Relative Performance List. But we can simply say that we can list the number of attributes for each company and associate each with every company in the industry. We calculate the average (arithmetic mean) of each set of attributes is calculated for each, and then we subtract each attribute of each company from its mean and divide by the mean. We now discover which are "above", which "below" and which the same as their means.

All this really amounts to a decision to arrive at which companies in an industry have done best in terms of our criteria. In particular it supplies:

(a) The mean value over the last ten years as well as whether this mean is "above", "below" or "equal to" the mean for this attribute for the other companies in this industry.
(b) The mean rate of growth over the last ten years as well as whether this mean is "above", "below" or "equal to" the population mean for this attribute.
(c) The expected rate of growth over the coming twelve months as well as whether this expected rate of growth is "above", "below" or "equal to" the mean of the population of expected rates of growth.
(d) The mean, expected rate of growth over the next three to five years as well as whether this mean rate of growth is "above", "below" or "equal to" the mean of the population of mean, expected rates of growth.

THE RELATIVE VALUE LIST

Clarkson now computes the Relative Value of each company's stock. As noted above, each company has an attribute that records a three-to-five-year forecast of its earnings per share. Although this is only an estimate, the figure is assumed to be reliable and is used, for each company to form a price earnings (P/E) ratio of the forecast earnings. As the model already contains the values for the current price earnings ratio and the historical mean of the prices earnings multiple for that company, the entries for the Relative Value List are as follows: The difference between the mean P/E ratio and the P/E ratio of the forecast earnings. This difference is taken as a percentage of the mean and is recorded as "above," "below" or "equal to" the historical mean. The second entry consists of the difference between the historical mean and the current P/E ratio. As before, this difference is taken as a percentage of the historical mean and is recorded as "above", "below" or "equal to". We use the notation in the same way as Clarkson:

P = current market price
E = expected earnings per share for the current year
E^* = forecast earnings per share three to five years from now
$\bar{P}/E^*$ = ten year average of price earnings ratio

Then for each company the calculations are as follows, the results of each being recorded as "above", "below" or "equal to".

(i) $$\frac{(\overline{P/E}) - (P/E^*)}{P/E}$$

(ii) $$\frac{(\overline{P/E}) - (P/E)}{P/E}$$

The Relative Value List contains these results, plus their value on the three point scale in the order that they are produced. Thus, for each company the Relative Value List is a pair of "aboves", "belows" or "equals to", which may form a pattern of only A "aboves" or "belows".

INTERRELATIONS

The methods and data Clarkson uses, and which we have described briefly, are, of course, not really independent. This leads us to the use of what he calls the scanner and the selector. The scanner accepts information on:

(a) The desired amount of growth.
(b) The desired amount of income.
(c) Whether current income is sufficient.
(d) The necessary stability of income.
(e) Income tax bracket.
(f) Profession of investor, etc.

The scanner checks whether (a) - (f) are above or below average, so each investor has a record of success (adequacy). He then uses the selector which takes the output of the scanner and converts the output into an investment policy. As Clarkson puts it:

(i) Growth Account. In these accounts assets are expected to appreciate at an average rate of 10% per year over a ten-year period. Income is not stressed and fluctuations in principle are tolerated.
(ii) Growth and Income Account. Here assets are expected to appreciate at 5-6% per year, while dividend yield should approach 2-3% per year.
(iii) Income and Growth. In this type of account assets are only expected to appreciate 3-4% per year. The desired dividend yield is 3-4% per year and the stability of the income stream is stressed.
(iv) Income Account. Here the size and stability of the income streams are stressed with the expected dividend yield being 4-6% per year. In this type of account,

growth (capital appreciation) is not stressed.

The final stage is called the Growth-Portfolio Discrimination net and can be seen in Figure 1, chapter 12, where it is drawn as a Testolog tree, in the context of expert systems.

The main criticism of the Growth-Portfolio Discrimination net, as will be clear on careful consideration of both testrologic technique and expert system is the over strong emphasis on acceptance or rejection.

A testrolog tree will be prepared to accept a high proportion of "passes" and some (only a few) "failures". This way it comes up, as in our examples shown, in terms not of "accept" or "reject", but rather with:-

* Ideal Investment

* Good investment

* Borderline Investment

* Bad Investment

or some such priority list appropriate to the circumstances and the context of the customer's requirements.

We show though on the next page the questions involved in the Growth Portfolio Discrimination net, which we repeat on page 197, with the testrolog tree.

There are various ways of drawing such a flow chart, but the testrolog tree is almost certainly the best, and such a testrolog tree is provided on page 198.

We should think all the time of a testrolog as a highly-specialised method of tree-searching, which allows the user to work top-down or bottom-up and see actually how we got where and where we came from.

There are, of course, many tree-representations of hierarchies; some grow as you pass along from branch to branch, others are wholly explicit and fully grown before the search starts.

Most tree, and certainly testrolog, as it is normally used, are explicit.

Q1 = Is mean growth in (past) price $\geqslant$ 20%

Q2 = Is mean growth in (past) earnings per share $> K_1$

Q3 = Is mean growth in (past) sales $> K_2$

Q4 = Is forecast growth in earnings per share (1 year) $> K_3$.

Q5 = Is forecast growth in sales (1 year) $> K_4$

Q6 = Is mean growth in cash flow per share (past) $> K_5$

Q7 = Is mean growth in profit margin (past) $> K_6$

Q8 = Is $P/\overset{*}{E} - \bar{P}/\bar{E}$ (y) on Relative Value List.

Q9 = Is $P/E < (P/E)$ by 10%

Q10 = Is forecast dividend $>$ 0?

Q11 = Is forecast dividend = 0?

Q12 = Is price $>$ 10% below high?

Q7 refers to y on Relative Value List and this is defined by Clarkson as:

$$y = \frac{\bar{P}}{E} - \frac{P}{E}$$

Finally, it should be said that diversification is achieved by spreading investments over at least five industries and generally to one investment per industry. The second system of Method III which we shall describe briefly, is Hartley's COIN[3].

PROGRAM COIN

COIN is a computerised investment program which predicts the relative future performance of a number of shares in the Stock Exchange according to some pre-chosen criteria. Its input is in the form of quantitative (or qualitative) data on ten variables which affect the share's performance for each of ten discrete time periods in the history of the share. The eleventh variable is the share price for the same ten periods.

The variables chosen were from investment information service Moodie's and, in particular their "Investment Handbook". The listed variables at the time were eleven in number, although more are now used. They were:

1.	Sales	- the turnover of the company in one year.
2.	Total profits	- in one year, before tax, etc.
3.	Earned for Ordinary	- the amount of profit set aside for the dividend on ordinary shares.
4.	Earned income	- the amount, as a percentage, of the maximum profit that could be paid out as dividend (based on the latest year's capital).
5.	Dividend	- the actual percentage paid.
6.	Net assets per share	- the theoretical value of the company on liquidation averaged per share.
7.	Average share price	- average of the highest and lowest prices during the year.
8.	Yield ratio	- the ratio of the dividend yield (the percentage of the share-price paid as dividend per share) to the average yield on Moodies Equity index at the same date.
9.	Ordinary capital	- the amount of capital issued as ordinary shares at the end of the financial year.
10.	Capital employed	- the total capital reserves of the company.
11.	Pre-tax profits	- profits before tax etc. but after capital depreciation has been accounted for.

Values of these eleven variables were given for the past ten years in yearly intervals from 1961 to 1970 inclusive. Thus for each company there were ten values for each variable. All of this information was taken and used as data input.

The output consists, essentially, of an ordered list of the shares for which data was input, the order being that of relative performance over the next time-period. The top ten (or indeed any chosen number) could then form the basis for a portfolio which can be reviewed by repeating the same procedure with new data at the end of each period.

Hartley's method is to supply an algorithm for changing the weight of the variables under consideration whenever a wrong prediction has been made. It only corrects one prediction at a time though and will sometimes, as a result, change some of the previous predictions. This could (and sometimes does) mean that some predictions which were correct with the old weights become wrong with the new ones. The way around this difficulty is, according to Hartley, to cycle through history correcting any wrong predictions as they occur until the whole of the history can be predicted with one set of weights. Thus the method is a repetitive, or reiterative, one and is therefore a kind of "learning system". The training method, which is the weight-changing procedure outlined above, can be shown to approximate increasingly to a good solution to the investment problem.

The comparison of any two shares is the basic operation of the model. The end result (output) is, as we have said, a prediction of their relative performance over the next period of time under consideration. This unit is then utilised in the prediction of the performance of a whole set of shares, all of which are compared under similar conditions, each with each other. The values involved for the variables and constants in the model can be listed as follows:

(1) Performance criterion;
(2) Number of variables per share, and which variables;
(3) Number of periods and length of each period in history;
(4) Normalisation constant for weights; and
(5) Value of a particular constant A, which occurs in the formal model.

First of all we will mention the performance criterion, which is the method of comparing two shares' performance. The object in buying shares is to make a profit by selling them when their price rises. Whether or not the dividend is included in the profits depends on the period of investment and a number of other factors, but a basic principle to remember is that if the price drops the investment has failed. Therefore, as a sound basis for any more complex criterion an increase in share-price over the last period considered was chosen. In other words, the "critical variable" which is compared for different pairs of shares is the share price at different times - particularly the difference between the time of buying and the time of selling.

The only direct comparison available is with the Weaver and Hall successful programme, which we discussed briefly in the last chapter, which uses the following six variables:

(1) Dividend yield;
(2) Dividend payout ratio;
(3) Forecast earnings growth rate - short term;

(4) Forecast earnings growth rate - long term;
(5) Historical earnings variability; and
(6) Historical earnings growth rate.

The following eleven variables have been suggested by another well known investor, James Morell:

(1) Dividend;
(2) Earnings record;
(3) Dividend cover;
(4) Volatility of earnings;
(5) Dividend yield;
(6) Earnings yield;
(7) Management;
(8) Politics;
(9) Asset value/share.
(10) Expected growth in dividend; and
(11) Expected growth in earnings.

It can be seen that Weaver and Hall concentrate on the two "technical" variables, dividend and earnings which are quantitative and readily available for every share. Besides the asset value per share, Morell adds two qualitative variables which he refers to as management and politics. Clearly these are (or can be) of supreme importance. This is especially in, say, an acquisition situation and therefore is very relevant to what we said in the last chapter but one; they are, though, obviously very difficult to quantify. However, as emphasised earlier there is no need to quantify when only comparisons are used as in COIN; at least quantification is made much easier. Comparisons involving management and politics can be made and, indeed, are inevitably made by the method of (subjective) opinion. Since the program will throw out any useless or non-critical variables by assigning a low or zero weight to them. Then the correctness (or at least the pragmatic value) of the subjective comparison can be discovered.

The program allows for ten variables but this can be greatly extended as required An obvious point which it is worthwhile to make clear is that the "useful" variables are going to be those which are directly comparable, irrespective of which companies are involved. There may be cases where this is not the case, for example, it may well be that having a large board of directors is better than a small one. This clearly puts a premium on the overall size of the company, but, in general, variables like these should be made directly comparable by suitable means. This could be done by expressing the number of directors as a percentage of the number of employees. In fact such an example should not be taken too literally, since a company's effectiveness is not to any great extent highly correlated with the size of its board.

A feedback method has been suggested to ascertain the most effective subset of variables used from all the possible variables. This can be done by normalisation of weights (as already mentioned).

The normalisation constant (the sum of all the weights) is a compromise between accuracy and running time. The larger the number, the better the accuracy, i.e. there is more resolution between individual weights, but there is also increased complexity in the arithmetic involved in the weight-changing processes.

A constant A is the other important matter. The value of A affects the time of the learning period and it would seem that the smaller the value the shorter the time in learning to describe the history. In other words, since A is some sort of 'search distance' over and above the minimum required, it would seem unnecessary to search too far. However, in practice this was found not to be the case and the inference is that the learning time depends more on the complexity of the history being described than the value A. In COIN, A is fixed constantly at 100, the initial value of each variables was 100, and the sum of ten gives a constant 1000.

COIN depends very considerably on the <u>form</u> of the data with which it is presented. If there are any inconsistencies in the data then the program breaks down and produces an arbitrary prediction. This can be paralleled in any learning situation when a disturbance or inconsistency in the environment tends to degrade the learning process or even stop it altogether. This leads on to what is probably the central problem in investment and portfolio analysis - the choice of the key variables; which variables are the ones which mainly explain the movement in share prices?

The answer to our problem lies not in applying one approach rigidly, but using a combination of many different techniques already in use in other fields. Problem solving and forecasting in general, seem to offer much more scope than other methods in providing an understanding of the subject of investment as a whole. The problem of building a useful model has been approached with COIN in mind. It is hypothesised that the data for COIN can be manipulated, using a logic method in such a way that the performance of COIN becomes optimal, although it will never be perfect. Some success has been achieved by this technique; the success rate going up from 35% to a maximum of 70%. Thus the quality of data has been improved from not very good to quite good with minimal change. In fact, the only changes made in the data are to reverse some of the correlation signs (it is as well to add that correlations vary between + 1 (perfect) to 0 (no relation) to -1 (completely negative)), of the ten variables chosen (they are all assumed positive *a priori*). However the technique clearly has a maximum success rate at any given time with any given set of variables. What is required is that background research goes on continually to try to acquire new information as to key variables.

In chapter 11, we shall be greatly influenced by both Clarkson and Hartley, in trying to lay down clearly what we believe is the best approach to investment.

REFERENCES CHAPTER 9

1. G.P.E. Clarkson, 'A model of the trust investment process', In Computers and Thought E.Feigenbaum and J.Feldman (Eds) McGraw-Hill, 1963.
2. F.H.George, Precision, Language and Logic, Pergamon Press, 1979.
3. R.T.Hartley 'COIN: A computer simulation of Trust Investment'. Brunel University, Monograph, 1972.

CHAPTER 10
THE WORLD OF COMMODITIES

We have said that commodities would not be a major theme in this book, but the measure of the commonality they have with stocks and shares encourages the inclusion of at least one chapter devoted to the commodity markets.

The field of financial investment is very wide and can include Premium and Government Bonds, antiques, etc. Up to now we have been talking solely about stocks and shares, but now we move over into our other main field of interest which is commodities. This is a less well known field than the Stock Exchange, but one that has some advantages and certainly many differences which must be explained.

Commodities have been surrounded by an unusual amount of jargon - rather like the specialist fields of science - and some of the terminology must be explained in this chapter. We are now trading, for example, in futures; rather than physical entities (although share certificates are not exactly physical entities). The field of commodities includes what are sometimes called "soft commodities" such as sugar, cocoa, barley, wheat and the like and what, by implication, are sometimes (or should be) called "hard commodities" such as rubber, gold, silver and various metals. Whatever the commodity, the principles involved are basically the same.

Investments can vary in three ways: 1) in their degree of liquidity, 2) in the return one can expect and 3) in the level of risk involved in the investment. An investment is said to be liquid if one can convert it into cash almost immediately whenever one wishes. Examples of liquid assets are shares and Premium Bonds. However some assets are not liquid; some life insurance policies are very non-liquid as one cannot regain the deposits until an agreed number of years have passed. An investment in a physical object such as an antique or a picture or some other "personal" property is not necessarily liquid, as one cannot always find a buyer at exactly the right moment. The ability to sell such investments with little delay is known as the marketability of the commodity.

Investments such as shares in most large companies are liquid only because there are so many people involved in the market that they are therefore easily marketed, but a large holding in a minor company may well be difficult to sell at any given moment. The same is true of commodities; most are easily marketed, but some are not so at all times. Thus if one is particularly concerned with liquidity it is better to invest in the more popular commodities, which are generally the most liquid.

A commodity market was originally merely a place where commodity producers could meet with users of the commodity and, by means of an auction, reach a current selling price. However it was soon obvious that there was a need for futures selling so that the producers and users and also various other traders, particularly "middlemen", could reduce the risks and uncertainty that arose from the natural fluctuations in prices. A "buy" futures contract is an intention to buy a set quantity of some commodity at a previously agreed price at a certain time in the future, known as the terminal date or month. Such a contract can be completely eliminated by later taking up a "sell" futures contract for the same trading position. Thus the investor in futures need not be involved in actual physical trading of the commodity, but almost inevitably trades only in "intentions" or futures. There are thus three viewpoints that can be taken of a commodity market - that of a typical investor, that of a producer and that of a businessman who has to buy his raw materials on the market. We shall only be concerned with the first, although some mention will be made of the third (none of the second).

RISK AND RETURN

The return on an investment is usually taken to be the gain (or loss) over some stated period measured as a percentage of the capital involved, i.e. to quote Granger[1])

$$\text{Return} = \frac{\text{Final value - Initial value of investment}}{\text{Initial value}} \times 100$$

We naturally prefer an investment that gives a high return to one that gives a low return, but unfortunately comparison of investments is complicated by the fact that there is also a level of risk to consider.

But enough has been said on the mathematical technique of risk analysis as such, particularly bearing in mind Appendix II, so here we shall take a much wider view of what is entailed in decision making (the conceptual process) and decision taking. (the implementation of the conceptual process). Again in Appendix II we say something of the mathematical methods involved, but we do not only want to think in mathematical terms, since they supply a precise procedure which requires interpretation. They are models that can often be made to fit particular situations, but still the model has to be interpreted as part of a theory or in ordinary common sense terms. This inevitably means that if, for example, a computer is to be used in investment, (in its very broadest sense) we should chain together a series of tests which would seem sufficient to ensure that the correct choice was made.

All the above is excellent as far as it goes, but there may be many things which are not embodied in these tests which could play an important part in decision making. One example is "inside information". If all the formal tests operate on whatever public data is available then it cannot be expected to use public data that is not available. A parallel with horse-racing occurs here. You can run through your program using data such as weight, distance, going and previous results and the weights, distance, going and speed figures for those previous results and so forth. But if a horse has been specially run at slow speed or in any other way where its public performance data is misleading, then our computer (or indeed our human expert) fails to make the correct assessment. He may though have suspicions, while the person who actually arranged the dissimulation would <u>know</u> the situation. So it is our scientific approach to investment in either stocks and shares or commodities that certain facts may simply not be available, and we ought to look at more informal methods, which can be much more easily embodied in what are called expert systems and are the centre of discussion in chapter 12.

Consider the type of problem where a military commander has to make a decision as to whether to attack or defend, or attack by air, sea or, if on land, to the left or to the right and so on and so forth. He must work out the consequences of each tactic in the light of all his available information, coupled to the need to consider the possible outcomes in the light of taking one particular course of action. This looks like involving the minimax regret principle, so you have to consider the upshot of failure and may wish to ensure that you choose the decision which is least likely to "upset the apple-cart" the most if you are wrong. To use mathematical models in such circumstances can become unrealistically complex and furthermore usually depends upon what the other person (e.g. the enemy) does.

Similarly you may have to decide a question where you want to do such-and-such but it requires a great effort and perhaps a doubtful chance of success. It therefore may be that to do so-and-so, with lesser effort, and a better chance of success might be better. This will though depend upon the difference between such-and-such and so-and-so, the relative effort and the relative probability of success. It will look neat and tidy if we put numerical weightings into our matrices and use standard decision making methods, but the chances of these numerical weightings being anything more than a subjective estimate - little different from what you (as a human being) would make anyway - is all too apparent. The assessment of probabilities is such that they can only be subjective since their uncertainty springs from the uncertainty which is inherent in any string of causal events where the complex chain is uncertain partly through the interaction of people and companies, partly through lack of knowledge and partly through the intrinsic uncertainty of the causal relationships intrinsic to the world.

The upshot of this generalised argument is that complete faith should not be vested in mathematical techniques in isolation, anymore than a physicist at an elementary level would rely on his computations in dynamics or statics, say, out of the context of their application.

This sort of situation can be seen clearly in investment, where an asset whose price fluctuates a great deal is riskier than one whose price does not. That this is sensible can be seen by noting that, if the price changes a lot, then over some set period a rather large loss can result, particularly if one buys in a bull market and sells in a bear market. It may be thought that this problem can be overcome by choosing the most opportune time at which to sell, but this could result in one's capital being tied up in a low-return asset for long periods. Exactly the same argument holds for fluctuating profits on a product in a business market. Because of the high risk levels associated with commodities, a person who plays the market is sometimes called a "speculator" rather than an investor. Although a speculator is involved with risk, he should not be equated with a gambler, although he is only one step removed.

The main differences between the investor and the gambler are that the investor gains or loses by degrees while the gambler tends to win or lose, since the pools either come up or they do not, and a horse either wins or does not. Investment, as we have treated it (very broadly) involves not just the stock exchange but every aspect of business, while even casino games are relatively simple and narrow in concept.

COMMODITY MARKETS

The economy of nations, indeed of the whole world, depends heavily on the act of trading. There may be numerous reasons why it is more economical to produce some goods at one place rather than another, including physical, climatic, social and political reasons. The transportation of these goods from their source in response to some consumer demand will raise their value. A tractor just leaving a factory in an urban area has one value, but if transported to the Far East it has much greater value. This simple example exhibits one of the most important aspects of commodity trading: transport, storage through time (and the longevity of the commodity) and the differing values placed on the commodity by buyers and sellers which are influenced by these and other factors.

It is clear also that where some commodity, such as oil or coffee beans, can be produced in a number of different countries, that trading in them should be concentrated on just a few main centres; such centres are precisely what are called commodity markets. This is obviously not true of competitive branded markets, where one is trying to sell something quite specific like a particular aircraft or motor car, or indeed any commodity that was only suitable for one (or perhaps two) countries. By implication any commodity that is universally useable, wherever produced, is one that calls for the commodity market. This indeed is where what is effectively an auction takes place; such auction sales fix the current commodity prices.

The current market price for the investor to purchase a commodity if he enters the market is called the spot price, or sometimes, more familiarily, cash price. But this is not, of course, the only aspect of the commodity market, since we have forward contracts (which led to futures).

The forward contract occurs where a producer or manufacurer, aware that he will need a certain amount of this or that sometime in the future, will contract with a seller at an agreed price, to supply the required commodities at the time required. We may want raw materials for steel manufacture in the future long before the raw material is available. Similarly the car manufacturer may want to place an order for steel well before the possible delivery time.

Such forward contracts reduce the risk both to the supplier and the customer. This in fact means that they do not pay the spot price at the time the transaction actually takes place. If the spot price changes in the meantime one of the two will benefit that much more. But such (probably small) changes in spot price are offset by the security to both parties. We can have the situation, with the odd name "Contango Situation" where forward prices are prices higher than current spot prices. If the opposite occurs, it is known as a "backwardation".

This led in turn to the replacement of dockside auctions (a feature of the earlier part of the last century to "cost, insurance and freight trading" usually known as c.i.f. trading) and this was the cost paid by the purchaser. This was the first step in forward contracts, since the whole procedure was agreed before the ship left its port of origin. This ensured security (the elimination of risk) as already mentioned and meant the minimisation of delays and no money to be spent on holding the commodity in warehouses.

THE FUTURES MARKET.

It was the relative lack of flexibility of forward contracting that led to the futures market. With forward contracting, it was difficult to transfer from one contractor to another, which might be desirable if circumstances changed. Purchaser A (the original contractor) may find he has a glut of the commodity, whereas someone else B has a shortage (in both cases unforeseen when the forward contract was made), so for B to replace A seemed the obvious ploy.

The futures contract remedied this defect and was no longer a contract binding on some two parties. The futures contract simply guarantees to deliver a commodity of a certain standard and amount. This naturally let in the investor (speculator) who undertook the contract in the belief (or hope) that the spot price would rise during the <u>lead time</u> (the time between agreement and delivery) when he could resale at the current spot price and make a profit. He can, of course, in the meantime (during the lead time) sell his option (futures contract) to a third party. This notion, which has the intention of never actually obtaining the commodity is called a "long position". It should be made clear that futures markets (terminal markets) can vary in their lead time from weeks up to two years or more.

The reverse of the "long position" is the "short position" where the speculator sells now, and he will usually agree to buy (at a later date) a futures contract for the same amount and the same terminal date. He will normally expect to cancel this futures contract by buying later and if he leaves this until the terminal date, he must buy on the spot market.

Let us give an example of the sort of thing we are discussing A speculator (Mr. Jones) buys 500 tons of coffe (due 9 months later) in January at £200 a ton. The coffee is then called "October coffee" since October is the contract's terminal month. If he sells in April at £210 a ton he has made a gross profit of £13 per ton, which is £5,000, and this has to have a commission deducted from it.

If in the above example he had sold, rather than bought, 500 tons of coffee and then bought it as before, he would have lost, from his "short position", exactly what he won from his "long position". To avoid greater losses he has cancelled the original with a buy contract and although he loses, he supposes that to go to the terminal date in October would have lost him even more.

It is clear that the terminal date, like "full-time" in a football match which marks the end of the game, is crucial. He must always be keeping his eye on this terminal date and in the meantime carry out his forecasting with the greatest care. This is one thing that makes commodities different from shares.

There are one or two important points that the investor must bear in mind. That his futures should be conducted on an original margin of between 10% and 50%. This is bound up with the fact that whereas he can make a large profit he could also make a very large loss. This is common sense, in that he must, as he would in any casino game or betting on horses and dogs, ensure that he has not risked at any time his total capital, or even too high a percentage of it.

Secondly he should bear in mind that future prices with a fixed terminal date and spot prices tend to approach each other as the terminal date approaches. This will obviously influence his investment policy.

Thirdly, he might as a bookmaker might, hedge his bets by buying and selling, and then selling and buying to cancel the hedge. This occurs, for example, when he uses the futures market to "get in" and "out" at the right time and thus limiting losses when the spot prices change.

The business man (i.e. the producer of the goods or the industrial manufacturer) is closely related, since a producer can use the futures market in the same way as the forward contractor. This therefore ensures that he will get a set price in the futures and thus avoid (or reduce) risk. Furthermore he can make up any short fall in production by purchasing himself in the futures market.

At the other end of the proceedings the manufacturer can ensure a regular supply of raw materials at relatively constant price and again he does this by buying futures contracts. The producer and users thus use the futures market as an insurance, whereby the speculator acts as a "middle man", hoping to achieve a profit as a result, in effect, of helping to guarantee the insurance.

The market itself is very much like an auction of the kind where the dealers are on opposite sides of a ring and bid by simply shouting out their bid or offer. Subsequently, when the deal is made, it is recorded and reported in the financial pages of the press.

To get into the commodity futures market in the first place you need a broker. This is made available by the secretary of the association for each commodity exchange. Before we move on to a brief description of types of commodities, let us just mention in outline one basic aspect of trading, it is called options.

Options are in a sense quite the opposite of receiving a commodity. They offer the limiting of risk in both the Stock Exchange and the commodity futures market. The well known phrase "I'll give you first option" is the key. The granter of the option writes an option to the taker as a hedge against the future. The taker pays the premium (like a down payment on a house) to ensure that he will not have the chance to buy some commodity and stands to lose only his premium, if it is inconvenient to do so.

We should note the difference between commodity and stock options. First, the life of a commodity option, which can vary from thirty days to three years is more flexible, and generally of longer duration than share options, which are usually for three months.

Secondly, the price of a commodity option is usually lower with all costs considered, and this is most important, share transactions are subject to stamp duty; those in commodities are not. A share option might run to 8 to 20 per cent of the share price. Over the year this represents from 32 to 80 per cent of the share price. In contrast, a commodity "put" or "call" option costs around 5 to 15 per cent of the price of the commodity and can be negotiated for a delivery month up to eighteen months or more away.

The main attraction of options, however, arises from the fact that, although the investor's risk or liability is limited to the amount of his premium, the potential profits to be gained can be substantial. Purchasing options means that the investor is buying time. For this privilege a premium over an agreed "basis" or "striking" price is paid. It follows that the cost of this premium depends upon how far forward the investor wishes to deal and it varies between markets.

Options are traded in three forms: "calls", "puts" and "doubles".

1) A "call" option gives the buyer the right to buy at the basis price at any time between the date of purchasing the option and the expiry date. This option would suit an investor who expects the market to rise but wants to limit his loss should things go wrong.

2) A "put" option is the reverse, giving the buyer the right to sell at the basis price at any time between the date of purchasing and the expiry date. It is taken out when a decline is expected.

3) A "double" option works both ways, when the investor expects to make money whichever way the market moves - although, as the name implies, the premium is usually twice the amount of that for the other options.

For example, suppose an investor expects to see a rise in the coffee market by the end of the year. He negotiates through his broker to buy a call. Assume that the current market value for December coffee is £2,000 per ton. The buyer agrees to pay a premium of £200 a ton over the current market value to secure the call. For two lots, 20 tons, the purchaser pays £4,000 plus commission. If, between the day of striking and the expiration of the option, December coffee trades above £1,750 per ton, a profit is made by declaring the option. Where upon the granter of the option must send him a contract for December coffee purchased at £1,500 per ton. For a put option to be profitable, the market would have to fall by a similar amount, and the seller of the put would then send a contract for December coffee at £1,500 per ton.

A further advantage of trading in options is the ability to convert without incurring risk. In the above example suppose that after the investor has purchased two lots of call, the market rises to £1,850 per ton. The investor will be showing a good profit and if he thinks that a fall is imminent he can sell one lot to protect himself. This secures an automatic profit.

The commodities we shall consider next are the range of soft commodities covered. So-called "soft commodities" are any and every commodity (other than metals, rubber and bullion) which are traded in a commodities market. The most important are those with a large and also active, futures market.

The only soft markets actively trading in London today are those for cocoa, sugar, coffee, wheat, barley and soyabean meal. There are large markets in other soft commodities such as tea, cotton, jute, hides and furs ect., but in these cases they deal in the physical commodity itself thus they have no futures markets. We shall therefore be thinking only of the former list.

Commodity exchanges came into existence during the nineteenth century as a result of the rapid expansion of national economies. Improved methods of communication, scientific and technological developments, coupled to the rapid growth in population, caused a vast increase in international trade. Business became more international and there was increased competition between primary producers for markets and an extension in the time-period between initial production and final sale. This last point had a great bearing on the whole development of the commodities and futures market. Merchants, dealers and manufacturers, as a result, held a much larger stock of raw materials which inevitably exposed them to greater financial risk, and as companies normally operated on borrowed capital, any adverse price movement could have a disastrous effect on their liquidity. It was therefore necessary to find a means of limiting the risks to which producers and users of raw materials were constantly exposed. This led, after local informal dealings, to the opening of Commercial Sale Rooms in 1811, when all such commodity trading took place in a single centre.

The start of futures trading was in the "soft commodity" of cotton, which was largely traded in Liverpool. The large majority of cotton exported to Britain was imported from the Americas by mercahnts to Liverpool, hence the market place was situated there. The merchants were stockholders who kept large supplies not far from the spinners' mills. A large proportion of the spinners were small businessmen and as a result they were not able to carry large stocks and were very dependent on the credit given by the dealers. This led to people dealing in cotton "yet to be shipped" and it is this phase that clearly suggests the beginnings of the futures market. A cotton futures market was developed but subsequently government intervention in the physical market killed the futures market to the detriment of the whole industry, and at the moment there is no active cotton futures market in Britain. There are active cotton futures markets in the U.S.A. and Hong Kong. In Britain, although cotton has faded and still not recovered, cocoa provides an active futures market.

Cortez when he landed in Mexico discovered cocoa for the Western world, since it had been used in the form of a "hot chocolate" type of drink there for many years. It seems that it was imported to Mexico from South America, probably either Brazil or Venezuela, and spread by way of Spain to Europe and the Western world. Interestingly enough it was only after the introduction of another soft commodity sugar that cocoa took on its appeal in Europe. Cocoa itself is also the source of chocolate and therefore plays a primary part in the confectionary markets of the Western world.

Today cocoa comes mainly from Africa and after the Africas, Brazil is the largest exporter. The main cocoa crop is harvested in the winter months, and there is a smaller crop harvested in the summer, most often in the case of the largest African producers (Ghana and Nigeria) in the early summer, or late spring. Successful cocoa growing is much dependent, as one might guess, on climate. A hot humid atmosphere with plenty of rain is ideal, and there is, of course, the need to exercise great care to protect what are delicate crops from a whole variety of diseases. Before considering the market place aspect of our selected soft commodities, we shall look at each soft commodity in turn. The next is sugar.

We can quite briefly say that sugar had its origins in the form of cane sugar and originated from the West over two hundred years ago. Since that time sugar was grown at home, not from sugar cane but by extracting sugar from beetroot. This led to Europe producing the bulk of its own sugar.

Coffee comes next and is a really very old discovery going back over 1,000 years. It is mostly produced in Brazil, although it suffers from cycles of gluts and shortages which partly reflects the state of the purchasing country's economy. Coffee production, like cocoa, depends upon climatic conditions and rain and heat are essential. In the case of coffee, geographical conditions are also important. So it is that you need to grow the coffee in the hills, or at least at altitudes of anything from 2,000 to 6,ooo feet above sea level, and in essentially tropical conditions.

The other soft commodities we mentioned: soyabean meal, barley and wheat and vegetable oils and wool are not so explicitly located in the tropical or near-tropical types of climate. In fact they are not climatically dependent. But one associates wool with New Zealand, wheat with the U.S.A. and Canada, and finally the other soft commodity, tea, with India, Ceylon and China. Let us now look briefly at the markets for soft commodities.

In the case of cocoa, it is in Ghana (currently the largest of the cocoa producers) that the cocoa is grown by small holding farmers and controlled by, and the marketing for the farmers carried out by,the Ghana Cocoa State Marketing Board. The board issues a weekly purchase figure which is a good indicator of the production state of cocoa there.

Futures trading in cocoa began after World War I; the Cocoa Association of London being formed in 1926. In 1928 the London Cocoa Terminal Market Association was opened, and trade in cocoa was extremely brisk.

One example of a London Commodity Futures Contract is quoted by Conticommodity Services Ltd. as follows:

> "10 tonnes (metric tons) of cocoa at a "recent value" of £2,000, gave a total contract value of £20,000 with a minimum initial margin of £1,400, A margin (see Glossary) being the amount of money deposited by traders of futures contracts to ensure the proper performance of the terms of the contract; it is a performance bond and minimum initial margins must be maintained at all times".

A table showing the expansion of the futures market in London has been provided by M.E.T.Davies[3].

Cocoa: London Futures Transaction
1951 - 78

Year	Transactions (in long tons)	Transaction (in tonnes)
1951	52,265	
1952	121,850	
1953	146,420	
1954	284,795	
1955	191,225	
1956	211,920	
1957	222,290	
1958	365,110	
1959	292,850	
1960	257,890	
1961	420,410	
1962	459,395	
1963	901,550	
1964	712,210	
1965	1,243,680	
1966	1,946,155	
1967	2,085,000	
1968	3,540,000	
1969	4,970,000	
1970	5,646,260	
1971	5,144,740	
1972	5,026,830	225,690
1973	1,951,390	9,647,280
1974		9,543,700
1975		7,425,770
1976		11,717,060
1977		11,477,270
1978		9,826,310

Source: International Commodities Clearing House Ltd.

FIGURE 1

The Daily Sheet records all transactions and International Commodities Clearing House Ltd. (ICCH) fulfil the function of ultimate control and act as guarantor of all such commodities and futures exchanges, whether in London, Liverpool, Avonmouth, Hull or Teeside etc. The lot size is 10 tonnes.

Figure 2 shows the monthly range[4] of spot prices for the years 1969-1978 in £ per tonne (Granger):

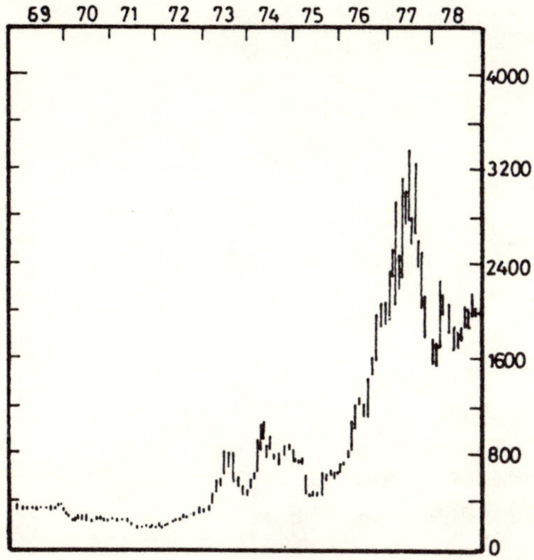

FIGURE 2

Cocoa: monthly range of spot prices. 1969-78 (in £/tonne) These should be compared with sugar spot prices (Granger)[5] for the same period (figure 3).

Sugar: London Futures Transactions
1959-78

Year	Transactions (in long tons)	Transaction (in tonnes)
1959 (Oct-Dec)	605,050	
1960	1,148,900	
1961	2,257,250	
1962	3,967,300	
1963	15,121,000	
1964	13,092,900	
1965	10,132,700	
1966	8,602,300	
1967	22,874,550	

1968	19,777,850	
1969	28,973,950	
1970	26,543,500	
1971	33,807,300	
1972	43,951,000	
1973	42,702,250	
1974	47,829,900	
1975	41,213,150	
1976	42,878,350	
1977 (Jan-Feb)	7,817,600	
1977 (Mar-Dec)		30,852,300
1978		34,641,700

Source: International Commodities Clearing House Ltd.

FIGURE 3

Much the same situation pertains here as the dealings in other soft commodities, and the ICCH is again the responsible board of control. The present raw sugar contract is for lots of 50 tonnes net (landed weight) with basis 96 degrees outturn polarisation; cost, insurance and freight (c.i.f.). Trading in futures and contracts are up to fifteen months ahead.

Now to the coffee market. The Coffee Terminal Market Association of London opened in 1958 with a lot size of 5 tonnes, although a Coffee Trade association had existed since 1888. The contract is for up to fifteen months forward with delivery months in January, March, May, July, September and November. As with cocoa and sugar the market is in the Corn Exchange building in Mark Lane. Dealing is in various standards, with some limited amounts of coffee below the official standard, as well as Robusta coffee.

The "killer" Brazilian frost in July 1975 caused cash and futures coffee prices to soar to unprecedented heights. It had a trade figure of 50c lb prior to 1975, and by 1976 it was trading at $1.55 lb and by 1977 it went to $3.40 lb. The frost in Brazil killed or damaged 1.5 billion of the 2.9 billion trees amd diminished the crop from 23 million bags to 6.5 million bags; a bag being 60 kgs (132 lbs). The following table shows the coffee production, exportable production, consumption, stocks and prices for period 1965-78.

WORLD GREEN COFFEE PRODUCTION, EXPORTABLE PRODUCTION, CONSUMPTION, STOCKS AND PRICES - 1965-1978
(million 60 kilogram bags)

Crop Year	Production	Exportable Production	Consumtion	Stocks in Producing Countries	Avg. Price c/lb. (3)
1965	81.6	66.3	62.9	87.2	40.37
1966	60.6	44.5	66.4	81.4	39.61
1967	68.6	51.7	70.6	79.4	37.22
1968	61.1	43.4	70.4	70.6	37.36
1969	66.4	48.1	71.8	65.2	38.71
1970	58.3	40.1	70.9	52.6	50.52
1971	71.8	53.1	76.6	47.8	44.66
1972	76.6	57.3	79.0	45.4	50.40
1973	62.5	43.7	76.2	31.7	62.16
1974	81.1	62.4	75.2	37.6	67.95
1975	73.7	55.5	74.7	36.6	71.76
1976	58.4	41.2	69.2	25.8	142.48
1977	68.7	51.3	69.6	24.9	256.38
1978	74.6	57.1	71.3	28.2	150.00

SOURCES:
USDA, Foreign Agricultural Service, January, 1978.
Pan American Coffee Bureau, Annual Coffee Statistics, No. 38, 1974, p.32.
International Coffee Organization, General Statistical Document.

FIGURE 4

A similar picture can be drawn up for all soft commodities, and the interested reader should aquire more detailed information from Granger[4] and look at the figures provided by International Commodities Clearing House Ltd., Conti Commodity Services Ltd., or any other of the reputable companies who specialise (usually world wide) in commodities.

RUBBER, METALS AND BULLION

We shall now look briefly at the "hard commodities" - rubber, metals and bullion. Rubber suggests rubber trees and rubber trees suggest Brazil or Malaysia, although Sri Lanka and West Africa also produce rubber. The development of motor cars (automobiles) had made tyre manufacture a major user of rubber, although there are multifarious other users. The usual factors of increasing financing and warehousing led to the setting up of the London Rubber Terminal Market Association on 1974, although a trade association had existed since 1913. The attempt has been made to standardise the quality of rubber by what was called

Standard Malaysian Rubbers (SMRs) and this has been widely, although not universally adopted. The size of futures contracts in rubber is indicated by an example. 15 tonnes of rubber at £550 per tonne gives a total contract value of £6,750 and a minimum initial margin of £600.

Now we go on to metals.

METALS

The London Metal Exchange (LME) was officially born in 1881, although traders had met and discussed their problems formally for some years before that. Unlike other commodity markets, the LME stands on a principals contract. There is no clearing house, nor any clearing house guarantee.

Copper is the largest "metal" commodity; at least in terms of turnover. Tin goes back as far as copper trading in time and lead goes back a long time too. More recently 1979 aluminium and nickel were added to the commodities traded.

Let us, as our example, concentrate our attention on tin, Malaysia produces over 30% of the world's tin concentrates, and is still increasing its output, but because of the use of water-intensive mining methods, tin production is sensitive to drought and as a result tin production is liable to considerable fluctuation.

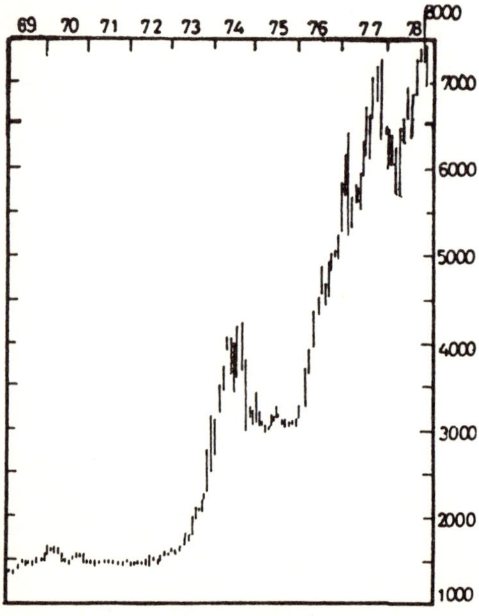

Fig. 5 Tin: monthly range of spot prices, 1969–78 (in £/tonne).

There are two contracts available in tin; one for high-grade tin and the other for standard tin.

For the investor involved in any of the LME controlled commodities, it is important to know the amount of stock in the warehouse at any particular time, since this is a major factor in determining market prices. It is a fact of life that high prices and turnovers and simultaneous lowering of (or falling of) stocks may increase the extent of backwardisation. Similarily the opposite state of a contango will occur with high or increasing stocks.

Let us finish this discussion of the range of commodities with a brief word on the bullion market.

BULLION

The bullion markets are even further from the bulk of commodity markets than are the metals. In thinking of bullion we are thinking of gold and silver. There are no existing formalised organisations for bullion, comparable to the LME and the Mark Lane exchanges. We shall concentrate our attention on gold and the London Gold Market (LGM) which is made up of five companies who meet twice daily to decide upon the price of gold. The "fixed price" being quoted in £s and $s per ounce. This price is fixed by establishing supply and demand in the outside world. The five companies making up the Gold Market are Mocatta and Goldsmid, N.M.Rothschild, Samuel Montague, Sharpe Pixley and Johnson Matthey.

Gold is unique in that it is used as a yardstick for money prices and other commodities. It is also, of course. of value in its own right as jewelery, watchmaking, electronics and other industries besides.

It should be noted that Americans are permitted to purchase Mocatta gold options through selected agents. The Mocatta gold options cover 200 oz and are issued with contract prices set in $5 intervals. At this point we terminate this brief survey of the range of commodities.

METHODS AND MODELS FOR TRADING

The basic principles of trading in commodities involve:

1) Making the best use of working (trading) capital.
2) Forecasting the markets correctly.

The reader will no doubt guess that it is the second on

which we shall focus the bulk of our attention. Capital Mangement, as it is usually called, involves the extent to which you have capital available to risk. This is exactly what a good horse racing punter should do: to decide how much they have available to put at risk.

A study of the state of the trading markets is essential to producer, manufacturere or speculator in futures, since he must know the demand and supply situation for any commodity with which he is involved. He must also know the current and forecast exchange rates, particularly the dollar-sterling ratio, as well as the rates of inflation, in the USA and Britain. Over and above these facts of trading life he still has to know the strategies of investment.

The basic principle of investment is bound up with two considerations:

1) Detecting a trend.
2) Detecting a change of trend.
(maxima and minima)

If we start from a well-defined base area, a perfect up-trend would proceed as follows: an initial rise is followed by a smaller setback, followed by a new rise to higher prices, followed by a smaller setback, follwed by another rise to a new, higher peak, followed by a further smaller setback and so on indefinately, in such a manner that the minor setbacks fall on a regular straight line which defines the up-trend, joining two or more of the minor lows. The price will not normally move in the same direction every day since sales will occur as prices rise and this will lead to the temporary setbacks. Trends have to be anticipated in terms of daily price, and it is much more difficult to decide whether the up-trend or down-trend has stopped. It is not unusual for a major trend to be interrupted by a substantial pause as a new, temporary, equilibrium is established. This could be mistaken for a change of trend.

We must now consider reversals. They are essentially of two types - "spearhead" and formal patterns. By "spearhead" we mean a situation where a previous trend, which will probably have been steepening, is abruptly reversed on one day. The most dramatic example was in silver up to May 1967. The major supplier (the big mining groups and the US Treasury) had "fixed" the price: when the supply ran out, the rise was quite dramatic. In three weeks silver had risen from 215 to 260 and then dropped back to 240. This was still a level of very substantial support: over 5000 lots of 10,000 ounces had been traded on the day it was reached (December 29th. 1967). The reaction was reversed on this support, and in the next fortnight the position advanced through the level of the spearhead top, and was traded for two days above 270. In this fortnight volume never exceeded 2000 lots in a day. The top was reached on May 20th., a Monday; and on that Tuesday there was a trading range of 10 points and the position closed at the bottom of it. Volume rose over 2000 lots. The subsequent rally was feeble; even when an upward gap appeared on May 24th. the volume contracted. A breakaway gap downward then appeared, between the dealings of May 27th. and 28th.: this was followed by a break for a holiday. The downward movement turned out to be quite short; it terminated at 246 on June 4th. The rally lasted only five trading days; and subsequent reaction which lasted as long traversed an even shorter distance. The whole character of trading had changed at this stage. The old patterns, in which inner trend lines had been extremely useful, had been superceded by a new pattern of shorter and ever shorter movements. The strong rises and deep reactions before had formed parts of a rising trend. The movements and counter-movements now were quite short.,and so the story goes on. We shall, since we promised only an "aside" on commodities, draw a veil over the rest of the story and simply remind the reader that the problem here, as with stocks and shares, is still mainly one of accurate forecasting.

One should add though that experience and familiarity must be conjoined with scientific method generally to ensure the maximum chance of success.

REFERENCES CHAPTER 10

1. C.W.J.Granger (Ed.). Trading in Commodities, Woodhead - Faulkner, 1974.

2. R.C.Jeffrey. The Logic of Decision. McGraw-Hill 1965.

3. M.E.T.Davies. Soft Commodities. In Trading in Commodities C.W.J.Granger (Ed.). Woodhead - Faulkner, 1974.

4. Granger opus citus page.

CHAPTER 11
A PLAN FOR INVESTMENT

Let us now outline a theory of investment. In taking the lesson from forecasting methods it is necessarily a "many-pronged" attack, and it will by no means be argued that this is the only way of proceeding. All one can say is that such techniques have been used with considerable success and in saying this we are talk -ing mainly of the Stock Market, although with certain reservations it may be extended to commodities.

In broad terms we are suggesting a multi-stage approach based explicitly on the application of scientific method. This involves forecasting and assessing demand trends, and this will suggest the most promising industries to look at first in the light of the customer's need (this follows much the same path as Figure 1 of Chapter 1). We are looking for "possibilities" then "probables" and then re-cycling our choice procedures until we are happy that all (or most) of the conditions we have imposed are met. The conditions are really tight constraints, others are desirable conditions which can in the light of other favourable circumstances be loosened or even waived. This is one reason why testrologic is appropriate as a modelling method. It could also though involve Expert Systems as we shall see in the next chapter.

We shall first use a Delphi type study with Cross Impact Matrices. This will not necessarily be done "algorithmically" but most usually be done "heuristically". The idea would be to get an informed view of likely changes of demand in the market place in the light of changing world events. This implies a fore-cast in broad brush terms followed by a scenario (John Chandler and Paul Cockle[1]) wriiten in the light of the forecast with each alternative made explicit.

Again we would say that this whole process can be carried out in a relatively informal manner ("heuristic" is almost too demand-ing a term in the limit). But the informality of the study should not alter the need to involve other people - as expert as possible - to pass opinion on the proposals. Here on the short term we are talking not of technological advances of the kind we talked about earlier as an example of Delphi, but the more immediate belief that a British company may no longer be able to compete in world markets, or that a general recession will occur and lead to a change of demand patterns. An example here would be that luxuries, especially in the form of expensive but non-useful articles, will give place to the necessary commodities for survival, or "luxuries" that provide holidays and entertainment (the"leisure industry") or such activities as gambling.

All the above should encourage the investor to look to see what "history" tells him about the correlation between patterns of demand and political social and economic occurrences. No complete theory of these matters yet exists, but a good deal of information can be accumulated from the record book and gleaned from experience - both one's own and other peoples'. It is the other peoples' experience that suggests Delphi and scenario writing at whatever level and with whatever precision. But the idea will be that the lead time will be short term and the forecasting narrow and to the purpose. It was Chandler[2] who has made the point, with special emphasis, that history is the basis for extrapolation to the future, and this becomes forecasting.

Let us assume next that having acquired a few clear glimpses of what the more or less immediate future has in store, we can work out some tactics. We seek first though to justify this forecast by formulating hypotheses and seeking to find evidence to support these hypotheses and provide an explanation of a causal kind so that "understanding" is superimposed upon prediction. This is scientific method at work and the idea is to provide a backcloth for the actual choice of a portfolio.

It should be explained at this point that the view is being maintained that we cannot sensibly start any investment analysis, even for"possibles" until we have a clear picture of what seems likely to happen. Such an analysis, it could be argued, is implicit in investment methods and this is partially true, but just as we have (like many others) warned that forecasting methods devoid of a background theory or understanding are dangerous, so too is the use of any investment method, before the climate in the market place has been tested.

The backcloth having been established and subsequently monitored to pick up any signs of change, we can proceed to a fair number of applications of the investment analysis itself.

We have been keeping our charts all this time. All these processes of forecasting run more or less parallel since we are considering the system not just as it starts up, but when it is in full swing. Having, in effect, made up our charts on a daily basis, then we are now confronted with the problem of providing the actual trend analysis.

Our first method of dealing with this situation, where we are under some pressure to use a reasonably simple mathematical method is to use a Moving Average. It is of interest that this loses very little if anything by comparison with a random walk model. The random walk measures prices at a precise moment of time and can be tranformed by using the average of the high and the low over some specified period of time, and the result becomes almost identical with a simple moving average.

It will be remembered that in chapter 6 we used the measures:

Q = quarter

T = takings

and we used, purely for computational convenience:

q = Q-8 and t = T-3

We then derived q^2, t^2, qt. t' represented takings based on the trend line.

so now, t' = T'-3 and q = Q-8 as before.

We next calculate (T-T') = (t-t') and $\frac{(T-T')}{T'}100$

$$\bar{t} = \frac{\Sigma t}{n} \quad \text{and} \quad \bar{q} = \frac{\Sigma q}{n}$$

and this leads to:

$$(t'-\bar{t}) = b(q-\bar{q}) \qquad \text{--- (1)}$$

where

$$b = \frac{\Sigma qt - \frac{\Sigma q \Sigma t}{n}}{\Sigma q^2 - \frac{(\Sigma q)^2}{n}} \qquad \text{--- (2)}$$

Substituting for $\bar{t}$ and $\bar{q}$ in the last 2 equations (1) and (2) leads to the equation:

$$T - 3 = b(Q-8) + 0.165$$

which is

$$T' = bQ + k \qquad \text{--- (3)}$$

where k is computed from (1)

We can then, using the values found, derive our trend, which we graphed in Chapter 6 for the example shown there. This is our longer term trend, we then derived our short term trend as a moving average and our average trend.

Let us now look at this sort of Trend Analysis more closely, if we start from a well-defined base area, a perfect up-trend would proceed as follows: an initial rise is followed by a smaller setback, followed by a new rise to higher prices, followed by a smaller setback, followed by another rise to a new, higher peak, followed by a further smaller setback and so on indefinitely, in such a manner that the minor setbacks fall on a regular straight line which defines the up-trend, joining two or more of the minor lows. The price will not normally move in the same direction every day, since sales will occur as prices rise and this will lead to the temporary setbacks. The three charts we shall use as illustrations all contain trends. It is much more difficult to decide whether the up-trend or down-trend has stopped. It is not unusual for a major trend to be interrupted by a substantial pause as a new, temporary, equilibrium is established. This could be mistaken for a change of trend. This now really requires the use of a computer.

THE ROLE OF THE COMPUTER

The computer is programmed in a suitable compiler language and its data base stores prices. It then makes calculations and displays the results to the user on a printout or VDU. These results are shown in the following format:

1) Tables that group together important information for following the market.

2) Graphs.

3) Analysis of market developments divided into the three following areas:

3/1 Trend
3/2 Strength of trend
3/3 Trend analysis
3/4 Exceptional activities

Following each day a projection (or kind of forecast) of the present is made for the two days to follow. This is not a forecast or prediction in the ordinary sense, but a simulation. One should note the difference. The computer provides rapid calculations and the possibility of following simulations that allow one to know in advance what position to take in a market if the price should reach a given value. It is therefore a trend analyser and it clearly implies a forecast. We are not here referring to any one program but talking in general terms.

DECISION MAKING

The key to any such program consists of a number of values each of which are calculated to today's price and according to previous prices.

These values are

Y1 - is calculated according to the most recent prices, and is the most sensitive of these three daily trend predictions.

Y2 - is calculated according to a larger number of prices, is more sensitive but also more closely approximates to the "fundamental" trend.

Y3 - is calculated over the longest period of time of all and should show the fundamental trend of the price change.

Y4 - any special or exceptional activity which may be involved (Chandler and Cockle[3]).

We also need to measure the strength of the price movement registered during the day call this X. It is important to realise that price incline (as we shall call it) does not represent the slope of the price trend but rather the strength of the price trend movement. As an anology one should not think of the price incline as representing the speed of a rising or descending price, but rather as a measure of the accerleration of the movement. The price trend (bullish or bearish) is calculated according to the sign of the price incline (positive for bullish, negative for bearish). Y1, Y2, and Y3 above are also calculated on the basis of price inclines. A price trend is confirmed when these three inclines achieve the same sign as X.

A second set of information is given under the title "price trend". This second set consists of comparing the price inclines and then evaluating their magnitude and importance (very weak, weak, medium, strong, or very strong, say). This information can be of a great assistance for making decisions in the short term. In effect, a strong or very strong price incline in a confirmed price trend (whether bearish or bullish) is often followed by a "technical reaction" (feedback) which tends to bring the price back to more normal levels after one or two price closes. These feedbacks (stabilizers) can occur even in the case of steadily rising prices.

We should here mention the point about Y4. Any attempt to make predictions must take into account the exceptional situation. We cannot do better by way of illustration than provide the example of Chandler and Cockle.

> "The following example concerns another business that we recently reviewed (see Table 1).After a first, hal -hearted, attempt to rationalize in year 2, a major shake-up in selling policies was introduced. The activity underwent major surgery in its distribution outlets, inventories and labour force. The graph of indices for the two profit lines (fig.1) shows that, not only are the absolute values markedly affected, but in two years out of the five, the direction of the profit trend is also changed by the extraordinary items. So the inclusion of exceptional factors that would obscure the trend in trading performance of the activity is avoided. They have to be stated, of course, and may represent most important factors in assessing the future of the business. But they should be kept separate".

Table 1

Year	1	2	3	4	5
	£m	£m	£m	£m	£m
Activity profit	11.4	15.3	14.3	16.1	20.3
Index	100	134	125	141	178
Extraordinary Items	-	1.9	-	7.8	5.7
Adjusted profit	11.4	13.4	14.3	8.3	14.6
Index	100	118	125	73	128

This table illustrates the problems that can arise which are not wholly predictable. The following graph (figure 1) illustrates the point.

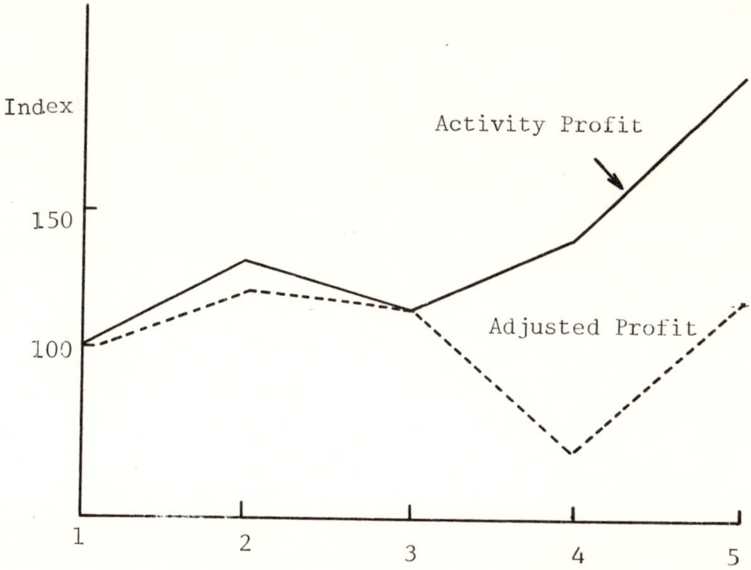

Figure 1

Comparing activity profit and profit after exceptional items.

We now illustrate the value of the three variables Y1, Y2 and Y3. We can use, as an example, a confirmed "bull" trend.

Y3 - which is long term with respect to prices is least effective because it refers back furthest in time.

Y1 - what is most recent will, by implication, be strongest as a predictor.

So a possible graph would be as follows:-

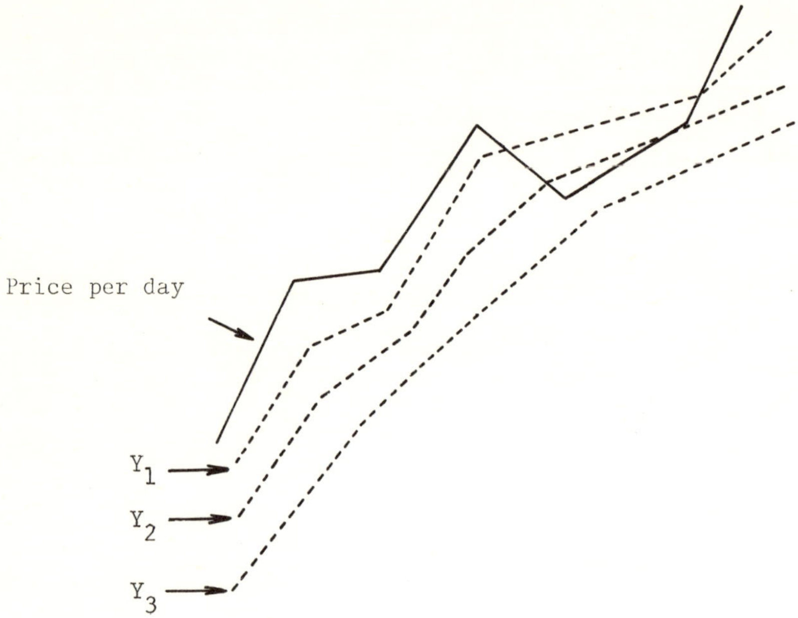

Similarly a "bear" trend might be as follows:-

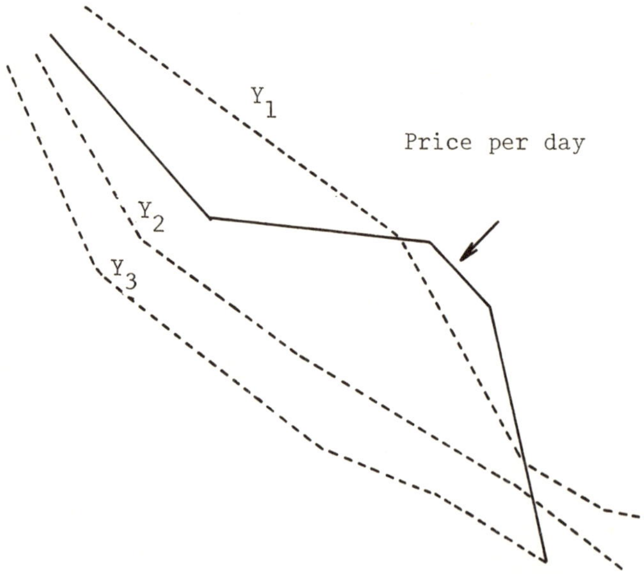

Figure 3. Three estimates of price trends for a "bear" market.

Clearly we could now combine figures 2 and 3, in either "direction", and this would then illustrate the change by way of detecting the "changeover" of Y_1 with Y_2, Y_1 with Y_3 and Y_2 with Y_3. For this purpose we are assuming the absence of a Y_4. factor, which would, of course, change the predictions, because of a causal knowledge of the reasons for the change taking place, while understanding that change might be wholly misleading.

Another technique which could be used in this situation, which we have suggested earlier (chapter 6) is a better one for a short term forecast. It is the Exponential Smoothing model and for this we need the smoothing constant A, as we mentioned earlier, A lies between 0 and 1 in value; we can estimate at the start and modify its value after a few readings. A is then normally constant for a "long period". All we do now is calculate:

$$MA_t = X_1 A + MA_{t-1}(A-1) \qquad \text{--- (4)}$$

which means that the moving average at the present is the latest production figure $(x_1) \times A$ added to the previous moving average $(MA_{t-1}) \times (A-1)$. The error is the difference between the forecast production and the actual production and the forecast and we can estimate the standard deviation (chapter 4) from the mean range (this is called the Mean Standard Error or MSE) and this shows us how much error we are likely to find in our predictions.

$$\text{So MSE} = \frac{e_t^2}{n}$$

where e_t is error at time t and n is the number of readings.

A third method which we could adopt is to use Adaptive Exponential smoothing. This involves reaction to a change after, of course, it has occurred. This means that the constant A of exponential smoothing in method two now becomes a variable in method three. There are various ways of developing this but the easiest and also one of the best is the tracking signal method. first developed by Trigg and Leach[4].

The method is essentially a two-stage smoothing. An arbitary response rate B is used as the smoothing constant and $\bar{e}_t$ is the smoothed error at time t, so: (it lies normally between 0.1 and 0.3)

$$\bar{e}_t = Be_t + (1-B)\bar{e}_{t-1} \qquad \ldots(5)$$

The mean absolute deviation m_t at time t is:

$$m_t = Be_t + (1-B)m_{t-1} \qquad \ldots(6)$$

The tracking signal T at time t is the ratio between $\bar{e}_t$ and m_t (i.e. given by (5) and (6)).

$$\text{i.e.} \quad T_t = \bar{e}_t/m_t$$

and A updated in

$$Y_1 = Y_{t-1} + Ae_t \text{ as } A_t = /T_t/$$

We can apply this method as an example (Ghosal[5]) to daily forecasts for 53 days of day values in the ceramic factory. The mean square error (MSE) is 34.5. The following figure shows clay values graphed against time:

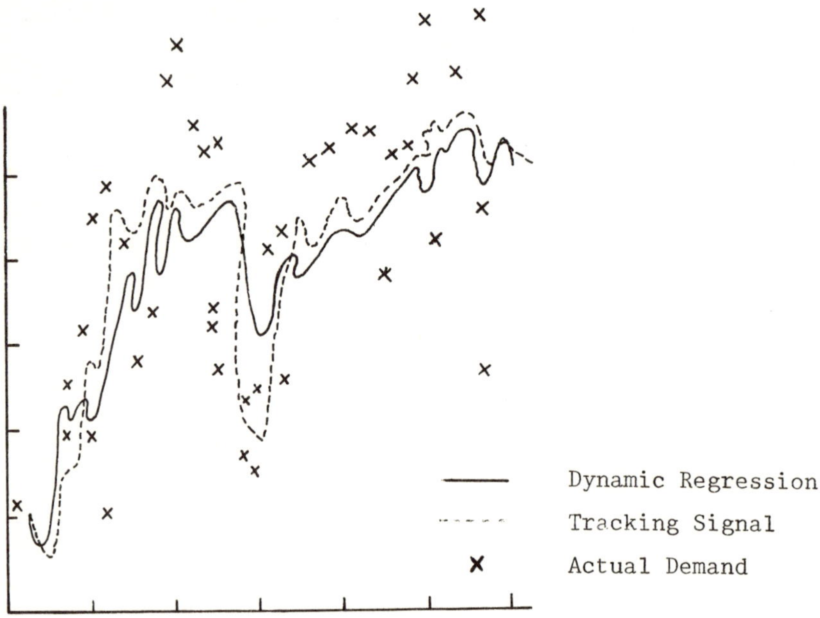

FIGURE 4

The table below (Table 2) shows the actual and forecast clay values for each of the 53 days.

*i*th day	1	2	3	4	5	6	7	8	9	10	11	12
1. Actual clay values	260.6	259.6	260.4	257.0	266.0	262.0	264.8	266.8	270.4	263.4	273.8	277.0
2. Dynamic regression method												
(*a*) Forecasts	260.0	260.1	259.8	260.2	257.0	266.0	265.9	265.8	266.0	266.9	266.6	268.1
(*b*) Value of α	0.2	0.666	0.611	1.0	1.0	0.120	0.143	0.182	0.212	0.217	0.204	0.270
3. Tracking signal method												
(*a*) Forecasts	260.0	260.6	260.2	260.3	257.6	261.6	261.8	263.7	266.0	269.6	268.2	271.2
(*b*) Value of α	1.0	0.351	0.198	0.802	0.470	0.492	0.632	0.729	0.815	0.320	0.530	0.667

*i*th day	13	14	15	16	17	18	19	20	21	22	23	24
1. Actual clay values	278.8	275.0	269.6	285.1	268.0	286.0	273.0	283.0	261.2	282.0	273.0	271.8
2. Dynamic regression method												
(*a*) Forecasts	270.5	273.6	274.2	272.0	278.4	273.2	278.3	276.7	278.3	278.9	279.5	278.4
(*b*) Value of α	0.375	0.445	0.486	0.485	0.434	0.363	0.301	0.252	0.221	0.199	0.179	0.169
3. Tracking signal method												
(*a*) Forecasts	275.1	277.8	276.5	276.4	279.4	277.9	279.0	278.6	279.0	279.3	280.0	279.4
(*b*) Value of α	0.730	0.470	0.005	0.338	0.133	0.137	0.068	0.083	0.160	0.252	0.078	0.323

*i*th day	25	26	27	28	29	30	31	32	33	34	35	36
1. Actual clay values	269.2	263.8	262.2	267.0	267.6	275.2	280.4	276.4	281.2	268.4	282.2	282.2

TABLE 2
Forecasts for the clay values in a ceramic factory

2. Dynamic regression method												
(*a*) Forecasts	277.3	275.9	273.8	271.6	270.6	269.9	271.2	273.5	274.3	276.2	274.0	276.3
(*b*) Value of α	0.166	0.174	0.191	0.210	0.226	0.239	0.252	0.265	0.276	0.284	0.288	0.293
3. Tracking signal method												
(*a*) Forecast	277.0	273.1	267.2	263.8	265.4	266.2	266.7	272.2	274.2	278.3	276.7	278.3
(*b*) Value of α	0.494	0.633	0.690	0.501	0.370	0.049	0.400	0.475	0.583	0.163	0.294	0.380

*i*th day	37	38	39	40	41	42	43	44	45	46	47	48
1. Actual clay values	276.8	277.2	278.0	281.6	282.0	285.0	875.0	288.6	282.8	286.4	281.2	277.8
2. Dynamic regression method												
(*a*) Forecasts	278.1	277.7	277.5	277.7	278.9	279.9	281.5	279.4	282.3	282.5	283.7	282.9
(*b*) Value of α	0.297	0.301	0.305	0.308	0.311	0.314	0.316	0.317	0.317	0.318	0.318	0.318
3. Tracking signal method												
(*a*) Forecasts	279.8	279.1	278.8	278.7	279.4	280.3	282.7	282.6	284.1	283.9	284.6	284.4
(*b*) Value of α	0.237	0.144	0.099	0.233	0.343	0.504	0.004	0.247	0.169	0.277	0.046	0.274

*i*th day	49	50	51	52	53
1. Actual clay values	286.0	289.6	279.4	280.6	272.0
2. Dynamic regression method					
(*a*) Forecasts	281.3	282.8	285.0	283.2	282.4
(*b*) Value of α	0.318	0.319	0.318	0.318	0.319
3. Tracking signal method					
(*a*) Forecasts	282.6	282.8	284.5	284.4	283.7
(*b*) Value of α	0.065	0.243	0.022	0.184	0.503

These methods of forecasting are all closely related to each other and we say a little more about the whole matter in appendix II. But we have to deal on one hand with anticipation of the future based upon the past and present, or only on the present, and sometimes where we have some understanding of the process (a causal explanation and other times where we have none). Prediction may be possible in either case, but is clearly much safer where understanding exists.

In the table that follows we show the Tracking Signal method compared with the actual amounts of clay produced and also compare it with the Dynamic Regression which we describe on page 216.

It should be emphasied that the various methods of forecasting that have been developed have usually been developed individually by forecasters to meet their own particular needs and which one to use for what is often a fairly arbitrary choice. As the following table shows the two methods used are both fairly accurate.

We could consider more complicated mathematical models for our forecasting purposes, and some mention of them is made in Appendix II, but little, if anything, is lost by sticking to the fairly easy (mathematically speaking) methods we have already used.

One should say next that what we regard as our next step could be sufficient in itself <u>without</u> any prior analysis of the kind we have been advocating (these would perhaps be followers of the Investment Method III), while some would regard us as having completed our job at this stage of forecasting with respect to the "possibles" to acquire the "probables", and thus by, say, adaptive exponential smoothing to have decided on our portfolio (supporters of Investment Methods I and II may argue this point). We shall argue that ideally we should do both and we will thus proceed to the last phase which could be regarded as a straight repeat of Clarkson's methods. We will though spell out the steps involved with a few interpolated words of explanation, which could make the methods and their relevence and purpose clearer now than when originally outlined Clarkson's approach in chapter 9.

The steps of our portfolio finding (Method III) are as follows:

1) The analysis and selection of a list of stocks for current investment. These are obviously expected to appear plausible and we then test them in the light of the customer's

need for suitabilty. This is the A list.

2) We formulate an investment policy and this links the client and his needs to the investment. It will consider laws, taxation and the like.

3) A set of criteria that guides the selection process (under admitted conditions of uncertainty) to the portfolio.

These three steps are broken down into sub-steps, where 1 above is broken down into economic state of country and the industry (and the companies within that industry) under consideration in the light of the economy and the customer's needs.

Each company is then examined with respect to the following attributes, each of which has a numerical value:

Sales
Earnings
Cash flow per share
Profit margin
Working capital
P/E ratio
Dividend payout ratio
Dividend per share
Dividend yield
Prices

This goes well beyond the consideration of prices alone, which was so roundly condemned by Granger and Morgenstern.

From this basic list three sublists are developed:

1. Trend: this contains the last 10 annual values of each attribute.

2. Average: this is a ten year moving average of values in the trend (1 above).

Recent form: rate of change of each value in trend list.

There is a further computation to consider:

4. The average rate of change of Trend and Average form lists.

Then the Expectation lists are formed which show whether the forecast value and rate of change for each value is above, the same as, or below the average for the economy and the industry. This leads to Company Expectation lists which use:

Sales
Earnings per share
Cash flow per share
Profit margin
Dividends per share

and these are derived by way of 1 and 3-5 year forecasts and give expected rates of change.

We next set up the Relative Performance list by considering the mean of each company within a particular industry. We now take the means and calculate as above, equal or below the average mean, the mean of each company.

The method then moves over to consider the Relative Value list and this means the P/E ratio, and we shall not set up again (see chapter 7) this calculation, but remind ourselves of the relative value, as a percentage of the historical means, in terms of above, equal to or below.

The next steps involve the interrelations in terms of growth, stability, tax, income etc., and finishes with the final coup de grace as the Growth portfolio discrimination net (Figure 3), chapter 9. This leads to the actual portfolio and leaves only a question of the amount to be invested and the issue of diversification.

COMMODITIES

We shall regard the above methods as more or less appropriate to the commodities market as well as the stock market. The regression analysis phase is identical. The preliminary forecasting is methodologically the same and this leaves the heuristics of Clarkson and here we can see the need to replace the word stocks by commodities and supply the same trend analysis in terms of performance and expectations (using average, long term and short term trends) for commodities. The terminal date intervenes here as a bar to indefinite holdings and this is, as we have made clear, a major difference between the stock market and the commodities market, but it must not cloak the fact that the general methods to be used are very similar.

It should be added that experience is a major factor in any investment and no amount of science can wholly replace experience.

It is therefore advisable to get to know and understand the workings of the market place. You should do the equivalent of a football pool or horse racing forecast and try it out on previous results first. This means, or could mean, using the current state of affairs and investing on paper and see how the results work out. This way you can test your methods carefully before you put them to the real test. No waiting or on line experimentor research is required; that can all be performed on data from the past.

Finally it should be added that forecasts at all levels will be continually monitored and changed (adaptively) as necessary in the light of experience.

REFERENCES CHAPTER 11

1.	John Chandler and Paul Cockle	McGraw-Hill.
2.	John Chandler	<u>The Science of History</u> Gordon and Breach (1983).
3.	John Chandler and Paul Cockle	Opus Citus
4.	D.W.Trigg and A.H.Leach	Exponential smoothing with adaptive responses rate, <u>Oper.Res.Qtly, 18,53</u>. (1967)
5.	A.Ghosal	<u>Applied Cybernetics It's Relevance to Operations Research</u>. Gordon and Breach. (1978).

CHAPTER 12
EXPERT SYSTEMS & INVESTMENT

In this chapter we shall take another approach to investment methodology through the field of artificial intelligence, and in particular through the use of Expert Systems. First then we should provide some general guidelines to the building of Expert Systems. In building an expert problem solver, it is always necessary to decide the knowledge program it should have and how that knowledge should be expressed and in particular the following factors are listed:-

1. Clusters of knowledge. By clustering facts together, a particular problem solver can say "apply this cluster" rather than having necessarily to know exactly which particular fact to use.

2. Levels of Abstraction. In addition to reasoning with chunks, experts also need to reason about larger, more abstract chunks of information.

3. Qualitative Analysis. Some kinds of abstraction involves qualitative knowledge, this is bound up with the need to make deductions at the highest levels of abstraction.

4. Metaknowledge. In addition to being able to reason about the problem domain, we need to reason about the reasoning process; this was true especially of META-DENDRAL (Feigenbaum et al[1],) and MECHO[2].

EXPERT SYSTEMS

The name Expert System has been coined relatively recently to operate retroactively, to depict various computer programs that have been designed in broad terms to solve problems. The term "solve problems" will be used in its broadest sense to include diagnosis, the information of plans, decision taking and so on,and included or may be include any of specialist features such as tree -searching[3], mini-maxing[4], alpha-beta pruning[5], or some type of resolution principle[6] which involves the setting up of assumptions and the subsequent search for contradiction. There is, even among this apparently diverse set of activities, a commonality that merits our attention. But in this chapter we shall be primarily concerned with those relatively simple Expert Systems that deal with Corporate Startegy, in its various forms, within the business field, and with an eye to investment as our immediate goal. With something like a problem solving capacity (including the variety of methods mentioned above) available for conversation (asking and answering questions at the very least) and the ability to draw inferences of every kind from classical logic to practical reasoning, we have the basic ingredients of an Expert System.

There are already in existence whole sets of well known Expert Systems some of which we have already mentioned (Michie[7]). Among the best known of which are DENDRAL, PROSPECTOR, MYCIN, MECHO and PUFF. But we shall be saying something later of these. I have myself been involved particularly in three such systems GOAL (George[8], SCHEDULER[9], and CRIB[10], and am currently operating on Expert Systems which are particularly concerned with Corporate Strategy (George[11])).

GOAL is a program for practical reasoning. A goal is specified by the end state and the method of reaching the end state is specified on a step-by-step basis. The only question is to the method of weighting the steps to make choice possible at each point. This can be done as a result of experience: A, is more often associated with B_1 than B_2, and the generalisation on this for a whole sequence A,B,...,N will produce a Markov net. Alternatively we may have <u>a priori</u> probabilities based on "design considerations" with respect to the complete (or part of the) "set up".

In any event if:-

$$A_1 \supset B_1, \text{ let us write this } A_1 1 B_1$$

and

$$A_1 1 B_1 1 C_1 1 D_1 1 G$$

then $A_1 1G$

where G is the goal. So given choices

$$A_1 1 B_1 0 B_2 0 B_3 0 B_4 1 C_1 0 C_2 1 \ldots 1 G$$

where 0 is 'or' in the exclusive sense then it is the relative weighting which will determine the goal route taken. Since multiple choices

$$A_1 1 B_1 0 B_2 0 B_3 0 B_4$$

can always be reduced to binary choices we can have

$$(A_1 1 B_1 0 B_2) \text{ A } (A_2 1 B_3 0 B_4)$$

where A is 'and' and the whole process can be put, as we shall see, into testrologic form. This in essence is GOAL.

SCHEDULER was concerned with heuristic scheduling for a production line, and the problem here was to maximise orders throughout and minimise cost (and waste). This starts with a priority ordering of contracts, so the most important client is dealt with first (or on some such principle) and then follows the filling up of the schedule so that as far as possible no machine was not fully occupied and the machine's state change (which may be involved) was minimised.

This was done by use of both forward and backward scheduling over a period such as a week so that given m/amount of As(mA), n amount of Bs(nB), and so on, we could form a schedule in the light of available capacity, so that given rA capacity, where r = m/2 say, then we can load all As for the week, is sB and S = 2n,then we can load all B, subject in both cases that C,D, ... there is no change of state needed for rA and sB. We continue, ensuring maximum number of orders are completed each week, to "juggle" the schedule without necessarily achieving an optimal. If the program involved cutting materials e.g. (a Trim Loss program) then we should, of course, be concerned with minimising waste.

So much for the forward schedule. The backward schedule is responsible for maximising completed jobs, and will work its "juggling" against the forward schedule and with the "delivery date" in mind. An alternative version of SCHEDULER, called SCHEDORD (Hind[12]) was also developed but is in essence sufficiently similar not to merit separate discussion here.

The third system to be mentioned is CRIB (Computer Retrieval Incidence Base) and this operated when a fault occurred on the computer. First the symptons were reproduced (intermittent faults presenting a specially difficult problem) and then a hypothesis was formed on the information from the data base; this represented a model of the "patient" computer and sets of symptom-fault pairings, derived either experimentally or a priori. In general, experience took too long to gain - especially on modern computers - to provide an adequate base.

The sympton-fault pairings determined (heuristically) the route to be taken down the decision tree, and the location of the fault found, or a retreat and re-entry to the tree used. The "package" being located, it is replaced and sent for repair.

The whole system is adaptive, so that the symptom-fault pairings can change their weightings as a result of accumulated "global" experience on that particular patient computer.

It goes without saying that this type of heuristic diagnostic program can be applied to other machines and indeed involves the same logical construction as is required in medical diagnosis. A more recent version of CRIB called RAFFLES (Addis[13]) is also in existence, but as in the case of SCHEDULER and SCHEDORD, the differences are not so great as to merit a discussion if only in the interests of relative brevity. Let me turn now to the main set of programs with which this section is concerned.

For any corporate plan there must be, apart from an assessment of the past and present, some forecast regarding the future state of the economy and the market place. This introduces a new uncertainty area and over and above the uncertainty implicit in the actual process, we need the system to be investigated heuristically e.g. the medical diagnostic situation, machine fault finding and the like. Nevertheless, in spite of the additional uncertainty the only additional features involved are in the form of additional hypotheses.

There are questions first of all that must be asked about the methods to be used in this case. We have recently found the use of Testrologic of considerable help and have used it in studies of Investment Acquisition and Diversification. We shall outline the methods used and give a specific indication of the Testrologic features with one part of the Investment problem. The problem is, as always to find the appropiate portfolio for the stated goals.

Problem one involves forecasting the future of the demand in the economy, the possibility of the occurrence of certain vital events, e.g. joining the EEC, a world war, the setting up of OPEC, a change in the law. There are a number of things which need to be considered and your decision will ultimately, as well as initially, be tested for its sensitivity to such changes as are at least envisaged as possibilites. Let us assume that given this sort of information and the weighted forecasts for the relevant future, then we can infer which are the likely fields for investment may be spread over a few - theoptimal varies a little with size of investment - different shares.

Within the field of activity, remains the important decision as to which shares should be the chosen ones. We repeat roughly the same process now of conjoining the past, present and future. We set up hypotheses, draw inferences (by "practical logic") and derive consequences which can be tested for sensitivity, or where more than one set of outcomes is derived, by comparison, and then a decision is taken.

The processes can all be done in a variety of ways, but to be definite, and also to illustrate a method under current use, the hypothesis will be embodied in the programming of the Testrolog. Here the programming involves three important steps:

1. The wording and ordering of questions.
2. The nature of the questions.
3. The relative weighting of the answers.

In a sense, the programming is heuristic and the resultant program is algorithmic, in much the same way as a computer language (probabilistic say) would translate into machine code (deterministic).

A NOTE ON TESTROLOGIC

To remind the reader of our earlier comment on Testrologic let us here repeat the basic process. A decision tree of the conventional kind is such than for n questions, there are 2^n end states. A search of this sort of tree can be in breadth or depth or, as is usual, some combination of the two. This is where mini-maxing and alpha-beta pruning comes in. This sort of tree can also be put in the form of a tabulation. We find that trees with 2^n branches for large n are unwieldly and when the effective outcomes are substantially less than n, we can merge branches as we depicted in Testrolog.

So for n = 3 we may have 4 rather than 8 nodes, for n = 4 we have 4 rather than 16 at the 4th. level, at the 3rd. level and so the streamlining can be continued where we have the values of Y (Yes) or N (No) or "do not care which" and this latter value most often means the question is not applicable. So for the set of Questions Q_1, Q_2, Q_3, we might have:

Q_1 = Are you in London?

Q_2 = Are you in Birmingham?

where clearly an answer of Y to Q_1 eliminates any need to answer Q_2, which only applies to those who say N to Q_1, and so on for Q_3 and Q_4, etc. The use of testrologic in our Expert program will become apparent later, but in the meantime we can say that wherever Practical Logic (e.g. GOAL) can be used testrologic can be used as an alternative. This omits the question of drawing of inductive inferences, which is clearly also possible.

So far we have mentioned the use of logic (of whatever kind) to formulate hypotheses and to derive their consequences in a goal-seeking situation. We should also add that all such systems can be made adaptive and the adaption <u>can</u> be built into the Expert program. We should add finally that language is also available, so that the whole process can be described in terms of questions and answers, which are asked by both the Expert program and the user.

A natural language such as English would seem ideal for this purpose, but the complexity of translation from "free-idiom" English ultimately to a "machine code" is too complex and costly to make it worthwhile. As a result a form of conventionalised English is used and there are a number of such languages in the process of being built up. The originals included NAMER[14], BASEBALL[15], SIR[16], and SAD SAM[17] and now we have SHDLR[18] and LIP[19] and others which show greater and greater flexibility. The advantage of using language is obvious and allows the Expert system to play its important role as a specialist-reminder. It can utter such comments (the spoken word is being researched but a video screen and the written word is currently used) "look again at H_S. as that has the highest cumulative weightings over the first three stages of the tree search".

Finally it should be said that the scope and potential of Expert systems is quite enormous and whereas they can obviously be used as "helpmates" it should be absolutely clear that they can also be used to carry through the whole process of decision making from beginning to end. They have already been used for many problems at different levels.

In our own case we should now exhibit the sort of steps we envisage and in doing so I shall follow Clarkson's methods as outlined in Chapter 9 and will concentrate attention on the choice of a particular company within a chosen industry.

We shall use attributes:-

Sales
Earnings
Cash Flow/Share
Profit Margin
Working Capital
P/E Ratio
Divided Payout Ratio
Dividends per Share
Dividend Yield
Prices

and normally have records over the past ten years, so we have the average and then increase (or decrease) for each of nine comparitive years:

$$Y = \frac{X_i - X_i + 1}{X_i + 1}$$

where i = 1...9, and x_i are the attributes, and average rate of change is given by Y. We can from this data calculate average rate of growth, etc for each company and compare each company with the average company in the relevant group.

The important point then arises as to the relative importance of our attributes, so that our hypotheses is that they have taken this or that order. We can then decide what attributes are crucial, what combination of attributes must necessarily be of sufficiently high standard, and in general how much each company considered compares with the rest. The sort of questions to be asked are:-

Q_1 = Are company's Sales increasing?

Q_2 = Are company's Sales average greater than industry's GTAI average?

Q_3 = Are company's Earnings increasing?

Q_4 = Are company's Earnings averaging GTAI?

Q_5 = Is company's cash Flow/Share increasing?

Q_6 = Is company's cash Flow/Share GTAI?

Q_7 = Are company's profit margins increasing?

Q_8 = Are company's profit margins GTAI?

Q_9 = Is working capital increasing?

Q_{10} = Is working capital GTAI?

and perhaps more; where GTAI means "Greater Than Average in Industry". These then should be repeated for the same attributes as forecasted. Initially, and here we show the Testrolog version, we have, when all else is decided a list of "probables" and then the final decision to take.

There are in fact 23 questions in our version of the Clarkson System prior to this last stage, as they involve twenty questions as above (the ten repeated) plus three others on P/E and dividends; there could of course have been others, but these were hypothesesed to be sufficient.

The last stage (where F means Forecast) is as follows:-

Q24 Is Mean Growth past price $\geqslant$ 20 per cent?

Q25 Is Mean Growth past earnings/share $> K_1$?

Q26 Is Mean Growth past sales $> K_2$?

Q27 Is F (Growth earnings/share) 1 year $> K_3$?

Q28 Is F (Growth in sales) next year $> K_4$?

Q29 Is Mean Growth is past Cash Flow/share $> K_5$?

Q30 Is mean Growth in Profit Margins $> K_6$?

Q31 Is y on Relative Value list?

Q32 Is $P/E^* < \bar{P}/E$ by 10 per cent?

Q33 Is Forecast Dividend > 0?

Q34 Is Forecast Dividend $= 0$?

Q35 Is Price $>$ 10 per cent below high?

We need then to choose levels for K_1-K_7 and the testrolog program is:-

Start

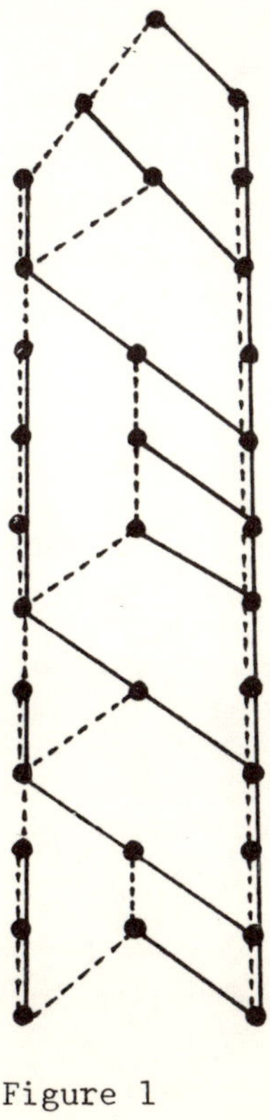

Accept

Reject

Figure 1

The hope is that we can simulate, or synthesise, expert systems which will play the role normally played by the human being. By such means we can make the human being's role more explicit and by careful testing improve on it. This can be achieved in the same manner as ordinary scientific hypotheses can be tested by experiment and then become laws when the evidence in their favour is overwhelming and there is not a single contrary instance. A contrary instance may not destroy the law, but change it to a probablistic rather than deterministic law, so that instead of a implying b, we need to say a probably (almost always) implies b. This is true of many weather forecasts for example, so that "red sky at night is shepherds' delight" is true most, but not all, of the time.

Testrolog's role in all this is that of a practical logic which tells us what follows when certain choices are made or certain observations made. But cannot provide "certain" results, any more than any inductive influence can.

Such methods are extremely powerful, whether testrog is used or not, and we expect that the future holds enormous potential for such genuinely Expert systems.

IN SUMMARY

Throughout this chapter we have built up progressively from simple to complex systems over a period of time. Not many years ago a large academic institution offered a substantial prize to anyone who could write a computer program which learned to play OAX (Noughts - And - Crosses) in the apparent conviction that such a thing was impossible. Since then we have progressed through all sorts of domestic game playing from draughts (checkers) up to chess and have developed heuristic methods so that today no one would question the possibilty of a computer being programmed to learn to play chess and play it better, eventually, than any human chess player. All this has helped to clarify our psychological theories regarding learning and thinking, and sharpened our awareness of the need for greater semantic precision in our usage.

At the same time as the above has taken place, great strides have been made in widening the range of problem solving. We now look at any and every problem - well defined or not - and think in terms of optimisation as well as explicit solutions. Expert systems (in a sense better described as Special purpose problem solvers) have now been widely accepted as methods that can be used to tackle any problem whatever.

Involved in this progression, we naturally have seen progress in the use and understanding of logic and a broadening of our view of classical logic and above the classical systems of deduction and induction.

In particular, we have seen the use of decision tables, first cousin to decision trees game trees and semantic nets, and also testrologic. The power of testrolog trees, as they might be called is very considerable, and all such methods are capable of use within the compass of an Expert system. That mathematics, probability theory and statistical methods can also be so used goes without saying.

The technicalities as one might call them of modern Al work, and here one thinks of the methods of tree-searching, alpha-beta pruning, chaining - both forward and back - and the use of situation - action rules, are all tings we have briefly remarked on. But my purpose is more with the general conclusions for investment, rather than with the intimate details of Expert systems.

CHAPTER 13
IN SUMMARY

We set out to make investment a scientific process and not just a lottery. This has entailed some mathematics and some logic, but perhaps most important of all an awareness of scientific method. Then, more specifically, the use of the systems approach and explicitly the methods which are characteristic of artificial intelligence, such as heuristic, testrologic and Expert systems. We also set out to make the whole process as easy as possible, commensurate with the need for some precision, and this precision mainly depends upon methods of assessing and forecasting the value of shares in different industries in the market place. Over and above that it also depends upon locating the best companies in those more successful industries. This all entails looking at business and business houses, the market place and the world economy.

It must be noted that it is perfectly possible to discover an excellent investment in a "decaying" or depressed industry. As a market contracts, so often the relative market share of some few companies (perhaps even one only) may increase substantially, so that one can sometimes find very good opportunities where primie facie one would least expect to find them.

On the positive side we have moved from fairly simple to more complicated investment methods. Theories of investment so called, are concerned with the means of forecasting change of share price. The first of the group really includes Chartism which is the direct application of scientific method to the stock market. It presupposes the possibility of curve fitting and is an example of the direct application of scientific method in the simpler cases where the behaviour of the share price is assumed to be periodic or nearly so, in its fluctuations. In fact a more sophisticated view would attempt to predict changes as a function of the world and home markets.

Chartism grades over to forms of Technicalism (is in fact a form of technicalism) where we go to other related methods. The first is Markowitz's model and this relies on more sophisticated analysis than mere curve-fitting. It depends upon a statistical model and the prediction of future dividends and price changes. The name 'Technicalism' springs from the fact that one only considers "technical" variables such as share price in one's forecasting methods.

Fundamentalism goes beyond Technicalism in that it includes additional information on companies and the economic state of the country and the world. These models are often implicit. Weaver and Bray developed one of the best known Fundamentalist models and based their model on regression analysis, which in turn is one of the best known methods for statistical forecasting.

We also considered the Random Walk model of Granger and Morgenstern which is really a range of models which, among other things, makes the future share price depend upon the present rather than the past.

We then come to what seems the most promising field of investment analysis to be developed so far; it is what has been called Theories of Investment and we illustrate this by two methods: 1) Clarkson's heuristic method and 2) Hartley's COIN.

Clarkson's method depends upon simulating the behaviour of the best of the trust investment officers and has perhaps shown the greatest promise so far. It is a fairly lengthy method to apply but it is not especially difficult. It does though, like some of the other methods discussed, lend itself to the use of the computer. In the days of the mini-computers and microprocessors, this need present no problem.

Hartley's COmputerised INvestment (COIN) program was based on the perceptron which is a pattern recognition system described in terms of logic, and makes its prediction in an adaptive manner. It has yet to be shown to be successful, but one may guess that there is still scope for further developments in forecasting models of all kinds. Indeed I see this as a field for considerable future developments. Since writing this monograph I have dabbled in models of stochastic kind not altogether different from the football pool forecasting methods mentioned, and with some fair degree of success.

It should be made clear that one needs a sort of data bank of past results (Moodie's Handbook, The Financial Times and so on and so forth) going back over the recent past - this ideally should be computerised. Then one should, by systematically going back over past results, see whether or not the methods are effective in much the same way as one can try out football pool and horse race forecasting over past games and past races. Exactly the same can, and should, be done with different forecasting methods in stocks and shares. You can then gradually discover the best available model. This may in turn imply different models for different situations. This is a fast changing field and you should always be aware of new ideas; you can perhaps add to these new ideas yourself, even if you also keep them to yourself.

As a science, investment is a part (a specialist part) of forecasting and it is this that has come of age in the last few years. Not only have new and more accurate methods of forecasting been developed but the methods of processing that forecast information for the purposes of decision making and planning have also been developed.

It is now recognised that statistical forecasting techniques are likely to be far more accurate if supported by hypotheses of a causal kind. This means that forecasting is seen to be an effective scientific procedure.

I have added three appendices (really one appendix divided into three parts) dealing with different aspects of forecasting. The second appendix especially says a little more about time series and the like brings out the important point that the mathematical methods used divide into those with and without causal hypotheses (or laws) as mentioned above, but also those which use past history and those which do not. In appendix II I have not attempted to be systematic because the full story from simple curve fitting and moving averages through exponential smoothing, stochastic processes to control systems, ARIMA and other relatively complicated time series methods demands a whole book. I have here depended upon references for further reading. Appendix I provides a brief account of just one econometric model and appendix III deals with a selection of decision making techniques. These appendices are separated from the main text for reasons explained in the foreword, but also because, while useful, they are not a part of the methodology of the whole argument *per se*, increasingly like a scientific prediction. Indeed it is the scientific method applied directly to business activities such as investment that has made the subject a science.

Over and above this general recipe for success in developing business science, has come the full weight of artificial intelligence. This, as we have seen, has led to *heuristic methods*, and, more recently *decision tables* and *trees*, which may be testrologic in form and involve a variety of different search procedures which may be heuristic in form. Such systems are dynamic and adaptive, and involve feedback and feedforward.

The application of the whole paraphernalia to investment, with the symbolisation, axiomatisation and formalisation and other model-making activities (all essentially part of scientific method) added onto, or rather being an integral part of, the whole approach, should soon I believe see the full flowering of the systems approach to the complex and wide ranging problem of investment.

Accepting House: a near synonym for merchant bank.

Algorithm: a precise method for arriving at conclusions as contrasted with heuristics.

Basis price: the price agreed between seller and buyer of an option to become the price at which the option can be exercised. The basis price is usually the current market price of the commodity, for the delivery month, at the time the option is sold. (Also "Striking price")

Bear: One who believes prices will move lower; a bear market.

Bull: One who expects prices to rise; a bull market.

Call: A period in which trading is conducted to establish the price for each futures month at a particular time.

Clearing house: the separate agency associated with a futures exchange through which futures contracts are offset or fulfilled and through which financial settlement is made.

Contango: price differential between nearby and forward quotation when near dates are lower than forward quotation. c.f. "Forwardation".

Debentures: a loan paid to the company on which a fixed interest is paid.

DELPHI Technique: a forecasting method based on the consensus of experts.

Discounting House: Business Groups who take a promissory note (like a post dated cheque) prior to actual payment.

Double option: a double option provides the purchaser the right to buy from or sell to the seller on the futures market a futures contract at an agreed price at any time during the life of the option.

Exponential smoothing: a method of assessing trends.

Fundamentalism: Investment method (Models) normally using statistical methods, and all available data on company, industry and economy.

Forwardation: see "Contango".

Futures: contracts for the purchase and sale of commodities for delivery sometime in the future on sn organised exchange and subject to all terms and conditions included in the rules of that exchange.

Heuristic: a method of using ad hoc rules, or hypotheses as a basis for solving problems and the like, as contrasted with algorithms.

Investment Analysis: the process of choosing a portfolio (collection) of shares.

Investment Theories: the methods of investment which depend upon features of the stock market, e.g. share prices.

Issuing House: groups who raise capital and sell shares for a company.

Least Squares: a statistical method of curve fitting which minimises the distance of points under consideration from the curve (line) that approximates the set.

Markov Nets: a stochastic process in which one value is conditionally related to previous values.

Motivational Research: research in terms of people's behaviour which leads us to infer what the real motive was for their purposes.

Moving Average: a method of assessing trends.

Normal Distribution: a statistical distribution of a bell-shaped character, e.g. heights and weights of people in society.

Operational Definition: a definition of some term couched in terms of how it is observed, e.g. the time is what your watch says.

Ordinary Shares: an investment in the capital of a business.

P/E Ratio: the ratio of prices to earnings.

Poisson Distibution: a statistical distribution with a die-away curve.

Preference Shares: ordinary shares which give certain priviledges to their owner.

Random Walk: a statistical method used for forecasting purposes.

Regression Lines: lines showing the correlation between variables.

Risk: the danger of loss that one faces in the light of taking any decision.

Sampling: the collection of information from a population which is used as typical of the population.

Scenario Writing: a method of writing possible outcomes in a forecasting situation.

Stochastic Process: a random series.

Stock-jobbers: the members of the stock exchange who decide upon share prices.

Synergy: common features between different systems.

Technicalism: investment method (Models) using statistical methods depending on "technical" variables (share price etc.) only.

Venture Analysis: a method of deciding on the probable best size of investment in, say, a new factory and fixing other features such as the price of a commodity.

APPENDIX 1
AN ECONOMIC MODEL

We now proceed to show one particular econometric model (Surrey, 1972).

The idea of an econometric model is, as with any formalised (computer) model, to show that one can specify relationships between variables which determine economic behaviour, at a fairly abstract level, and that this sort of model can be used for forecasting purposes. An econometric model should be capable of sufficient precision to be used predictively and modified as a result of experience.

The precision of such econometric models lends itself ideally to computerisation. The value of such computerised models lies in determining the behaviour of the market place with a certain amount of precision, thus providing essential information for the businessman and the investor. It is clearly vital, as has already been made clear, for the investor to take into his consideration the present and likely future state of the economy. This is true of all methods of investment whether technicalist (Method 1), fundamentalist (Method II) or heuristic and simulatory (Method III). Now let us consider the detail of the model.

The reader should always bear in mind that econometric models are amongst those forecasting models that can be self-falsifying. Forecasting the weather does not effect what actually happens, but forecasting the economy, like other social events, can change the forecast. This is so precisely because governments and other bodies listen to such forecasts and may take action to ensure that such forecasts do not materialise.

The present example is among the best of present econometric models, but there are now, in 1983, a large number in existence. Now to the system itself which may lay claim to be one of the most effective of its time and had a considerable influence on the construction of more recent econometric models.

The work of planners such as Jay Forrester have also gained greatly from such work and we shall mention his contribution later.

The system is not wholly linear, hence cannot be precisely depicted by a set of linear equations. One example demonstrates its non-linearity, and that is the relation between value on one hand and volume and price on the other; this relationship is multiplicative. Solutions to the equations are achieved by successive approximations. A trial solution for GDP is taken, the values of the endogenous variables based on this trial of GDP are calculated and the resulting GDP total compared with the initial trial value. On the basis of the discrepancy revealed, a second trial value for GDP is then taken and the process repeated until consistency is achieved.

In what follows we show the equations on which a computer model can be based.

There are behavioural relationships and national income accounting relating to the above exogenous to endogenous variables. The equations are:

IRSE = f(GDP, IRSE(-1))

DNI = f(GDP, DNI(-1))

WS = f(GDP,WS(-1), TIM)

TAXWS = f(WS, TIM)

TAXO = f(IRSE, DNI)

CEND = f(RDW,RDO,CEND(-1))

CPIFC = f(WS,GDP,MP,CPFIC(-1))

FCA = f(CE)

S = f(GDP,TFS,FCA,S(-1))

IMP = f(INV,TFS)

It should be noted that the use of a negative subscript (typed in brackets) means "lagged" and therefore IRSE(-1) means 'income from rent and self-employment lagged for one quarter'.

The following are the abbreviations of the behavioural equations:

IRSE = Income from rent and self-employemnt

GDP = Gross domestic product

DNI = Income from dividend and net interest receipts.

WS - Wage and salary bill

TIM , = Time

TAXWS = Tax on wages and salaries

TAXO = Tax on other income

CEND = Consimers' non-credit expenditure

RDW = Real disposable wage and salary income

RDO = Other real disposable income

CPIFC = Consumer price index net of indirect tax content

MP = Import prices

FCA = Adjustment to factor cost

CE = Consumer expenditure

S = Level of stocks

TFS = Total final sales

IMP = Import of goods and services

The identies are as follows:

CPI = X CPIFC + Y T

RDW = (WS + FP + NI + YCG + TAXWS)/CPI

RDO = (IRSE + DNI - NTA - TAXO)/CPI

CE = CEND + (DCR)/CPI

TFS = CE + PAC + GPI + EX

INV = S - S(-1)

GDP = TFS + INV - IMP - FCA

where the new abbreviations are:

T = Indirect tax component of consumer prices

FP = Forces pay

NI = Net insurance contributions

CG = Current grants to persons

CPI = Consumer price index

NTA = Net transfers abroad

CR = Consumer credit

PAC = Public authorities consumption

GFI = Gross fixed investment

EX = Exports of goods and services

INV = Stockbuilding

These behavioural equations have a complicating factor, in that each equation includes calculated values from the past, which vary from quarter to quarter from the actual values. They therefore involve errors which we (have to) presume are randomly distributed.

The difficulty is that in a complex situation, which is being represented by a set of simplified equations, there can be no certainty that the errors are in fact random; they may be systematic variations attributable to variables not included in the questions. A commonplace example may help here. We might say about our own football team that the errors it makes against a particular rival team are random and in the end we win as many games as we lose - we might find on looking at the records (and the teams!) that the reason we have in fact lost twice as many times as they have over the last two seasons is due to extremely poor defensive strategy which has accounted for seventy five per cent of their goals - no random effect this, but a specifically causal one in which the problem is to find the causal relations.

The important consequence of such factors for the computer model is that, on finding what appears to be an important variable factor, which was previously omitted, this should now, of course, be included. Such a change might well have consequences that go back through the causal chain of past events and lead us to reconstruct the past as a basis for the future. This is one reason why methods of formalisation are introduced. They are introduced in order to give greater precision to our planning, or at least minimise vagueness and imprecision.

We can test results against the past to see whether it predicts variables such as incomes, stockbuilding and outputs, and this in turn influences its future use.

Finally, the essential properties of the model are the impact which they have, given a change in one exogenous (primary) variable. Three effects occur with such a change:

1. Direct leakages, so that increases in consumer expenditure automatically raise imports, which in turn have other effects.

2. Accelerating effects, so that, for example, the stimulus to output raises employment which, in turn, raises earnings, and so on.

3. This accelerating effect is in turn lagged, so that its effects appear at some later time.

These are obvious factors for inclusion in our formalised models in axiomatic form.

There are in existence many different econometric models, so rather than trying to follow up each it would be more useful to look briefly at the general underlying principles involved in all of them, especially since they well illustrate cybernetic principles in action.

Figure 1 shows a straightforward econometric model in diagramatic terms:

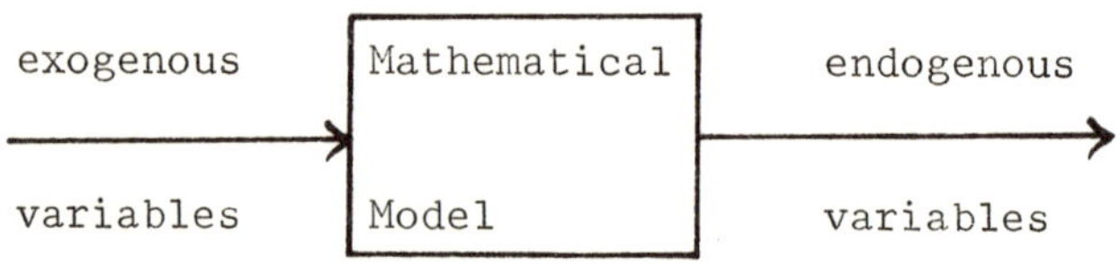

Figure 2

A straightforward Econometric model in diagramatic form.

and Figure 2 shows the same model from a more obviously cybernetic point of view (with feedback loop included):

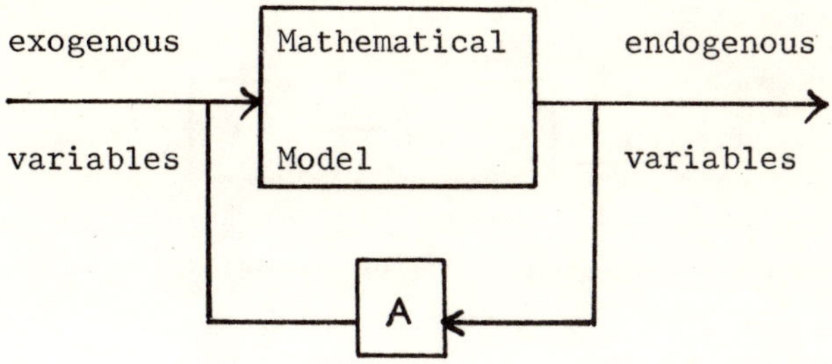

Figure 3.

The same as figure 2 with a feedback loop

In figure 3, A represents a matrix which contains all the coefficients describing the system and this relates vectors X and B (exogenous and endogenous variables respectively) in the following equation:

$$A \; . \; X = B$$

which lead to such equations as:

$$a_{11} + a_{12}j = C$$

and

$$a_{21}V + a_{22}C \;\; = J$$

where C,J and V stand for the Co-consumption, income and investment respectively.

In long-range economic growth models, there are often models such that of Figure 4:

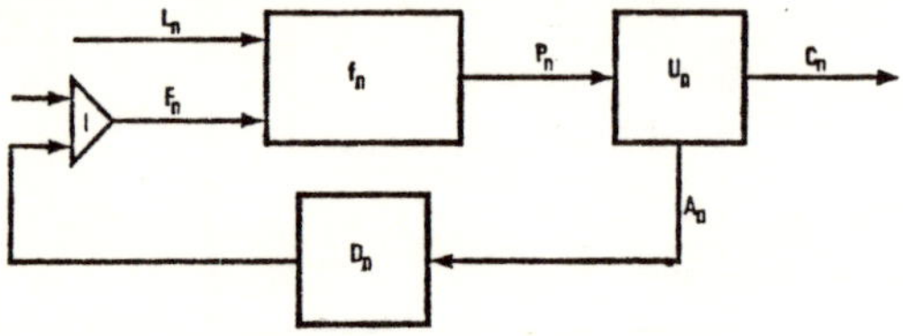

Figure 4

where:

P_n = Final social product

f_n = Production function

L_n = Labour force

C_n = Consumption

I_n = Gross investment (shown as an accumulation)

D_n = Depreciation rate

U_n = Control parameter

Figure 3 represents a one-sector economic growth model.

It is now possible to trace out model after model representing social, economic and business forces which are assumed to operate in various environments, finishing (in general terms) with the World Model which has been proposed by Professor Jay Forrester[2] and his team at the Massachusetts Institute of Tecnology. This, while exciting, as it now includes birth rates, death rates, population density, as well as business features such as capital investment, goes well beyond what is required by immediate business needs. Indeed very general models (such as long-term forecasts and the models they are based upon) become, in general, less reliable.

APPENDIX 1 REFERENCES

1. M.J.C.Surrey — The Analysis and Forecasting of the British Economy. Cambridge University Press, 1971.

2. J.W.Forrester — World Dynamics. Wright-Allen Press, 1971.

APPENDIX 2
MORE ON FORECASTING

In this Appendix we shall look in a little more detail at forecasting by the Time Series. This can provide a basis for economic and business planning, and especially investing. It should be noted that such methods are also used for (1) production and scheduling; (2) inventory and reproduction planning and control and (3) the control and optimisation of almost any industrial process. These are short term forecasts in the main and the lead time varies with each problem. The lead time, for example, in the inventory control problem is defined as a time period that commences when an order to replenish stock is placed with the factory and lasts until the order is delivered into stock. This indeed is always the case and is the time that exists between making decisions and taking decisions (the decision and its implementation).

It will be supposed initially that observations are available at discrete, equal intervals of time. For example, in a sales forecasting problem, the sales in the current month and the sales in the previous months might be used to forecast sales for lead times 12 months ahead, denote $Z_t(1)$ the forecast made at origin t of the sales Z_{t+1} at some future time t + 1, that is at lead time 1. The function $Z_t(1), 1 = 1,2,\ldots$ that provides the forecasts at origin t for all future lead times will be called the forecast function at origin t. The main objective is to obtain a forecast function which is such that the mean square of the deviation $Z_{t+1}-Z_t(1)$ between the actual and forecast values is minimal for each lead time t.

Risk Analysis (see Appendix III) may be associated with decisions based upon the forecasts. The accuracy of the forecasts may be expressed by calculating probability limits on either side of each forecast. They are such that the realised value of the time series, when it eventually occurs, will be included within these limits with the stated probability.

The next point to consider is the estimation of transfer functions. This depends inevitability on the ability to control as well as forecast, which is obviously not always possible, especially in investment. The concept of a transfer function here is in no way different, in essence, from the classical feedback theory. Such a study is made in order to:-

1) Achieve better control of existing systems and

2) Improve the design of new systems.

3) To anticipate events.

Several methods have been proposed for estimating the transfer function of plant units from process records consisting of an imput time series X_t and an output time series Y_t. We should be clear that there are two kinds of forecasting methods. The first methods are used where knowledge of the past is available and this includes time series analysis such as trend analysis and the Box-Jenkins ARIMA method. These do not require causal knowledge of what is forecasted. Regression applies where causal knowledge exists. In the absence of past knowledge exponential smoothing and control models are used. In the fourth case of no past knowledge, but where knowledge of causal factor exists, leads to Bayes rule in an empirical situation.

An important application of transfer function models in forecasting occurs for example, if the dynamic relationship between two time series Y_t and X_t can be determined. Then past values of both series may be used in forecasting Y. In some situations this approach can lead to a considerable reduction in the errors of the forecast.

The word 'control' above implies the use of both feedforward and feedback loops for the control of the stability of the system, and also of particular (special purpose) types of hardware to carry out the control. We have servosystems in hardware or at the theoretical level, TOTES which are pencil and paper feedback models with part of the input fedback as output.

In general we are concerned with a statistical approach to forecasting time series and to the design of feedforward and feedback control schemes. The control schemes we discuss in this book are appropriate for the periodic, optimal adjustment of a manipulated variable, whose effect on some output quality characteristic is already known, so as to minimise the variation of that quality characteristic about some target value.

The reason, of course, that control is necessary is that there are inherent disturbances in the process. When we can measure these disturbances it may be possible to make appropriate compensatory changes in some other variable. This is referred to as feedforward control. Alternatively, or in addition, we may be able to use the deviation from target or "error signal" of the output characteristic itself to calculate appropriate compensatory changes. This is called feedback control. As Box and Jenkins[1] have said"

> "Unlike feedforward control, this mode of correction can be employed even when the source of the disturbances is not accurately known or the magnitude of the disturbances is not measured. More generally, it may be desirable to use a mixture of feedforward and feedback control; feedforward control can be used to compensate for those disturbances that can be measured and feedback control for those disturbances that cannot be measured".

The approach to control adopted here is to typify the disturbance by a suitable time series or stochastic model and the inertial characteristics of the system by a suitable transfer function model. It is then possible to calculate the optimal control equation.

The precise nature of the stochastic and transfer function models which are appropriate in any given situation will not usually be known. Furthermore the appropriate numerical values for the parameters contained in these models will be unknown. Therefore we have to proceed iteratively. Whatever records and background information are available may be used to design a pilot control scheme which is then run on the process for a period.

An important class of stochastic models for describing time series, which has received a great deal of attention is the so called stationary models which assume that the process remains in equilibrium about a constant mean level. However, forecasting has been of particular importance in industry, business and economics, where many time series are often better represented as non-stationary and, in particular, as having no natural mean.

DYNAMIC REGRESSION

If exponential smoothing is used in a situation with a variable response rate then one method of several is Dynamic Regression. Dynamic Regression here is used with Adaptive Exponential Smoothing and an alternative to the tracking signal method used by Trigg and Leach. Chandra and Ghosal[3] have suggested a method of Dynamic Regression to update the values of a parameter of L^A at various points of time. The sum of squares of errors up to time t is minimised in order to estimate the value of A for arriving at y_t (the forecast for time t + 1).

$$\bar{A}_t = \sum_{r=1}^{t} (x_r - y_{r-2})(x_{r-1} - y_{r-2}) / \sum_{r=1}^{t} (x_{r-1} - y_{r-2})^2$$

where $\sum_{r=1}^{t} e_r^{\,2} = \sum_{r=1}^{t} (x_r - y_{r-1})^2$

$$= \sum_{r=1}^{t} (x_r - y_{r-2} - A(x_{r-1} - y_{r-2}))^2$$

A regression system can be envisaged in which we regress $d_r = x_r - y_{r-2}$ on $e_{r-1} = x_{r-1} - y_{r-2}$ This means that we regress in the two period ahead 'forecast' on the one period ahead forecast: the linear regression is given by

$$d_r = Ae_{r-1}$$

This provides a regression system in which the slope is updated as more information is acquired a mechanism is given by which the parameter learns at each time period and we call it a dynamic regression. The estimate A is applied at time t to obtain the forecast y_t for the (t + 1)th time period:

$$y_t = y_{t-1} + Ae_t$$

We may easily work out a few variants of the Dynamic Regression scheme proposed above. From practical studies it may be found that when t exceeds a specified limit, the parameter A attains a stationary level. Fluctuations of the system x_t may be very well represented through forecasts obtained with the help of such a constant level of A, the response rate; in some cases, however, the adaptive nature may not be taken care of. In such a case we propose the following modification. We set a limit n to the number of terms which should be included in estimating the adaptive rate A, when the length of the interval (1,t) exceedsn. Thus we get the modified version as follows:

$$\bar{A}_t = \sum_{r=t-n+1}^{t} d_r e_{r-1} / \sum_{r=t-n+1}^{t} e_{r-1}^{\,2}$$

Through a number of experimental studies it has been shown (Chandra and Ghosal[3], Bedi and Ghosal[4]) that the regression coefficient forecasts efficiently in many cases.

We can extend the scheme of Dynamic Regression in any problem of forecasting with the help of regression equations. When we estimate the regression coefficients by minimising the sum of squares over a past period of t years, it implies that this set of estimates gives the best fit over the past t years - it does not imply that the set of forecasts obtained with the help of these estimates will lead to small mean square errors in future. From the point of view of forecasting the dynamic regression approach seems to have a great potentiality.

In Dynamic Regression we also may take recourse to a scheme of discounted sum of square, in which we may attach more weight to the recent past and less to the remote past. If we have an exponentially weighted scheme here we also get:

$$S_t^2 = \sum_{t=1}^{n} b^{t-r}(d_r - e_{r-1})^2$$

and the estimate is obtained by equating

$$S_t^2 / A = 0$$

Some experiments with a value of b around 0.8 or 0.9 led to satisfactory results in adaptive forecasting.

With the availability of high speed electronic computers we may experiment with the above methods of forecasting. We give a few examples which will elucidate the usefulness of these methods. We now look briefly at a Linear Filter Model.

A Linear Filter Model is a stochastic model one of which we employ, and is based on the idea that a time series in which successive values are highly dependent can be usefully regarded as generated from a series of independent "shocks" a_t. These shocks are random drawings from a fixed distribution, usually assumed normal and having mean zero and variance 0_{11}^2. Such a sequence of random variables a_t, a_{t-1}, a_{t-2}, etc. is called a white noise process by engineers.

The white noise process a_t is supposed transformed to the process z_t by what is called a linear filter as shown in Figure 1:

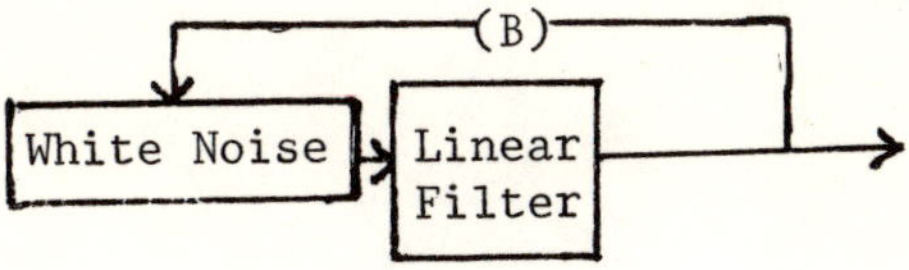

Figure 1

Representation of a time series as the output from a linear filter.

The linear filter operation simply takes a weighted sum of previous observations so that

$$z_t = s + a_t + k_1 a_{t-1} + k_2 a_{t-2} + \dots$$
$$= s + k(B)a_t$$

In general s is a parameter that determines the level of the process, and

$$k(B) = 1 + k_1 B + k_2 B^2 + \dots$$

is the linear operator that transforms a_t into z_t and is called the transfer function of the filter.

The sequence k_1, k_2, ... formed by the weights may, theoretically, be finite or infinite. If this sequence is finite or infinite and convergent, the filter is said to be stable and the process z_t to be stationary. The parameter s is the mean about which the process varies. Otherwise z_t is non-stationary and s has no specific meaning except as a reference point for the level of the process. Now to a brief discussion of autoregressive models which will bring us to the end of this introductory section on time series. It is a stochastic model which can be extemely useful in the representation of certain practically occuring series is called autoregressive model. In this model the current value of the process is expressed as a finite linear aggregate of previous values of the process and a shock a_t. Let us denote the values of a process at equally spaced times t,t - 1, t - 2,... by z_t, z_{t-1}, z_{t-2}, ... Also let $\bar{Z}_t, \bar{Z}_{t-1}$,... be deviations from s; for example,

$\bar{Z}_t = Z_t - 5$ Then

$$\bar{Z}_t = K_1\bar{Z}_{t-1} + K_z\bar{Z}_{t-2} + \cdots + K_p\bar{Z}_{t-p} + a_t$$

is called the autoregressive (AR) process of order p. The reason for this name is that a linear model

$$\bar{Z} = K_1\bar{x}_1 + K_z\bar{x}_2 + \cdots + K_p\bar{x}p + a$$

relating a "dependent" variable z to a set of "independent" variables $x_1, x_2, \ldots, x_p$, plus an error term a, is often referred to as a regression model, and z is said to be "regressed" on $x_1, x_2, \ldots, x_p$. In k(B) the variable is regressed on previous values of itself; hence the model is autoregressive.

If you consider a generalised autoregressive operator k(B) in which one or more of the roots of k(B) = 0 is unity, then we can write:

$$K(B) = K(B)\ (1-B)^d \qquad \text{--- (1)}$$

and K(B) is a stationary operator, and where an autoregressive model is one in which the currecnt value of the process is expressed as a finite, linear aggregate of previous values of the process coupled to a "shock" (perturbation) a_t.

The above equation (1) can be generalised to:

$$K(B)\bar{z}, = K(B)\ (1-B)^d \bar{z}_t = j(B)a_e \qquad \text{---(2)}$$

$$K(B)w_t = j(B)a_t \qquad \text{---(3)}$$

$$W_t = D^d\bar{Z}_t \qquad \text{---(4)}$$

where W_t represents a moving average and D is a difference operator.

The equations (3) and (4) are powerful models for describing both stationary and non-stationary time series and is called an autoregressive integrated moving average process (ARIMA) of order (p,d,q). We shall later be saying more about them. But we can say straightaway that the underlying principle is the same as with all mathematical forecasting techniques; it is that of extrapolation from the past and the present to the future. It is a search for a correlation (but more complex than an ordinary product-moment or rank correlation) between "then and now and the future". What gives rise to such a large number of different methods is the variety of possible forecasting situations: simple and complex; where there is control over the future (through feed-back or feedforward) or where there is no control but merely the ability to make the forecast (cf. econometrics and meteorology). After that there are methods which are qualitative, quantitative, logic, etc. The field is, as we are seeing, a very complicated one.

MORE ADVANCED TIME SERIES METHODS

So far we have dicussed Regression Analysis, Moving Averages (MA) and exponential smoothing and the beginnings of Trend Analysis generally as measured by Time Series; we also made a first mention of the Autogressive Integrated Moving Average (ARIMA) process.

Next we should mention the Poisson Process (Cox and Miller)[5]. The Poisson distribution relies upon the fact that the occurrences it describes are relatively rare by comparison with the number of times they might have occurred. Similarly it will be found that the binomial distribution approximates closely to the Poisson distribution where p or q is very small and n is relatively large. The Poisson distribution is in fact derived from the binomial distribution as the limiting form of the latter where the value of n tends to infinity. This is a very useful approximation since the Poisson terms are easier to calculate and in many industrial and other applications it is often a fact that p is quite small relative to n.

Now to a brief word on Stochastic Processes, where, a model which describes the probability structure of a sequence of observations is called a stochastic process. A time series of N successive observations $\underline{Z}' = (Z_1, Z_2, \ldots, Z_N)$ is regarded as a sample from an infinite population of such samples which might have been generated by the process. To make a forecast is to infer the probability distribution of a future observation from the population, given a sample $\underline{Z}$ of pay values. To do this we need ways of describing stochastic processes and time series, and we also need classes of stochastic models which are capable of describing situations actually occurring.

An important class of stochastic processes is the stationary process. They are assumed to be in the form of statistical equilibrium, and in particular, vary about a fixed mean. Useful methods for describing the behaviour of stationary processes (as we mentioned earlier) are the autocorrelation function and the spectrum (hence spectral analysis). Stochastic processes of special value in modelling time series are the autoregressive, moving average and mixed autoregressive moving average (ARMA) processes.

Because many time series that occur in real life (for example stock prices and sales figures) have non-stationary characteristics, the stationary models introduced in the last section are further developed here to give a useful class of non-stationary processes called autoregressive integrated moving average (ARIMA) models.

BOX AND JENKINS' METHOD

The large recent development in short term forecasting of time series has been largely due to Box and Jenkins[6] in their treatment of time series as a bivariate system and in their improvisation of ARIMA model. Box and Jenkins applied the concepts of multiple time series to the practical problems of fitting and prediction through time series data.

If we stipulate that a time series (x) is a multiple series the implication is it is a mixture of two linear systems: one of these is by an autoregrssive series (x) and the other generated by a moving average series (e). We can assume now that x is a stationary time series, and this means we have

$$a_0x^n + a_1x^{n-1} + \dots + a_rx^{n-r} = b_0e_n + \dots + b_se_{n-s} \quad \text{---(5)}$$

In the above the left hand side of the equation is an autoregressive series of order r, while the right hand side is a moving average series of the error terms e. It is assumed that e is a series of independent and identically distributed random variables with expected value zero and a specified variance. Then from the Kalman structure[7] it can be shown that we can generate the multiple time series defined in (5) from a system of errors e. This can be done as follows. Let us define a backward operator B such that $Bx_t = x_{t-1}$ or $Be_t = e_{t-1}$. Then we can write (5) in the following manner.

$$(a_0 + a_1 B + \ldots + a_r B^r) x_t = (b_0 + \ldots + b_s B^s) e_t \qquad \text{---(6)}$$

this gives

$$x_t = (a_0 + \ldots + a_r B^{r-1}) \; (b_0 + \ldots + b_s B^s) e_t \qquad \text{---(7)}$$

Of $a_i (i = u, \ldots, r) b_j (j = 0, \ldots, s)$ and values of r and s. The process of prediction would therefore be made up of two steps, one of which is a simulation of the series e_t as i.i.d.r.v's and the other the generation of x_t by use of the values a_i and b_j

$(i = 0, \ldots, r;\ j = 0, \ldots, s)$. This is in essence, autoregressive moving average (ARMA) model. If we define:

$$R(B) = a_0 + \ldots + a_r B^r$$

and

$$1(B) = b_0 + \ldots + b_s B^s$$

then we can write (6) and (7) as

$$R(B) x_t = 1(B) e_t \qquad \text{---(8)}$$

so that

$$x_t = R^{-1}(B) 1(B) e_t \qquad \text{---(9)}$$

In a further generalisation of multiple time series we can replace x_t by a vector X_t and e_t by a vector E_t (Quinouille[8]) If x_t is not a stationary time series, but a polynomial of order q - 1, then we can make it stationary by taking differences of order q. Box and Jenkins did this by use of a backward difference operator D:

$$Dx_t = x_t - x_{t-1}$$

$$D^2x_t = x_t - 2x_{t-1} = x_{t-2}, \text{ etc.}$$

Then they defined the autoressive integrated moving average (ARIMA) model as

$$R(B)D^qx_t = 1(B)e_t \qquad \text{---(10)}$$

so that

$$D^qx_t = R^{-1}(B)1(B)e_t \qquad \text{---(11)}$$

If x_t is non-stationary and shows an exponential growth process, we can make a transformation to make it a polynomial. Thus leaving out the error component we have

$$x_t = c \exp(kt) \qquad t \in (0.\infty) \qquad \text{---(12)}$$

then we can apply the transformation

$$y_t = \ln x_t$$
$$= \ln c = kt \qquad \text{---(13)}$$

error structure we can represent the process by

$$D^2y_t = L(B)e_t \qquad \text{---(14)}$$

The whole point of the ARIMA structure is that if a growth process can be made stationary through a transformation and taking of differences, it can be represented in the form (10). It must however be remembered that if the form of the trend is such that with any transformation and differencing we cannot make it stationary, we cannot apply the ARIMA structure. For example, if the growth trend is given by

$$x_t = ct^P \exp(kt) \qquad ---(15)$$

where p, c and k are constants, then a log-transformation and differencing will not make 11 stationary.

A substantial knowledge of past is required to identify an ARIMA structure of the form (10). Experimental studies made by Box and Jenkins and various authors indicate that we need to have past records of 30 - 40 time periods to do an ARIMA diagnosis. However, in cases where we detect a trend of the form say (12) through graphical analysis, we may do with data over a shorter period. Determination of the orders (r, s, q) in (10) is done by calculating serial correlations of various orders, partial correlations (see Box and Jenkins); a good deal depends on the interpretation of the analyser. For the practical purposes, it is always advocated to select the least values of r, s and q. The second stage of identification is to estimate the parameters q_i (i = 0, ...,r) and b_j (j = 0,...,s). This is done through the non-linear least square method or by numerical approximation.

In Box and Jenkins' analysis we work in three steps: (1) we identify the appropriate ARIMA model on the basis of past data; (2) we fit the best fitting model over the best and test the goodness of fit; (3) we make forecasts for the future. Sometimes, we also test the efficiency of forecasting on substantial data of the past be dividing it into two periods - a fitting period comprising 30-45periods, and the subsequent forecasting period. It has been remarked by various workers that a specified model or technique may be excellent for the purpose of fitting, but the forecasting efficiency may be low. The reason is that we get a good forecast on any model derived on the basis of past data only if the past pattern of behaviour, with respect to a set of characters, remains unchanged in future. Besides, no model other than the control models discussed earlier enables us to make an adaptive forecast for a situation where we have to predict before a deterministic change takes place. The ARIMA technique leads to a good fit over the fitting period - in many cases the mean square error is significantly less than that obtained through univariate methods.

At this point (and with reference back to earlier chapters) we bring our brief summary of this huge and unwieldly subject to and end. Suffice it that to set up as a forecaster without any knowledge of some of the methods merely referred to under the general heading of <u>Time Series</u> is unthinkable. Any particular application though may involve a very deal of hard work.

In Appendix III we turn to Decision Making.

APPENDIX 2 REFERENCES

1. G.E.P.Box & G.M.Jenkins. Time Series Analysis Decision and Control. Holdenday, San Francisco, 1970.

2. D.W.Trigg & A.G.Leach. Exponential smoothing with adaptive response rate, Oper.Res.Qtly,18,53.

3. B.Chandra & A.Ghosal. An adaptive procedure in exponential predictions. SCIMA (J.Management Science and Applied Cybernetics), 2, 63 - 75, 1973

4. D.N.Bedi & A.Ghosal. Adaptive Forecasting with non-linear control models, SCIMA, 6, 47 - 58

5. D.R.Cox & H.D.Miller. The Theory of Stochastic Processes, Methuen, 1965.

6. G.P.E.Box & G.M.Jenkins Opus Citus.

7. R.E.Kalman. A new approach to linear filtering and prediction problems.J.Basic Eng. Series,D82, 35.

8. M.Quinouille. Multiple Time Series, English University Press, 1957.

APPENDIX 3
DECISION MAKING

The first method which requires consideration is Bayes Theorem We start from an axiom set for the calculus of Probability and from this we can deduce Inverse Probability as well as Bayes Theorem; both of these techniques have been used in the firecasting context. We shall try to make both their derivation and their application clear (George[1]).

THE CALCULUS OF PROBABILITY

Let us write p/h for the phrase "the probability of p given h". The following axiom set is then sufficient to provide a calculus.

1. Given p and h, p/h is uniquely defined.
2. p/h in the closed internal (0,1) for all real numbers, i.e. 0 p/h 1.
3. If h p, then p/h = 1, where means "(logically) implies" and where 1 means'certainty.'
4. If h Np, then p/h = 0 where 0 means 'impossibility': (N = not).
5. p.q/h = p/h x q/h x p/q.h.
6. pvq/h = p/h = q/h - p.q/h.

We should note that p/h is a relationship between p and h, where p and h can be thought of as two propositions. So p may mean "A probably (measure) implies B" and h may mean "Most A's imply B's".

From axiom 5, we can directly derive the principle of Inverse Probability, which is:-

$$p/q.h = \frac{p/h \times q/p.h}{q/h} \qquad ...(1)$$

Where (1) follows directly from axiom 5 by simply dividing each side of the "second part" of the formula by q/h.

Axiom 5 is sometimes called the conjunctive axiom and can be very simply exemplified. What is the chance of drawing two spades in succession without replacement from an ordinary pack of playing cards? p is the statement "the second card is a spade" and h is the fact that there are 13 spades in a set of 52 cards.

$$p/h = 1/4$$

$$q/p.h = 12/51$$

$$p.q/h = \frac{1}{4} \times \frac{12}{51} = \frac{3}{51}$$

Axiom 6, the disjunctive axiom, can be similarly exemplified. So in the above example, the chance that at least one card is a spade is given by

$$\frac{1}{4} = \frac{12}{51} - \frac{1}{4} \quad \frac{12}{51} = \frac{87}{204}$$

Inverse probability is interpreted in terms of the above example as giving the probability p in the event that q is known to have occurred. So for the example of choosing two successive spades from a pack of cards we get

$$p/q.h = \frac{3}{51}$$

We can interpret inverse probability in more general terms so we say that if p is a theory and q is some statement relevant to p, then we can think of p as being changed by q (either in terms of confirmation or disconfirmation). The special case where $p \rightarrow q$ and therefore where $q/p.h = 1$ reduces (1) to

$$p/q.h = \frac{p/h}{q/h} \qquad \ldots(2)$$

The issue now is to decide where we can find an application to shares and commodities, and the answer lies in the need for some hypothesis or theory of the change of a share or commodity value.

The next step is to derive Bayes Rule, since this is the basis of so many decision processes and especially where new evidence is available and the need arises to modify the original estimate (forecaster decision). Bayes Rule is usually written

$$P_r/q.h = \frac{q/(p_r.h).p_r/h}{\prod_1^n q(p_r.h).p_r/h} \qquad \ldots(3)$$

Where p_1, p_2 ..., p_n are n mutually exclusive possibilities, one of which is known to be true, and where $\prod$ means "the product of", i.e. $\prod^3 y_i = y_1 x y_2 x y_3$, a convenient alternative rendering of

(3) is

$$P(H/D) = \frac{P(D/H)P(H)}{P(D)} \qquad ...(4)$$

where P(D/H) is the conditional probability of an event D given another event H and where P(H) / 0.

In terms of our above example of drawing two spades in succession from a pack of playing cards for H = "drawing one spade" and D = "drawing a second spade", Bayes in (4) gives:-

$$P(H/D) = \frac{\frac{12}{51} \quad \frac{1}{4}}{\frac{1}{4}} = \frac{12}{51}$$

This gives the conditional probability of the second card being a spade granted the first card actually was a spade. We say P(H/D) is an _a posteriori_ possibility.

Let us give an example of Bayes Rule. Two people toss a coin, without having given it any prior examination. They agree after one toss (which is heads) that it either has two heads (A_1) or is normal (A_2), so they agree that the situation is defined by

$$P(B/A_1),\ P(B/A_2)$$

for the proposition B, which refers to A_1 and A_2 and describes the outcome of tosses. If a tail occurs $P(B/A_1) = 0$ and if all tosses give heads $P(B/A_1) = 1, P(B/A_2) = \frac{1}{2^n}$ in any case. Now suppose the first five tosses yield hhtht then $P(B/A_1) = 0$ and $P(B/A_2) = \frac{1}{32}$. But the two people may disagree about the possibilities of the probabilities (_a priori_ probabilities) A_1 and A_2. One of them (X) says A_1 and A_2 are equally likely while the other (Y) thinks A_2 is twice as likely as A_1. This can be written:-

$$X\text{: } P(A_1) = P(A_2) = \frac{1}{2}$$

$$Y: \; P(A_1) = \frac{1}{3} \; . \; P(A_2) = \frac{2}{3}$$

Now after five tosses the evidence B allows them to reconsider these initial notions about A_1 and A_2.

Bayes Theorem is:-

$$P(A_1/B) = \frac{P(A_1) \; . \; P(B/A_1)}{P(A_1)P(B/A_1) + \ldots + P(A_m)P(B/A_m)}$$

which gives

$$P(A_1/B) = \frac{0}{0 \; . \; P(A_2)/32} = 0$$

For both X and Y and the case for A_2 (the coin is not double headed) has collapsed, i.e. the coin does not have two heads. But if it gave the first 5 tosses as hhhhh, this means by Bayes:-

$$P(A_1/B) = \frac{P(A_1)}{P(A_1) = P(A_2)/32}$$

$$\text{Then X:} \quad P(A_1/B) = \frac{32}{33} \; ; \quad P(A_2/B) = \frac{1}{33}$$

$$\text{Y:} \quad P(A_1/B) = \frac{32}{34} \; ; \quad P(A_2/B) = \frac{2}{34}$$

So in fact there is little disagreement here between X and Y, and the possibility of the coin having two heads remains. This example allows the easy change of a priori probabilities in the light of new evidence, although the question at issue in the above example is not wholly resolved. We now turn to the use of Bayes Theorem in decision processing.

DECISION PROCESSING

We have maintained that the main purpose of forecasting (at least for us in this context) is, apart from its use as a control, the making of decisions (of what to invest in and how much to invest, being our main concern). The concept of forecasting is rooted whenever possible in past history and (or at least) an understanding of what casual principles are involved. We therefore need hypotheses and models to aid in both prediction and understanding. We need also to bear in mind all sorts of factors (concepts) such as ambiguity, choice, knowledge available, preference, decidability, and many other concepts besides.

We have already derived inverse probability Bayes Rule in one version. Let us derive an alternative version of Bayes and show one example. Bayes Rule can be written:

$$P(H/D) = \frac{P(D/H)P(H)}{P(D)} \qquad \ldots(5)$$

where P(D/H) is the conditional probability of an event D given another event H and where $P(H) \neq 0$.

In terms of our earlier example of drawing two spades in succession, for H = "drawing one spade" and D = "drawing a second spade", Bayes in (5) gives:

$$P(H/D) = \frac{\frac{12}{51} \cdot \frac{1}{4}}{\frac{1}{4}} = \frac{12}{51}$$

This gives the conditional probability of the second card being a spade granted the first card actually was a spade. We say P(H/D) is an *a posteriori* probability while P(H) is an *a priori* probability. We now illustrate its use in a computer context. Ward Edwards[2] has designed a series of computer programmes to test out the effectiveness of Bayes Rule in man machine situations. He used a version of Bayes Rule that is a modification of (1) above. This version is called the odds-liklihood ratio form.

Given two hypotheses H_A and H_B and some datum D (comparable to h in the earlier part of the last section):

$$P(H_A/D) = \frac{P(D/H_A)P(H_A)}{P(D)} \qquad \ldots(7)$$

Similarly for H_B, Bayes odds-likelihood ratio form is:

$$P(H_B/D) = \frac{P(D/H_B)P(H_B)}{P(D)} \qquad \ldots(8)$$

Dividing (2) by (3) gives:

$$\frac{P(H_A/D)}{P(H_B/D)} = \frac{P(D/H_A)P(H_A)}{P(D/H_B)P(H_B)} \qquad \ldots(9)$$

we will write (5) as

$$L_1 = L_o \qquad \ldots(10)$$

L_o is the ratio of the a priori probabilities for H_A and H_B, and L_1 gives the liklehood ratio, and $P(D/H_A)$ and $P(D/H_B)$ are both a posteriori probabilities. Only the likelihood ratios are needede for the application of Bayes Rule (Edwards, Lindman and Savago[3]). Ward Edwards uses this Bayesian property of aggregating information to set up a probabilistic information processing system which he called PIP. PIP works on the assumption that "men can serve as transducers for P(D/H)"; this means that a given situation where information is to be processed and predictions or diagnoses made, then the predictions are evaluated.

Ward Edwards[4] made up a 50 page summary of the "imaginary history of the world from 1964 to 1975". It was such that eight hypotheses were plausible as a result. They were of the form:

"Russia and China are about to attack North America".

Then at a later date additional information was supplied by sensors to the computer as a result of which the eight hypotheses would be reassessed in characteristically Bayesian fashion. Several likelihood ratios were assessed for each datum, and training occurred with the processing of vast amounts of information over a lengthy period.

The most important result to come out of this experiment was that PIP achieved a greater degree of certainty from the data than did the equivalent human group who acted much like a group of military or political leaders might. The ad hoc human group was called POP, and two other variants were called PEP and PUP respectively. The results indicate clearly enough the advantages of using Bayesian methods over mere human judgement.

We also notice here the resemblance to Scenerio Writing. We shall now look at Baysian Models from a slightly different point of view. We can think of Baysian Models as models of deliberation (Jeffrey,[5]).

DECISION PROCESSING

In this section we shall look at such methods as Bayes Rule (Jeffrey[6]) from a slightly different standpoint than above. In the first instance we define a desirability matrix as describing the ideal combination of events. For example, if we wish to have fish with chips, this will have a greater rating than having fish with boiled or roast potatoes; similarly the wish to swim goes better with a seaside holiday than one in the country. The desirability gives the relative weighting of some quality with respect to some others. Thus we might from our first example, write a desirability matrix for fish in column 1 with beef in column 2, with chips in row 1 and boiled in row 3 and roast in row 4. We shall assume that boiled and roast potatoes are equally acceptable to go with the beef. We thus have:

$$\begin{bmatrix} 1 & 0 \\ 0 & \frac{1}{2} \\ 0 & \frac{1}{2} \end{bmatrix} \quad \ldots(11)$$

In practice, of course, an empirical analysis of tastes in a community might throw up something totally different. A matrix such as the following seems quite likely:

$$\begin{bmatrix} .88 & .08 \\ .08 & .48 \\ .04 & .46 \end{bmatrix} \quad \ldots(12)$$

Alternatively, and considering the idealised desirability matrix, we might have included negative numbers giving:

$$\begin{bmatrix} 1 & 1 \\ -1 & 1 \\ -1 & 1 \end{bmatrix} \qquad \ldots(13)$$

where -1 means completely unacceptable.

Suppose now we think of the probability matrix as suggesting beef and fish as equally likely (we obviously do not control the choice). Then we have probability matrix:

$$\begin{bmatrix} \frac{1}{2} & \frac{1}{2} \\ \frac{1}{2} & \frac{1}{2} \\ \frac{1}{2} & \frac{1}{2} \end{bmatrix} \qquad \ldots(14)$$

Now we multiply equivalent entries in the probability matrix (we shall use * to symbolise this unusual type of matrix multiplication)

$$\begin{bmatrix} 1 & -1 \\ -1 & 1 \\ -1 & 1 \end{bmatrix} * \begin{bmatrix} \frac{1}{2} & \frac{1}{2} \\ \frac{1}{2} & \frac{1}{2} \\ \frac{1}{2} & \frac{1}{2} \end{bmatrix}$$

$$= \begin{bmatrix} \frac{1}{2} & -\frac{1}{2} \\ \frac{-1}{2} & \frac{1}{2} \\ \frac{-1}{2} & \frac{1}{2} \end{bmatrix}$$

Adding the row gives:

$$\begin{bmatrix} 0 \\ 0 \\ 0 \end{bmatrix}$$

Here no one choice of potatoes is better than any other in this case. If we had a desirability matrix

$$\begin{bmatrix} 0 & 1 \\ -1 & 1 \\ -1 & 0 \end{bmatrix} \qquad \text{...(15)}$$

then we should have had:

$$\begin{bmatrix} 0 & 1 \\ -1 & 1 \\ -1 & 0 \end{bmatrix} * \begin{bmatrix} \frac{1}{2} & \frac{1}{2} \\ \frac{1}{2} & \frac{1}{2} \\ \frac{1}{2} & \frac{1}{2} \end{bmatrix}$$

$$= \begin{bmatrix} 0 & \frac{1}{2} \\ -\frac{1}{2} & \frac{1}{2} \\ \frac{1}{2} & 0 \end{bmatrix}$$

giving

$$\begin{bmatrix} \frac{1}{2} \\ 0 \\ -\frac{1}{2} \end{bmatrix}$$

So that now the choice of chip potatoes in row 1 becomes the best choice according to this type of Bayes application.

We can of course deal just as easily with events which are not equiprobable, and we can deal with desirabilities which are not completely specified. In any case, of course, as with all applications of probability theory, it seems that the greatest single difficulty lies in establishing the appropriate numerical probabilities. Justification for the technique is easy enough to understand, since to put the matter crudely, highly desirable and very likely events are the first choice. Then we weigh desirability against probability of occurence and omit altogether the undesirable and the unlikely, and try to avoid the highly undesirable and fairly likely. If I wish to eat a good meal at a restaurant I would choose a very good meal at a very convenient restaurant as opposed to a superb meal at a hopelessly inconvenient one. In terms of stocks and shares I would go for the likely (probable) and the convenient (desirable), where ease of disposal, minimum risk, etc. are part of 'convenience'.

Bayes Deliberation method presupposes the methods of discovering (deciding upon) the numerical probabilities and desirabilities that constitute the data for deliberation. Let us look at Ramsey's method for dealing with this.

Given the probabilities we can find out what the desirabilities must be. We give an example of Ramsey's method. The probability matrix is:

	Die before 65	Live beyond 65	
Smoke 40+ cigarettes per day	.41	.59	...(16)
Smoke only pipes/cigars	.25	.75	

The desirability matrix is:

$$\begin{bmatrix} d + c & d + L + C \\ d & d + L \end{bmatrix} \quad \ldots(17)$$

where C is measure of preference for cigarettes, L is his preference to live beyond 65. (17) is obviously reducible to:

$$\begin{bmatrix} C & L + C \\ 0 & L \end{bmatrix} \quad \ldots(18)$$

Expected desirabilities of the two acts are:

$$.41C + .59\ (L + C)$$

and

$$.75L$$

If we assume indifference bewteen the two acts, we get:

$$C = .16L$$

substituting .16L for C in (18) gives:

$$\begin{bmatrix} .16L & 1.16L \\ 0 & L \end{bmatrix}$$

and since L o, we multiply each entry be 1/L and get:

$$\begin{bmatrix} .16 & 1.16 \\ 0 & 1 \end{bmatrix}$$

so we have a scale of desirabilites:

1.16	1	0.16	0.0
Live to 65+ & smoke 40 cigarettes +	Live to 65+ & smoke only pipes/cigars	Die before 65 & smoke 40 cigarettes	Die before 65 inspite of only smoking pipes/ cigars

A very similar method (see Jeffrey[7]) works in the opposite direction, so that given the desirabilities one can compute the probabilities. Jeffrey also gives an account of a more rigorous and more general approach to this same subject.

We shall not discuss further the technical apparatus which occurs in the full range of possible applications. We can though make the point that such methods which are closely related to forms of probabilistic logic are open in many people's eyes, to all sorts of difficulties (Hintikka and Suppes[6])

Another type of decision processing sometimes called "Games against Nature", very similar to that discussed by Jeffrey was previously discussed by Thrall, Coombs and Davis. They consider various strategies under various conditions of uncertainty, subjective estimates of probability and the like. At this point we come close to psychological theories of estimating.

A simple example will illustrate the approach. Consider that the rows of the following matrix represent states of nature which are equally likely. Consider next the choice of column you would make, in ignorance of the relevant correct row. Here is the matrix:

$$\begin{bmatrix} 0 & 2 & 1 \\ 3 & 2 & 1 \\ 0 & 0 & 1 \end{bmatrix} \qquad \ldots(19)$$

If we use <u>Laplace's strategy</u>, we take the arithmetic mean of each column and select the column with the highest mean; in this example, column 2 is selected. If, however, we were playing the <u>optimist's strategy</u> we would select the column with the maximum pay off, and that gives colum 1 as the solution. If you play the <u>pessimist's strategy</u>, you consider which column loses you least in the event of your being wrong, and the answer now is column 3.

The matrix above does not supply a means of losing, since all the payoff elements are non-negative, but by reducing each element of the matrix by 1, we do not alter the logic of the argument, but change the payoff by making the decision taken more realistic. Thus for the following matrix you may also actually pay out money as well as receive it:

$$\begin{bmatrix} -1 & 1 & 0 \\ 2 & 1 & 0 \\ -1 & -1 & 0 \end{bmatrix} \qquad \ldots(20)$$

A further factor which affects the choice of strategy followed is the size of the units involved. If the integers about refer to single pounds (sterling) then your maximum loss is £1. If they refer to a thousand pounds each, then you could lose £1,000. As the size of the prize and the risk goes up, so the decision may change along a sort of continium between extreme optimism and extreme pessimism.

Let us look at the matter again now explicity as risk and analysis leading up to what has sometimes been called venture analysis. In general, as far as choice is concerned in Gaming Theory ("against nature"), we have the following:

Laplace: aQmax (1(a,e))
eE

Wald: aQmax (eEmin (1(a,e))

Hurwicz: aQmax (eEmax (1(a,e)) +
(1 -)eEmin (1(a,e))

Savage: aQmax (eEmin (1(a,e) - bQmax
(1(b,e))))

a_1, e_j are alternative possible acts and e_j are alternative possible events, 1(a,e) is the value of taking act a when event occurs.

Q is a column vector of sets of a's, i.e.

$$Q_1 = \begin{matrix} a_1 \\ a_2 \\ \vdots \\ a_n \end{matrix}$$

As an example, take Savage's method of choice and define Q_1, Q_2, Q_3 as:

$$Q_1 \equiv \begin{array}{c} \\ A \\ B \end{array} \begin{array}{c} e_1 \quad e_2 \quad e_3 \quad e_4 \\ \begin{bmatrix} 2.5 & 2 & 0 & 1 \\ 1 & 1 & 2 & 1 \end{bmatrix} \end{array}$$

$$Q_2 \equiv \begin{array}{c} \\ A \\ C \end{array} \begin{array}{c} e_1 \quad e_2 \quad e_3 \quad e_4 \\ \begin{bmatrix} 2.5 & 2 & 0 & 1 \\ 0 & 4 & 0 & 0 \end{bmatrix} \end{array}$$

$$Q_3 \equiv \begin{array}{c} \\ B \\ C \end{array} \begin{array}{c} e_1 \quad e_2 \quad e_3 \quad e_4 \\ \begin{bmatrix} 1 & 1 & 2 & 1 \\ 0 & 4 & 0 & 0 \end{bmatrix} \end{array}$$

The choice from Q_1 is B

The choice from Q_2 is A

The choice from Q_3 is C

This violates the principle of transitivities between the rows A,B,C (here) and leads to no unique solution. These methods often involve difficulty and entail the reconsideration of values, especially when applied (as mainly intended) under conditions of uncertainty. When "certainty" pertains and it is simply a matter of choice, we can still encounter the above difficulty (among others) which might entail a change of values. To put it more simply, we may wish to change our choice of method, we might need (or be able to) include risk factors or we might simply toss a coin, seek a second opinion (consider our example of the food and the restaurant) or take a consensus rather as in a Delphi Study (White[9]). We now look at Risk Analysis itself.

RISK ANALYSIS

We shall indicate in quite simple terms the nature of risk analysis, since the ideas have already been partially explained. In intuitive terms, we are concerned with the taking of a risk, such as a gamble on a horse. Clearly we may be prepared to risk a few shillings and not worry if we lose; equally clearly, if we are instructed to put several hundred pounds on a horse, we should worry considerably, and lacking any other information, we might be tempted to back the favourite, because of the odds which would imply a minimum risk. If we were allowed to back more than one horse, we might put a substantial amount on three different ones in an attempt to minimise the risk entailed. We are supposing in this latter case that we are not so much concerned with winning - since we are being forced to place our bet - but are more concerned to avoid losing, since we cannot really afford the money; the risk is really too great.

The above situation, which may occur in a whole variety of ways, is the key to such things as business investment, launching a new product and similar activities. Our aim is to show how, while making a decision to carry out a business undertaking, we can minimise our risk. Let us first look at a simple example in matrix form:

$$\begin{array}{c} \\ A_1 \\ A_2 \end{array} \begin{array}{c} \begin{array}{cc} B_1 & B_2 \end{array} \\ \begin{bmatrix} 0 & 100 \\ 1 & 1 \end{bmatrix} \end{array} \qquad \ldots(21)$$

Suppose we take a "utility payoff" view of these numbers, and suppose we say that the numbers represent £0, £1 and £100 respectively. Suppose you have to play for A and your choice is between A_1 and A_2, and you do not know whether B_1 or B_2 is correct, which would you choose? We say that to maximise your utility you choose A_1 because then you can win £100 which is clearly the maximum possible payoff. But if we think of this problem in terms of regret (at loss) as in the last section, i.e. the extent we shall regret the loss if we are wrong, the matrix becomes:

$$\begin{array}{c} \\ A_1 \\ A_2 \end{array} \begin{array}{c} \begin{array}{cc} B_1 & B_2 \end{array} \\ \begin{bmatrix} 1 & 0 \\ 0 & 99 \end{bmatrix} \end{array} \qquad \ldots(22)$$

which is derived by subtracting each value from the maximum value in the same column, i.e.

$$\begin{array}{c} \\ A_1 \\ A_2 \end{array} \begin{array}{c} \begin{array}{cc} B_1 & B_2 \end{array} \\ \left[\begin{array}{cc} 1-0 & 100-100 \\ 1-1 & 100-1 \end{array}\right] \end{array} \quad \ldots(23)$$

which, of course, gives you the above values from (21) and still leads to the choice of A_1.

In general, of course, we can consider cases of varying probabilistics, whereas those above were considered to be equiprobable. This argument is identical with that of the last section viewed from a slightly different point of view. But if (19) were substituted for (24) the arguement would be more or less the same. Many different strategies are possible, and we must make a comparison between three of them to show how this choice may occur.

$$\begin{array}{c} \\ A_1 \\ A_2 \\ A_3 \end{array} \begin{array}{c} \begin{array}{ccc} B_1 & B_2 & B_3 \end{array} \\ \left[\begin{array}{ccc} 0 & 3 & 0 \\ 2 & 2 & 0 \\ 1 & 1 & 1 \end{array}\right] \end{array} \quad \ldots(24)$$

Suppose the columns B_1, B_2, B_3 are all equiprobable, which A would you choose where the payoff is in the £'s? Maximum utility suggests A_1, since £3 is the maximum payoff, minimum regret is derived as before, giving the matrix (25):

$$\begin{array}{c} \\ A_1 \\ A_2 \\ A_3 \end{array} \begin{array}{c} \begin{array}{ccc} B_1 & B_2 & B_3 \end{array} \\ \begin{bmatrix} 3 & 0 & 3 \\ 0 & 0 & 2 \\ 0 & 0 & 0 \end{bmatrix} \end{array} \quad \ldots(25)$$

so you would clearly choose A_3 to minimise your regret. A third strategy might be to choose A_2 since this (this again is Laplace's Strategy) could be supported by the view that it gives the maximum average payoff. The average of the three rows of 24 being 1, $1\frac{1}{3}$ and 1 respectively. There are other more complicated strategies but these are sufficient for our purpose. Now if we take matrix 24 and change the value of the payoff from £'s to millions of pounds much as we changed (21) to (22), we may whether we would still bet the same way. You now stand to lose - or fail to win - up to £3 million. If you now translate (24) into a new matrix (26), which satisfies all the same conditions, the point becomes even more obvious:

$$\begin{array}{c} \\ A_1 \\ A_2 \\ A_3 \end{array} \begin{array}{c} \begin{array}{ccc} B_1 & B_2 & B_3 \end{array} \\ \begin{bmatrix} -1 & 2 & -1 \\ 1 & 1 & -1 \\ 0 & 0 & 0 \end{bmatrix} \end{array} \quad \ldots(26)$$

The same strategies exist and the payoffs are relatively the same but now you may have to risk losing £1 million. This will almost certainly have the effect of moving your choice from A_1 as first choice, overlooking A_2 and moving to A_3 where you cannot lose anything. The fact that you cannot win anything is no longer the most important factor.

To summarise the situation, we shall say that it is fairly obvious that the choice of strategies to be used is a function of the size of the risk, and we must use this technique as a result of some quantification of the data where possible, whenever we are asked to take any decision which entails risk. With the minimax approach to risk in mind, let us look at a technique which has been derived from such beginnings.

VENTURE ANALYSIS

We now turn to venture analysis; given that we need to do something such as market a new product, we are faced by market uncertainties. We are unsure of the rate of market penetration and yet need to build a factory of some size. If we choose a fairly arbitrary measure such as the "net cash position", which is defined as the cumulative net earnings plus depreciation reserve less the permanent investment and working capital, we may choose to maximise this. Rather than predict market penetration, it is often easier to minimise regret (Stage 1).

For a particular factory size, say £5 million, £10 million and £15 million respectively, we could forecast in terms of, say, rates of market penetration: great, medium and small. So if our payoff is in terms of "net cash" at some later date (this is a function of budgeting), then we can construct a utility matrix as follows:

Factory size	Forecast	"net cash"	at time t
£5 million	(60	40	20)
£10 million	(70	50	10)
£15 million	(90	42	18)

which gives a regret matrix

$$\begin{bmatrix} 30 & 10 & 0 \\ 20 & 0 & 10 \\ 0 & 8 & 2 \end{bmatrix}$$

so the minimum regret, given the lowest maximum value of a row, is given by the last row whose maximum value is 8. We therefore can say that our factory choice (on this basis) must be the largest one.

Fixing the price of the commodity now takes us into the second game-theoretic phase, and we repeat the procedure and find a solution to the game in the light of the customer's and competitor's likely action. The difficulty with all these methods is to select the best budgets and various estimates in the first instance. Success depends on seeing which are the most relevant features and optimising them in the manner suggested.

For the last phase we can think of the firm's price for the product as against the customer's price for the product. He is now considering what price of product maximises his market penetration. Suppose we consider profits to the firm as a payoff defined in £'s as:

$$\text{Profits payoff} = \frac{\text{Firm's profits}}{\text{Customer's profits}}$$

Now make up the matrix:

$$\begin{array}{lc} & \\ \text{Customer's price for product} & \begin{array}{c} 225 \\ \\ 200 \\ \\ 175 \\ \\ 150 \\ \\ 125 \end{array} \left[\begin{array}{ccc} \frac{14}{62} & \frac{26}{50} & \frac{38}{38} \\ \\ \frac{28}{96} & \frac{50}{74} & \frac{72}{52} \\ \\ \frac{43}{113} & \frac{76}{80} & \frac{109}{47} \\ \\ \frac{58}{119} & \frac{101}{71} & \frac{143}{29} \\ \\ \frac{73}{100} & \frac{126}{47} & \frac{178}{-5} \end{array} \right] \quad \ldots(27) \\ & \begin{array}{ccc} 50 & 75 & 100 \end{array} \end{array}$$

Firm's price for raw material

Although $\frac{178}{-5}$ gives maximum payoff it is gained at the expense of financial loan to the customer, so that if we choose the marked diagonal we find in fact that this provides the minimax solution; and since $\frac{76}{80}$ is the ratio which maximises the profit to the firm, we choose this as our solution to the game, the graph then tells us (by tracking back along the ordinates and abscissae) what the firm's and customer's price must be. The firm's price is 75, which could be some such measure as £75 per unit (such as a lb or cwt).

We are presupposing in this example some part of the principle involved in the theory of _n_-person games, but we shall not take the matter any further.

APPENDIX 3 REFERENCES

1. F.H.George — Precision, Language and Logic, Pergamon Press, 1977.

2. W.Edwards (Ed.) — Revisions of opinion by men and man-machine systems. IEEE Trans on hum. Facts in Electronics.1. 1, 1-63 (whole issue).

3. W.Edwards, H.Lindman & L.J.Savage — Bayesian Statistical inference for psychological research. Psychol Rev, 70,193-242, 1963.

4. W.Edwards — Opus Citus

5. R.C.Jeffrey — The Logic of Decision, McGraw-Hill, 1965.

6. R.C.Jeffrey — Opus Citus

7. R.C.Jeffrey — Opus Citus

8. R.M.Thrall, C.H.Coombs & R.L.Davis — Decision Processes, Wiley, 1954.

9. D.J.White — Decision Theory, Allen and Unwic, 1969.